you can't take it with you

you can't take it with you

Common-Sense Estate Planning *for* Canadians

fifth edition

Sandra E. Foster

John Wiley & Sons Canada, Ltd.

National Library of Canada Cataloguing in Publication Data

Foster, Sandra E., 1955-
You can't take it with you : the common-sense guide to estate planning for Canadians / Sandra E. Foster.

Annual.
[1996]-
Includes index.
Published also in French under title: Partez l'esprit en paix.
ISSN 1498-4970
ISBN-13: 978-0-470-83846-4 (5th edition)
ISBN-10: 0-470-83846-9 (5th edition)

1. Estate planning—Canada—Popular works. 2. Inheritance and succession—Canada—Popular works. I. Title.

KE5974.Z82F67 2000- 346.7105'2 C2001-300814-5
KF750.Z9F67 2000-

Production Credits:
Cover design: Jason Vanderberg
Interior text design: Natalia Burobina
Printer: Printcrafters

John Wiley & Sons Canada, Ltd.
6045 Freemont Blvd.
Mississauga, Ontario
L5R 4J3

Printed in Canada
1 2 3 4 5 PC 11 10 09 08 07

contents

preface

I AM PLEASED TO ANNOUNCE the tenth anniversary of *You Can't Take It With You* and to offer you the fifth edition.

Estate planning. Just the words are enough to intimidate many Canadians.

Planning your estate may be one area of financial planning you put off for as long as possible. After all, almost half of all Canadian adults have never taken the time to prepare a basic will. However, your estate plan does not have to be difficult or complicated. It could be very straightforward—making sure your paperwork and financial details are organized so your executor or representative can pull together your financial life on your behalf after your death.

I worried about my own estate plan early. At one point, my four children were all under the age of six. It turned out that twins ran in my family! Like most parents, we wondered who might best raise our children should something happen to us. But our family members and friends were all in various stages of their own lives. Were they really willing and able to take on the responsibility of guardianship for four very young children, who would ultimately become teenagers? I also worried that they might have to go to separate homes should anything happen to us.

More recently within our family, I was reminded how important it is to have an up-to-date estate plan in place and to have discussed your wishes with your family. If you should fall ill, I personally believe the priority then is to be able to put time and energy into your health and your family and not worrying about your estate plan or money in the last few days.

Here's the bad news.

When it comes to your estate plan and death, there is one thing I know for sure. Death will affect each and every one of us. It's not something that "might happen." It's not an "if." We just don't know when. So it's better to have your estate plan in place sooner rather than later.

Another aspect of estate planning that makes many people uncomfortable is that some day they might be here, but be unable to make their own decisions. By preparing pre-estate documents, you can appoint someone to act and make decisions on your behalf.

Now, here's the good news.

While many things may seem more important on a daily basis, I believe estate planning—preparing your will and pre-estate documents—is very important. These documents have a great deal of power and give you the opportunity to put your instructions in writing and speak for you when you can't.

If you have put together your estate plan, congratulations. However, you still need to make sure your instructions stay up-to-date. This does not mean you have to change your documents every year, but many things can affect your estate plan—changes in your family, the tax rules, and various provincial legislation. If it's been some time since you reviewed your documents, it's probably time to dust them off and reread them (assuming you actually read them before) to see if the instructions are still appropriate.

When you developed your first estate plan, the focus may have been on writing a will indicating who would get what and who would care for your children. Today, an estate plan involves much more. First, it involves not just your will but also those documents that will speak for you if you are alive but not able to speak for yourself. Of course, your will indicates who gets what, but your estate plan should consider all your assets (not just those distributed through your will) and whether they are taxable or non-taxable. For example, life insurance distributed outside the will is not taxable. An RRSP left to a non-spouse or partner and any capital gains on other assets will create a tax bill that will have to be paid. Your estate plan should not only consider who gets what, but also how much tax will be due and how much each beneficiary will receive according to your estate plan.

SO IF NOT, WHY NOT?

I'm not surprised that planning your estate is not on the top of your "to do" list. But it should at least be *on* your list somewhere.

Over the years, I've heard a number of reasons why people avoid putting an estate plan in place.

1. **I'm not old enough.**

   This is a complete fallacy. While statistically-speaking, most people die when they are older, some people die in middle age and young adults have a number of fatal accidents (this is one reason car insurance is not cheap for young drivers). Age is not an excuse for not having an up-to-date will and power of attorney documents.

2. **I'm young and healthy.**

   This is not just the converse of "I'm not old enough." Being young and/or healthy today does not excuse you from having valid pre-estate planning documents in place, in particular a document naming a representative who will make decisions on your behalf if you cannot make them for yourself. Terri Schiavo was only 26 when she collapsed. With no written instructions naming a representative to make decisions on her behalf, hers became a very public battle that went all the way up to the U.S. Supreme Court, and the president of the United States flew in wearing his pajamas to sign controversial legislation in 2005.

   Accidents and illnesses happen at any age.

3. **The government has a will in place, so I don't have to worry about it.**

   Haa! From what I can tell, the only reason each province has intestacy rules—read "I didn't bother" rules—is so that an estate can be distributed according to a formula. However, these intestacy rules have no flexibility and may not represent the needs of the traditional or modern family. For example, there is no guarantee that your spouse or partner will inherit all the family assets.

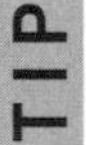

This is more than a Tip. At a bare minimum, I believe you need to have a valid, up-to-date will and pre-estate documents.

4. **My family will be able to figure it out.**

Another haa! While you may want your family to get along, or to be able to get along, it may not happen, no matter how much you hope it might.

And, unfortunately, I've also met the family who got along until there was a significant amount of money or assets of sentimental value to distribute (which may not have anything to do with their dollar value).

Although this may be too much to expect, a will that makes it clear how an estate is to be distributed could defuse potential family problems and preserve relationships. We all know instances where brothers and sisters no longer speak to each other because one feels the other received some sort of advantage.

Even in a family that gets along, trying to figure out what or how they should go about settling an estate is really not what they need to be doing when they are grieving. Even preplanning your funeral can help them get started.

5. **I don't know what to do.**

For the most part, estate planning is an area of specialization practised by some lawyers, accountants, and financial advisers. To develop an estate plan, you need to assess where you are, consider the strategies that would work for your situation and objectives, and then implement the plan. In addition, if you have a complex family structure, family members with special needs, or family dynamics that are not the most positive, your estate plan may also need to be structured to address these.

When some people say, "I don't know what to do," they sometimes mean they are afraid to consider their estate plan. After all, the reality of an estate plan is planning for the time when you are not here. And the reality of a pre-estate plan is that it is for a time when you are not able to make your own decisions. But planning your estate does not tempt fate.

If you don't know what to do, you may need advice or strong encouragement from a trusted legal, spiritual, or financial adviser in your life. Other people may not be willing to pull their estate plan together until their doctor tells them that "they should make sure their affairs are in order."

If you don't know what to do, I'm not surprised.

At this point, no one expects you to know what to do. If you did, you might not have picked up my book.

6. I don't like lawyers.

I know this can be a real stumbling block for some people—notice that I did not say roadblock. But some lawyers have always had it right and some are starting to get it. Much traditional legal training is adversarial (anyone been through a nasty divorce?) and some people have met lawyers only while dealing with something extremely difficult.

Eventually, my clients need to see their lawyer to have their documents updated or prepared. I've had people attempt to delay and delay this step to the point where I've had to refuse to see them again until they'd made an appointment with their lawyer. (They don't have to do this alone. I've prepared notes for the lawyer and have even gone to the initial meeting on occasion.)

Whenever you are looking for professional advice, you want a professional *you* can deal with. Ideally, having some understanding of estate planning will enable you to go to your appointments more prepared and use the time more effectively.

7. It will cost too much.

Yes, working with any professional will cost money. But doing it yourself also has its costs. Think about the last time you or your spouse tried to fix a leaking pipe!

When people tell me that a professional estate plan "will cost too much," it's sometimes because they don't know what they don't know. Other than for the most straightforward situation, there are cost benefits to having documents prepared by a lawyer or a notary.

Will it cost too much? For you, I don't know. But I do know from experience that there are different types of costs related to an estate: time, money, and stress. Some of these costs are immediate and some of the costs, or losses, are down the road.

Properly prepared power of attorney documents for finance and health that give your representatives the appropriate authority can save time and money should they have to act on your behalf.

A well-prepared will can save your executor time and money when settling your estate.

Here are just some of the very expensive missed opportunities from poorly prepared estate plans that I've seen:

- Extra time was needed to deal with the public guardian or trustee (curator) because a clause was missed.
- No appropriate temporary guardian was appointed for children, leaving the children unsure as to where they would be staying.
- No trust was set up for minor children and the children received a significant sum of the money when they turned 18. I'm not exactly sure how you might measure this cost or the loss when they went on a spending spree.
- The extra taxes that had to be paid each and every year because the opportunity to set up a spousal testamentary trust was missed.
- The taxes paid on the final tax return were higher than necessary because the assets with the most capital gains were left to children rather than a spouse.
- A spouse made the assumption that his second wife would look after his children from his first marriage.
- An individual gave his children a substantial amount of money when he sold his business, which triggered U.S. estate taxes since he was an American.
- The executor was not given the appropriate powers.
- Something was missed that became an expensive court matter.
- A charitable gift in the will was made using cash rather than securities, which had increased in value.
- The family cottage had to be sold because the deceased had not made purchasing additional life insurance a priority.

While it may not always be possible to put an actual dollar value on the cost or the amount saved, a well-thought-out estate plan makes a difference financially and to those who are important to you.

Years ago, I discovered I was relatively unique as a financial adviser in that I helped many of my clients integrate their financial plans and their estate plans (this was before estate planning was talked about much, if at all). At that time, I was frustrated that there was no handy reference source.

I spent hours trying to read the *Income Tax Act* (even now, I can't say I understand all of it) and hours in the law library (not trying to become a lawyer) to understand some of the estate planning solutions available to Canadians across the country.

The research I did for those clients, and the notes for the seminars from those early days, completely covered the top of the buffet in my dining room. It was clear to me—although not to a few publishers who sent me rejection letters—that this was an area where a readable, comprehensive source could make a difference.

When the book first started to take shape, I met my share of disbelievers—people who did not believe that estate planning was important or that it was a topic that would be interesting to enough people. Estate planning was truly in its early infancy. After writing, rewriting, and editing, the first edition was launched.

Since then, so much legislation has changed and so have the tax rules. So have I over the last 10 years. This edition is my commitment to bring you an up-to-date edition that reflects my current thinking and includes answers to many of the questions I have been asked recently.

It still seems that it is easier for Canadians to talk about sex than it is to discuss estate planning and money. Planning also just seems difficult, whether it is retirement planning or estate planning. Estate planning also requires us to admit that we or someone close to us may become very sick, get older, or will ultimately die.

But I have yet to find a documented case where putting an estate plan in place will itself tempt fate. Financially-speaking, many hard-working Canadians—even those who do not consider themselves to be wealthy—have accumulated estates during their lifetimes: homes, cottages, RRSPs/RRIFs, pension plans, jewellery, and so on.

Many people still think of a will when they think of estate planning, but a well-rounded estate plan can involve much more. Other aspects include ensuring that you will pay no more in tax and fees than necessary, life insurance, health care considerations, succession planning, and looking after family members. If you don't think any of these will affect you or your family, you are probably wrong.

Today, estate planning also involves preparing documents appointing people you trust to speak for you if you are alive and not able to speak for yourself, provided you take the time to prepare these documents.

While estate planning can be difficult to define, it involves caring for yourself, the people around you, and distributing the assets and property you have saved and managed most effectively.

I have seen—and heard many stories—many situations of families where the impact of the illness or death of a family member was horrendous or downright brutal. While doing nothing is one of your options, I do not believe that this is in the best interests of your family, business, and other relationships.

Everyone should put in place an estate plan and review it periodically to ensure their instructions are current. Putting an estate plan in place can help keep government out of our lives wherever we can and provide a roadmap for our beneficiaries. Yes, I know how difficult it can be. I work with clients on a regular basis who might bring me dusty will files and out-of-date power of attorney documents, if they have them at all. If you have assets and family you care about, you owe it to them (and to yourself) to have these documents in place. I've been saying it for a decade and I'm still saying it.

Does that decade make a difference? Yes. You, like your neighbours, are now 10 years older. If you haven't put an estate plan in place, now is the time. If your estate plan has been in place for a while, you know that nothing stays the same, so it's probably time to dust it off and give it a thorough review.

You Can't Take It With You was the first of its kind in Canada—a comprehensive, practical guide to estate planning for Canadians—and it continues to be a major success story and bestseller.

The information in this book continues to evolve from real-life experiences, research interviews with ordinary Canadians and other professionals (I'm pleased to acknowledge that there is more information available today than ever before), the interpretation of bulletins published by the Canada Revenue Agency (formerly Canada Customs and Revenue Canada), and the applicable federal and provincial legislation. I offer this information to help demystify some of this wording and help you better understand your estate planning choices, and what your lawyer or notary is talking about.

Your estate plan might be straightforward or complex, but there is probably no one perfect solution for you. Is your goal to design an estate plan that will meet your needs while you are alive and benefit your beneficiaries as you envision? How can your estate plan balance the tax and other financial issues with your family's dynamics (and any tricky family issues)? A successful estate plan would consider how effectively different strategies might handle any of these differences. As one example, someone in a second marriage might initially consider his adult child as the beneficiary of an RRSP, but soon discover that there are certain tax advantages if a spouse is the named beneficiary. So what to do?

Any particular strategy or technique, considered in isolation, may appear to make sense until it is combined with other objectives or considerations. And then it may be completely inappropriate. As part of developing your estate plan, you may consider a number of strategies, but some of them may never make it into your actual plan.

While it is important to design an estate plan that will be appropriate for your personal and business situation, as well as your family dynamics, it is also important to keep your plan as simple as possible so your representatives can understand and follow your instructions.

We will discuss ways you could distribute your estate, what happens on death, the issues that arise when assets are left to a spouse (same generation planning) or to children or grandchildren (inter-generation planning) or to charity. I could list all the issues we'll consider throughout the book, but they are also listed in the Table of Contents.

Self-assessment is an important phase in estate planning. I have a limited number of copies of the *Estate Planning Workbook* available for purchase (see the back of this book). Otherwise, your financial adviser or lawyer can help you with the self-assessment phase. However, as you work through *You Can't Take It With You,* you can complete the various estate planning checklists and quizzes, as well as making note of the tips and the examples.

After reading this book, I hope you will be more informed and willing to discuss your estate planning with a professional adviser to ensure you do not send Canada Revenue Agency any more than necessary, or sooner than necessary.

Because, as far I know, you *still* can't take it with you.

NOTES REGARDING THE EXAMPLES USED IN THE BOOK

I have used examples that would be as simple and realistic as possible to illustrate the concepts discussed. I've used a 40% combined marginal tax rate for federal and provincial income tax throughout except where noted. A 40% marginal tax rate assumes that for each additional dollar of income earned, 40 cents goes to the government(s). But tax rates vary across the country. The combined federal and provincial top marginal tax rate in some provinces is close to 50%. In other provinces it is closer to 40%. When assessing the cost or benefit of any strategy for your own situation, your adviser can assist you in calculating the tax cost or savings of any particular estate planning technique.

WORDS OF CAUTION

Legislation related to family law, wills, powers of attorney, trusts, succession, living wills, probate taxes, and fees, etc.—which can all affect estate planning—vary from province to province. However, there seems to be a similar theme—to help protect your assets after death and to help you protect your assets if you become mentally incompetent and ensure that any medical decisions made on your behalf are made by someone with the appropriate authority.

The rules and names of the Acts vary for each province and territory, and so do some of the terms for roles that are very similar. For example,

I might refer to an executor in this book when the full term for the person acting in the role if your province is Ontario is an executor and trustee or, in Quebec, is a liquidator. In Ontario, the person referred to as a power of attorney for finances is called a mandatary in Quebec. Throughout the book, I will use various terms, but for the term used in your province, please refer to table 7.1 in chapter 7 and table 15.1 in chapter 15. In addition, Quebec follows a civil code; there are additional differences and I invite you to refer to my book *Partez l'Esprit en Paix*, 1999, published by Transcontinental, for a more thorough discussion.

You should bear in mind that there are provincial differences if you are discussing your estate planning with friends and family who live in provinces other than your own and that legislation is updated periodically.

The information is offered for general interest and educational purposes to help you understand the language of estate planning and the more common estate planning strategies. The author, publisher, and distributor make no representations or warranties about the information in the book and are not liable for any claims, losses, or damages of any kind arising out of the use of this book.

The book discusses general issues to consider when preparing an estate plan. It is not designed so you can "do it yourself." It does not exhaust every consideration, all combinations, situations, scenarios or suggest ideas for every situation.

This book is *not* intended to be a formal estate planning guide for professional estate planners, lawyers, or accountants. (Hopefully, this book will help provide a foundation of estate planning information for Canadians who do not have their technical expertise.)

The analysis in this book represents the opinion of the author and the legislation in effect at the time of publication, as well as changes that have been announced by the government that may not have been formally passed into law. While care has been taken to ensure the accuracy of the information contained in this book at the time of publication, readers should obtain up-to-date professional legal, tax, and financial advice on how these ideas might fit their own situation before deciding on a particular course of action.

This book is *not* a legal document or a tax guide and does not provide legal advice.

acknowledgements

THIS BOOK REFLECTS THE KNOWLEDGE and insights that I gained from research and from dozens of discussions on estate planning with other professionals. I wish to thank all the dedicated professionals who went before me and those who are focusing today on providing leadership in their profession and the best advice to their clients.

I have also met many other professionals who are committed to the well-being of others and thank them for their dedication, care, and support.

I would like to acknowledge my husband, Dave, too, for his unfaltering faith and support, and my children for their patience.

the estate planning checklist

THE FIRST STEP IN DEVELOPING or reviewing your estate plan is to look at your current situation, to know where you are today, and to assess what you want to do. An estate plan, like any plan, reflects your situation and what you want to do at the time it is prepared.

Your estate plan will reflect your family dynamics as well as your financial and business circumstances. But you can't get where you want to go without starting at the beginning.

Take this quiz. Any *No* or *Unsure* answers may require special attention as you go through this book and consult with your professional advisers.

Yes	*No*	*Unsure*	
❐	❐	❐	Have you prepared and signed a will?
❐	❐	❐	Have you prepared documents appointing a representative who can make decisions on your behalf in the event of mental incapacity?
❐	❐	❐	Have you recently reviewed your will and pre-estate documents for financial and health matters?
❐	❐	❐	Are your will and pre-estate documents for financial and health matters up to date?
❐	❐	❐	If you are married or cohabiting, have you taken steps to protect any assets you brought into the relationship?

Yes	*No*	*Unsure*	
❐	❐	❐	Have you named beneficiaries and alternative beneficiaries for your RRSPs, annuities, life insurance policies, LIFs and RRIFs, pension plans, and/or DPSPs?
❐	❐	❐	Are your beneficiary designations up to date?
❐	❐	❐	Have you named a backup executor in your will and backup powers of attorney?
❐	❐	❐	Have you provided adequately for your dependants?
❐	❐	❐	Have you provided for your spouse so he or she will not have to make a claim against your estate under provincial family laws?
❐	❐	❐	Have you estimated your income tax due on death?
❐	❐	❐	If you are not a Canadian citizen, have you informed your advisers?
❐	❐	❐	Do you have any assets that can be rolled over tax-free to your spouse or partner?
❐	❐	❐	Have you considered the potential benefits of a testamentary or alter ego trust?
❐	❐	❐	Do you have enough life insurance in place?
❐	❐	❐	Have you estimated the cost to have your will probated after your death?
❐	❐	❐	Have you reviewed how best to register the ownership of assets?
❐	❐	❐	Do you have enough cash to pay the cost of dying—including income taxes and executor and probate fees—without forcing the sale of family assets, such as the house, cottage, or family business?
❐	❐	❐	If you have specific wishes regarding your funeral, have you left instructions with your executor?
❐	❐	❐	Have you prepared a living will or medical directive?
❐	❐	❐	Have you prepared a power of attorney for personal care or a health care proxy or mandate?

Yes	*No*	*Unsure*	
❒	❒	❒	Have you documented your wishes regarding organ donations or donating your body to science?
❒	❒	❒	Have you considered making a planned gift to charity?
❒	❒	❒	If you have a business, do you have a succession plan to ensure its future?
❒	❒	❒	If you have children from a previous marriage, does your will or other documentation ensure any specific bequests for these children?
❒	❒	❒	Does your spouse/child(ren)/executor know the names and addresses of your professional advisers?
❒	❒	❒	Does your spouse/child(ren)/executor know where to find your financial records, income tax returns, bank accounts, safety deposit box, and insurance policies?
❒	❒	❒	Have you prepared a detailed record of all your assets and accounts?
❒	❒	❒	Have you prepared all the necessary documents (including will, power of attorney for finances as well as for health care) for your estate plan?
❒	❒	❒	Do you have all the information you need to complete your estate plan?
❒	❒	❒	Is your estate plan integrated with your retirement and tax plan?
❒	❒	❒	Have you reviewed your estate plan with a professional competent in estate planning?
❒	❒	❒	Is your estate plan up to date?
❒	❒	❒	Are there ways to simplify your financial affairs so your estate can be settled more quickly?

chapter one

what is estate planning?

It is better to live rich than to die rich.
—*Samuel Johnson*

I BELIEVE ANYONE 18 OR OLDER WITH A FAMILY—parents, siblings, or children—a bank account, a house, or just a few personal possessions should take the time to write a will. And anyone who is 16 or older should also prepare pre-estate documents or power of attorney documents, for health care and finances, as well as make their wishes regarding organ donation known.

I used to say estate planning was about providing for others—your family, your business partners, favourite charities, and maybe even someone you've never met—and dealing with the final chapter in your life. I still agree with that. But it is also important to remember that a proper estate plan also includes providing for yourself.

The cost of working with professionals to set your estate plan in place may be relatively small when compared to what could be saved by having a properly documented estate plan.

If you have difficulty making decisions regarding your potential incapacity and death, you are not alone. In this book, we will consider many of the difficult questions.

One woman was very honest when she told me, "This is so difficult for me to think about, and to be sure I'm making the right decisions. But I don't want the government making these decisions for me or my family." It's amazing how keeping the government out of one's personal affairs is a powerful motivator.

Estate planning can help ensure the desired outcomes for your beneficiaries on your death. You don't need to be rich to do estate planning. Anyone with a few assets and a family has an estate. Your estate consists of everything you hold or own title to, such as your home, bank account, stocks, bonds, mutual funds, real estate, business interests, pension plans, insurance policies, car, jewellery, art and coin collections, and other personal items. Whatever the value of your estate, simple steps can help to ensure that those you want to benefit will.

BUILDING YOUR ESTATE PLAN

Your estate plan will reflect your family and financial situation, and any business interests. It is also a balancing act between your objectives, your family dynamics, and current legislation.

The result of a successful estate plan will preserve your assets as much as possible and enable the smooth transfer of those assets to your beneficiaries in a manner that satisfies your wishes.

But an estate plan is much more than just distributing your assets. It also addresses all of the issues relevant to your personal situation and priorities and ensures you have up-to-date documents so your instructions can be carried out. These could include:

- meeting your financial needs for the rest of your life
- documenting who will receive what after your death
- planning charitable donations
- appointing an executor to administer your estate
- protecting your financial affairs in case you become unable to manage your own affairs

- appointing a representative to make medical decisions on your behalf in the event you cannot make decisions on your own behalf
- providing direction to your family regarding your wishes for medical treatment, organ donation, and funeral arrangements
- ensuring your family will be able to manage financially after your death
- choosing a guardian to look after your children
- protecting the interests of the children from a previous marriage
- putting together a business succession plan so it can survive without you
- saving your estate fees and income taxes
- ensuring your beneficiaries receive the full value of their inheritance as smoothly as possible

Traditional estate planning is the process of taking stock, making decisions, considering the special needs any beneficiaries may have, and preparing your will, the key document for the orderly transfer of your assets to your beneficiaries.

In addition, there are documents I refer to as "pre-estate" documents that include the powers of attorney and living wills, which are powerful additions to a traditional estate plan. These documents allow you to decide who decides if and when you are unable to decide for yourself. These documents allow you to appoint a:

- power of attorney for finances who will look after your money
- power of attorney for health and personal care who can make health care decisions for you when you can't

In many households, one person may be actively managing the money. Part of your estate planning should ensure that the surviving partner (which could end up being you) is prepared to manage the money. Part of estate planning includes introducing your spouse or partner to your advisers and familiarizing him or her with the types of investment decisions that are being made. And you want to make sure that there will be enough in the estate or from insurance to maintain your family's lifestyle.

Your will and your total estate plan need not be complex. Indeed, some of the best estate plans are straightforward. Estate planning is really a personal matter, and what works for one person may not work for you and vice versa. It just has to be designed to meet your objectives, which requires communication between you and your advisers so your executor, beneficiaries, and advisers do not have to guess at what you intended.

WHEN SHOULD YOU PREPARE AN ESTATE PLAN?

I interviewed S., aged 66, a few years after the death of her husband. He had never been particularly interested in handling the family finances, so she was used to dealing with their money. At the time of his death, the family assets were registered either in her name or in both names and his will reflected his current wishes. On his death, the assets were transferred smoothly and with a minimum of expense. Her words of wisdom: "Educate yourself! Get advice! And use common sense!"

Some people think they are too young to do estate planning. Yet age is not the main factor. We all hope to live to a healthy old age; not all of us will. As soon as you have some assets or a family, you should have an estate plan. Estate planning is not something that you do at the end of the day. Rather, it should be part of your ongoing financial strategy. People in their late forties start to bury their friends, people who were in their peak earning years who hadn't stopped to consider that they might be mere mortals. Despite all of our medical and technological advances, we cannot escape death. Now, this does not mean that we should live in paranoia. It just means that every once in a while you should imagine what would happen if suddenly you were no longer in the picture and take the appropriate measures.

Like any other part of your financial plan, estate planning requires periodic tune-ups to keep it effective. If you marry, remarry, divorce, or are widowed, a review of your estate plan may indicate that changes are needed to reflect your new personal circumstances. If the people appointed in the will are unable or unwilling to act on your behalf, the documents should be updated. If your assets increase or decrease in value, the amount of income tax due on your final tax return will change. And importantly, your estate plan should reflect changes in tax legislation, succession law, and family law. If you retire at 60 and live to be 85, that's 25 years of changing legislation and family dynamics.

When it comes to estate planning, it is better to be too early than too late!

Do you want the government to be one of your beneficiaries? Governments—but we don't have any estate taxes—are waiting for you to die so they can collect those final income taxes building up in your RRSPs and RRIFs, as well as collect what's due on the profits you have made but not yet settled up.

Although technically Canada Revenue Agency (CRA) is not one of your beneficiaries, they stand to receive taxes from your estate based on the income reported on your final tax return. This will be different for each person. For example, if you don't have a spouse or partner, the value of your RRSP would be added on to page one as income on your final tax return, perhaps putting you in the highest tax bracket you've ever been in. However, if you pay attention to how the tax rules work, you may be able to keep a larger estate for yourself during your lifetime and your beneficiaries and reduce your tax bill. For example, certain types of gifts to charity legally avoid tax on any capital gains that might otherwise be taxable, and gifts to certain family members might decrease your taxes while the same gift to other family members may increase it.

Even Canadians who do not consider themselves wealthy by traditional standards have accumulated significant wealth during their lifetime. They also invested in property—property whose values rose rapidly through periods of high inflation. (You may remember when houses cost $50,000!) The values of personal real estate and other assets have increased the net worth of more than one generation of Canadians. Surveys reveal that more disposable wealth is about to change hands in the next two decades than ever before.

If leaving a large estate is not one of your priorities, you might look at ways to reduce the size of your taxable estate. You might spend more on yourself or give some away by taking money out of your RRSP (Registered Retirement Savings Plan) or RRIF (Registered Retirement Income Fund) today. Many people believe it is better to leave money in these registered plans for as long as possible, but this is not always the case. So let's say you are 62 and your husband dies. You transfer his RRSP to your own (tax free) and let it grow for another seven years until you are 69. At that time you start taking out the minimum amount allowed, and then you die at age 75. Without planning, up to half of your RRIF could be taxed on your death. Suppose your RRIF is worth $120,000 and you are not survived by a spouse or common-law partner. Your estate could face a tax bill of up to $60,000. Of course, you want to be sure that you have enough for your needs, but do you really want the government to be a major beneficiary? I'm not advocating that you run out and spend all of your RRIF, but you may want to see if the tax bill at death can be minimized and your income over your lifetime maximized.

Keep your beneficiary designations up-to-date on your RRSPs, RRIFs, life insurance, group benefits, etc. Why? The more accurate this information is, the more smoothly your estate can be settled and the less work and complications there will be for the estate trustee.

IS IT WORTH PREPARING AN ESTATE PLAN?

By the time you finish *You Can't Take It With You*, I hope you will agree that "*yes, it is worth it.*"

Some people say, "Why bother? Let the kids look after themselves." I think, in some cases, this is an attempt to avoid looking into the future or facing mortality. There are many questions to be asked and decisions to be made when you develop an estate plan; some are for the benefit of your beneficiaries, but some are also for you. If thinking about your own mortality seems morbid to you, think of the alternatives.

Most of us do not want some bureaucrat making decisions on our behalf if we are still alive and unable to. You may just want to make sure that your family does not have to report to some government official to justify their actions.

By planning your estate, and preparing the pre-estate documents that will speak for you while you are alive and your will for after your death, you can make your wishes known even when you are no longer physically able to. And by obtaining proper advice, you can avoid making major business, legal, investment, or tax blunders.

In addition to the dollars you may save by planning your estate, the financial plan can provide a sense of security. It can give you that peace of mind that comes from knowing that you have looked after your financial affairs the best way possible. John F. Kennedy said, "There are risks and costs to a program of action. But they are far less than the long-range risks and costs of comfortable inaction."

Here are some of the terms I'm going to use throughout the book.

Although I will use a number of terms interchangeably, the term most often used for someone who will make decisions on your behalf while you are still alive or represent you is representative or power of attorney. For the actual title of the person in your province or territory for financial matters, see the chart on page 108 in Chapter 7. For the actual term used for the person in your province or territory for health or personal care, see the chart on page 267 in Chapter 15.

I will use the term executor for the person who is given the authority to settle your estate. In some provinces this may be called estate trustee, executrix (if female) or liquidator (in Quebec).

THE SIX D'S OF ESTATE PLANNING

There are at least six D's to putting together your estate plan:

- decide
- design
- develop
- discuss
- document
- distribute

They are all important to your personal estate plan. When I'm asked which is the most important when putting together an estate plan, I think the most important three (not just one) are deciding what you want to do, making sure you discuss it with the people involved, and then documenting it.

A FRAMEWORK FOR YOUR ESTATE PLAN

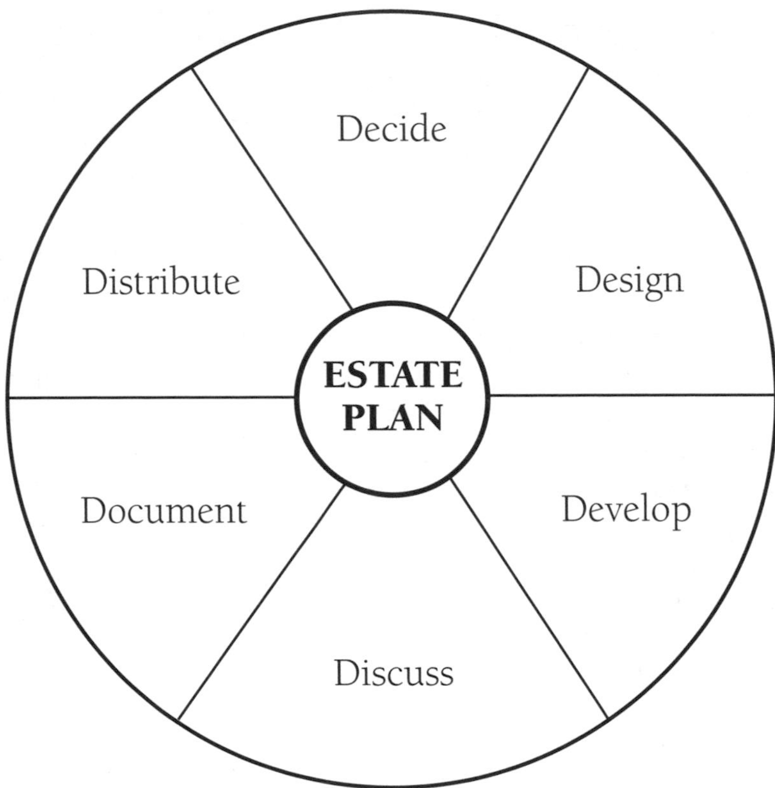

Decide

The beauty of your estate plan is that you can decide whether or not you want to leave as large an estate as possible, or whether you'd prefer to spend as much as you can before you go. (If you don't spend it, someone else probably will!) You get to decide who gets what (remember, that could be you), how much they get, and when.

While you cannot legally write anyone out of your will who is financially dependent on you, your estate plan truly is your statement of your wishes.

Your estate plan should reflect your values and priorities. The checklist in Chapter 18 will help you identify your personal estate planning priorities and values. Be sure to keep these values in mind as you consider different estate planning strategies.

Design and Develop

There are many ways to design your estate plan to achieve your estate planning objectives. There are ways to reduce the cost of dying by leaving an inheritance to a beneficiary in a tax-effective manner.

If you have been diligent about splitting income between you and your partner to pay as little tax as possible while you are both alive, you might consider setting up a testamentary spousal trust in your will, so you can continue some of this income splitting even after you're gone.

There are many ways to register your assets, and even to distribute your assets.

Your estate plan should also reflect the needs of your beneficiaries. For example, any beneficiaries who may still be minors at the time of your death would need a trust set up in your will to manage their inheritance until they are older—unless you want the public trustee of your province to manage these assets until they become adults. If you have beneficiaries who will never be any good at managing money, you might want to consider how much, if any, they should receive outright.

The estate plan you design and develop will be unique to your personal and financial situation.

Document

You also need to properly document your estate plan to ensure it will be carried out. If you fail to have valid estate planning documents, the government has a "default" plan that must be followed and that may not settle your estate the way you want nor make medical decisions that you would have wanted.

Naming beneficiaries on your RRSPs, RRIFs, life insurance, annuities, and company pension plans, as appropriate, is part of documenting your estate planning. If you need to revise your designated beneficiary, it's not enough just to e-mail your financial institution the new name or to tell them over the phone. You must put your request in writing. Your financial institution can provide you with the correct form to use. Complete it, sign it, and return it to them.

Discuss

Be sure to discuss your plans with your family and those people who are close to you. You should also discuss your estate plan with anyone you have assigned a job in your estate plan, including your executor, power of attorney, mandate, representative, guardians for any minor children, and the trustees of any trusts you establish. These people are not mind readers and will not be able to guess what you want done or why you want some things handled a certain way. They may not even be aware of all their duties and responsibilities. In the appendices, you'll find lists of the general duties and responsibilities of the executor and the representative for financial decisions and for personal and health care decisions.

They do not have to know all the details of your estate plan, but they should know enough to tell you if they would be willing to act on your behalf when the time comes.

Remember, you will not have the opportunity to explain your decisions after your death and may not have the opportunity in the event you become incapacitated. Take the time while you are able to ensure that those involved appreciate your decisions, even if they do not agree with you.

Distribute

It is the role of the executor and trustee to settle your estate and ultimately distribute the assets in your estate to your beneficiaries.

How easy would it be for someone to quickly pull together the personal and financial details of your life?

Many people, even if they haven't taken the time to prepare an estate plan, have statements and paperwork all over the place (they may even have trouble finding the paperwork needed to complete their personal tax return each year). Imagine how difficult it could be for someone else to access all the relevant information that is needed, not just to do your final tax return, but to wrap up all the details of your life. In the event you become mentally incapacitated, your power of attorney or representative needs to locate personal and financial information to make decisions on your behalf.

On your death, your executor needs to locate all your personal and financial information, your beneficiaries, and anyone else you have named in your will. If you are looking for worksheets to help you document all your personal and financial information—the people in your life, your assets and liabilities, as well as the location of all your estate planning documents—you can order a copy of the *Estate Planning Workbook* using the order form at the back of the book as long as the workbooks are available.

THE MODERN ESTATE PLAN

If you do not take the time to prepare the documents that are part of an estate plan and a pre-estate plan, the government has:

a) rules it must follow if you become incapacitated and cannot make your own decisions and
b) intestacy rules if you die without a will, which determine who gets what.

One simple definition of estate planning refers to those assets that are distributed according to the instructions in your will. But the modern estate plan involves more than determining what you want done with your assets on your death and writing a will. Today, many people have structured their estate so that some of their assets are distributed outside the will, for example, by naming a beneficiary (for their RRSP, RRIF, or life insurance), or by owning assets jointly (such as a joint bank account). Your estate plan should really consider all your assets and the different ways they can be distributed, not just the assets that will flow into your estate to be distributed according to your will. It should also include your pre-estate documents.

When I put all my estate planning documents and financial papers in one place (more or less), I also realized my executor or attorney would not automatically understand my filing system, so I re-organized my papers to help my representatives. I also realized no one would be able to access my laptop (or anything else) without knowing my passwords, so I added a note indicating where they would find them.

What's in Your Estate?

The court system, when it refers to an "estate," generally refers to those assets that are distributed according to the instructions in your will. Some people will set up their estate plan so that everything they own will be distributed according to their will. To do this, they designate their "estate" as their beneficiary on their RRSP/RRIF, pension plan, life insurance, etc. so that on their death, all these assets form part of their estate and are distributed according to the instructions of the will, after the debts and taxes are paid.

But your estate is not just what is distributed according to your will, nor do all your assets need to pass through your will. In fact, there are a number of ways to plan your estate.

As someone who has worked with real people with families for many years, "who gets what" is often now more complicated than a distribution according to the instructions in a will. Some assets are owned jointly with rights of survivorship; life insurance has beneficiaries designated to keep the value out of the "estate" so it is not subject to probate tax. On the other hand, some life insurance might have the "estate" designated so the life insurance proceeds flow into the estate to pay some debts.

There are many estate planning techniques that can expand the definition of estate planning for real people, including testamentary trusts, which are no longer just for the very wealthy.

In addition to spending your money on yourself while you are alive, there are a number of ways to distribute your estate:

1. give away assets while you are alive
2. designate beneficiaries on life insurance policies, pension plans, RRSPs, and RRIFs
3. own property jointly, including in common or with rights of survivorship (not in Quebec)
4. set up a living trust
5. set up an alter ego trust or joint partner trust while you are alive
6. include a testamentary trust in your will

7. follow the instructions in a partnership or shareholder agreement you may have for your business interests
8. make a specific bequest in the will or bequest a share of the estate residue, after all taxes and fees have been paid
9. according to the intestacy rules of your province if you die without a will. This default option is not a plan and is not recommended.

The strategies you use to distribute your estate will depend on your personal situation. Some estate plans are more complex than others, but many estate plans are not complex.

A beneficiary designation on an RRSP or RRIF is not automatically transferred when you set up a new account, even at a related financial institution. You are required to name a beneficiary on your application form, as appropriate, or in your will.

You may not be overly concerned about providing your children and grandchildren with a big inheritance. You may even have one of those bumper stickers that says "I'm enjoying my children's inheritance!" You've probably worked to provide for your retirement, not theirs. But many people in their forties and fifties are hoping to receive an inheritance as part of their own retirement planning!

Traditional estate planning assumes that your goal is to look for the most effective ways to distribute the investments, real estate, and money you have at the time of death to your beneficiaries. As you read through this book, you will see that there are a number of ways to register your assets and reduce taxes when planning your estate. But let's not forget that one way to reduce the amount of tax due on death is to give some of your money away while you are alive or spend some of it on yourself (my personal favourite). When it comes to money, some people were good savers, but did not learn how to be good spenders. If this might be you, remember, you are entitled to spend your money on yourself. Some people call this a retirement plan. Don't write yourself out of the picture prematurely.

When considering your estate planning, your first priority should be to ensure that you have enough to meet your own retirement income needs. Most people built their estate for their retirement, not so they could give away as much as possible. You should be your favorite beneficiary. For some people, retirement and estate planning go together.

But as I have said before, I believe that estate planning is important at all life's ages and stages. When you become 16 and responsible for your own health care, when you enter a relationship and/or marry, have children, separate, divorce, become a widow or widower, become ill, inherit money—there are many points in one's life where the estate planning documents enable you to put your wishes in writing so whatever happens, you are not subject to the government's default rules.

SUMMARY

I believe an estate plan is an important part of your family legacy. And not just the money part.

I don't care how much you leave for your beneficiaries unless they have special needs. Personally, I believe that leaving children of any age a large inheritance without teaching them (or life teaching them) where money fits into a successful life is a big mistake. It's important to be able to live without a lot of money because having a lot of money doesn't make you important.

Any plan should be reviewed every couple of years or so to ensure that it reflects your priorities and needs as well as changes to the relevant legislation. Economist Peter Drucker said, "The best way to predict your future is to create it."

The choices you make concerning your estate, the discussions with your family, and your ability to take care of your loved ones can mean the difference between saddling them with financial difficulties (on top of their grief), or sparing them of financial worries. The inheritance or insurance you have in place and the discussions you are able to have in advance with your family may help them deal with their grief, without also having to worry about money.

chapter two

dying intestate: distributing your estate without a will

Facts do not cease to exist
because they are ignored.
—Aldous Huxley

WHEN IT COMES TO ESTATE PLANNING, too many people think in terms of "if" rather than "when." Maybe this helps to explain recent survey findings that only about half of all Canadians over 18 have a valid will.

If you die without a valid will (or one that cannot be located), you are considered to have died intestate—that is, without a last will and testament. Provincial governments, quick to realize this could affect everyone, set out rules laying out who gets what for those who die without a will. These rules make no allowances for the needs of your beneficiaries or the size of your estate. They simply set out a formula to be followed.

Some people assume that their assets will go to the government if they die without a will. This is not true. The government is only the beneficiary of last resort and is sometimes called the "ultimate heir." Assets go to the government (not including the taxes you owe!) only if you die without a will and have no living relatives, a process called escheat. (Why does it have the word "cheat" in it?)

Let's look at what might happen if you die without a will.

WHO GETS WHAT

Under the provincial "will," assets are distributed according to the intestacy formula. There is no flexibility in these "one size fits all" rules. People you want to benefit may be left out, and those who do benefit may not be whom you would have chosen. If you would like to leave a bit extra to a family member to cover a special situation or to a relative who has special needs, these rules do not make allowances. If you are in a common-law relationship, different provinces have different rules under intestacy. Do not assume that intestacy rules will provide for your partner. No one should do estate planning by "default" regardless of their relationship status.

If you are married and have young children, your intentions may be like many others'—to have your spouse receive your entire estate and then on his or her death, to distribute any remaining assets to your children. It is incorrect to assume that if you are "married with children" that everything will go to your spouse even if you do not have a will. However, in most provinces, a spouse is entitled to receive a preferential amount from an intestate estate, an amount that ranges from nothing to $200,000 depending on where you live, before any assets might be distributed to your children.

Table 2.1: Preferential Share by Province and Territory

PROVINCE/TERRITORY	PREFERENTIAL SHARE*
Alberta	$40,000
British Columbia	$65,000
Manitoba	$50,000 or ½ of the intestate estate, if greater

New Brunswick	marital property
Newfoundland	$0
Northwest Territories	$50,000
Nova Scotia	$50,000
Nunavut	$50,000
Ontario	$200,000
Prince Edward Island	$0
Quebec	$0
Saskatchewan	$100,000
Yukon	$0

**as of October 2006*

If you die without a will, your spouse will receive the entire estate after the debts, taxes, and fees are paid only if you have no children.

In some provinces, a "spouse" includes a person who cohabited with the deceased for a period of time, such as two years in the Northwest Territories or three years in Manitoba; or with whom the deceased had a child. If you have children, your spouse will receive the entire estate only if the value of your estate is less than the amount of the preferential share. If you die intestate and your estate is worth more than the preferential share, your spouse will not receive the entire estate. If your children are under the age of majority, the public trustee will hold their share in trust on their behalf. While this may be appropriate, it is not always so. It can also result in more tax being paid than is necessary. If there is still money available when they reach the age of majority, the balance would then be paid out to them. Whoopee!

With a will, you can leave money to your spouse outright and any money you leave to your children can be put into a testamentary trust with instructions as to how and when it is to be ultimately distributed.

If there is no will, and you have no surviving spouse or children, your estate would be distributed to other family members according to a pre-set formula.

Table 2.2 illustrates the general distribution of the residue of an intestate estate for someone who died without a will outside Quebec. The residue of an estate is what remains after all taxes, bills, fees, and expenses have been paid.

Table 2.2: Dying Intestate When the Value of the Estate Is Greater Than the Preferential Share (Provincial Summary)

Surviving spouse with	
no children	Spouse receives 100% of residue.
one child	Spouse receives preferential share of the residue. If there is no preferential share, or for amounts over the preferential share, half of the residue goes to the spouse, half of the residue to the child.
more than one child	*All provinces except Manitoba:* Spouse receives preferential share, if there is one, plus one-third of the remaining residue. Children share the remaining two-thirds of the residue. *Manitoba:* Spouse receives preferential share of the residue. For amounts over the preferential share, half of the residue goes to the spouse, half of the residue to the children.
No spouse	
one or more children	Children share the residue equally.
no children	Parents share the residue equally.
No spouse, no children, no parents	Brothers and sisters share the residue equally. If no brothers or sisters are living, then all nieces and nephews share the residue equally. If no distant family can be found, the estate goes to the provincial government.

A spouse's interest in the family home or the estate may be protected even if someone dies intestate. For example, if you die intestate in Ontario, your spouse can make an election under the *Family Law Act* to receive no less than 50% of the net family property. In Manitoba, the *Homestead Act* protects a surviving spouse's interest in the family home. (See Chapter 10.)

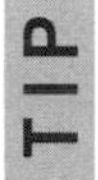

Some wills are incomplete and do not distribute all the deceased's estate. When this happens, the part of the estate not covered by the will could be distributed according to the intestacy rules. For example, a will might fail to distribute the residue and then the residue would be distributed according to the intestacy rules.

Table 2.3 shows the distribution of an intestate estate in Quebec.

Table 2.3: Dying Intestate in Quebec

Survived by a spouse with	
children	Spouse receives one-third of the residue. Two-thirds is split among the children.
No spouse	
one or more children	Children or their issue split the residue.
No spouse, children or other issue	One half to parents and one half to brothers and sisters. If there are no parents, then brothers and sisters and nieces and nephews share equally. If no brothers or sisters are living, then nieces and nephews share the residue equally. If no next of kin can be found, the estate goes to the government.

Table 2.4 shows the distribution of an intestate estate in Ontario. We will use this information in the two examples that follow.

Table 2.4: Dying Intestate in Ontario

Survived by a spouse*	
with no children	Spouse receives 100% of the residue.
one child	Spouse receives preferential share (first $200,000) of the residue. If the residue is greater than the preferential share, half the excess goes to the spouse and half to the child.
more than one child	Spouse receives preferential share (first $200,000) plus one-third of the residue over the preferential share. Children share the remaining two-thirds.
No spouse	
one child	Child receives 100% of the residue.
more than one child	Children share the residue equally.
no children	Parents share the residue equally.
No spouse, no children, no parents	Brothers and sisters share the residue equally. If no brothers or sisters are living, then all nieces and nephews share the residue equally. If no distant family can be found, the estate goes to the Ontario government.

*The *Income Tax Act* treats common-law and same-sex partners similarly to married spouses for tax purposes. Under the Ontario *Succession Law Reform Act*, "spouse" currently refers only to married spouses.

EXAMPLE Let's look at what might happen to John and Joan, who lived in Ontario.

John and Joan were married for 20 years and had two children, Robert, 10, and Elizabeth, 19. They had a mortgage-free cottage worth $140,000 that was registered in John's name; $100,000 in life insurance with estate named as the beneficiary; and $200,000 in stocks, bonds, and GICs in John's name. John had always been too busy with business to prepare his will and assumed Joan would receive everything. He thought there was lots of time.

When John died suddenly, his assets were distributed as follows:

His estate valued at $440,000 was distributed according to the intestacy rules of Ontario.

Joan was entitled to the preferential share, the first $200,000 of the estate, and she elected to receive the cottage ($140,000) and $60,000 of the investments.

Of the remaining $240,000 in investments, Joan was entitled to an additional one-third share so she received another $80,000. The children shared the remaining two-thirds, or $160,000. Elizabeth received her $80,000 immediately; the $80,000 for Robert was held by the public trustee to be paid to him when he turned 18.

You may say this distribution is fair because it gives the teenagers money to complete their education and meet other needs. But what if they used it to buy cars and to travel? If John had taken the time to think through his family's needs, would he have put this plan in place for his family? Would he have wanted to involve the public trustee for Robert? Or would he have wanted Joan to have received all the money to use as she saw fit?

So, would dying without a will and having your estate settled according to the provincial formula meet your family's needs? Most people, when they understand what could happen, write a will, or plan to write a will, or start to think about planning to write a will.

Not All Couples are Protected

Common-law partners are not treated the same as married spouses under all legislation.

Common-law partners of the same or opposite sex are not referred to, nor entitled to, receive automatic rights to property under the intestacy rules in most provinces. They may have rights to the matrimonial home or financial support if they were financially dependent on the deceased, depending on provincial family laws.

Intestacy laws focus on relationships by blood or by marriage, although changes are occurring. For example, in Nova Scotia, it is now possible to register a Domestic Partnership Declaration with the province. In Alberta, it is possible to enter a legal relationship referred to as an Adult Interdependent Partner (AIP) and the surviving partner may have partial rights, but not the same rights as a married spouse.

EXAMPLE Tom left his wife, Terri, years ago and after a not-so-secret affair moved in with Mary, who had her own career. Tom and his wife never divorced or legally separated. Tom's will named Terri his executor and the sole beneficiary. What happened on his death? In this case, Terri received everything.

If Tom had actually done some estate planning, he might have handled it differently. But when he first thought about planning, he and Mary had only been living together for a few months and he didn't want to formalize anything until he was sure. Well, time slipped away and he never got around to it and Mary didn't think it was all that important—until his death.

Don't depend on the goodwill of your family or wait for the legislation in your province to be changed. Here are some steps you could take to protect you and your partner now:

1. Prepare wills that clearly state your instructions, such as naming each other as executor and beneficiary.
2. Prepare pre-estate documents naming representatives to make financial and health decisions that clearly state your instructions.
3. Write a co-habitation agreement or prepare a partnership agreement appropriate for your jurisdiction.
4. Name your partner as the beneficiary on RRSPs/RRIFs, life insurance, annuities, and pension plan, where appropriate.
5. Register assets jointly with rights of survivorship, where available.
6. Purchase adequate life insurance with your partner named as beneficiary.
7. Set up a living trust prior to death for added privacy.

DELAYS IN THE DISTRIBUTION OF YOUR ESTATE

With a valid will, your executor receives the authority to act as the administrator of your estate after your death.

Without a will, expect it to take longer for your estate to be distributed to your beneficiaries. No one has the authority to act until the court appoints the administrator to distribute the estate according to the intestate rules. (In some provinces, this person is called a personal representative.) The administrator has powers similar to an executor's and the authority to administer the estate. Generally, the court issues Letters of Administration or a Certificate of Appointment of Estate Trustee Without a Will (similar to Letters Probate—see Chapter 6) to family members in a priority list that starts with your spouse, children, and grandchildren. The person appointed may not be anyone you would have picked, or even the most suitable family member to do the job.

Consider the stress this could place on your family. Your partner would likely suffer from the uncertainty and the wait—both of which can be avoided with a will.

As well, until the administrator is appointed, everything is held in limbo. Look at your own situation and ask yourself, "What would happen to my assets or business if no one had the authority to make decisions and to carry them out for a period of time?"

The Canadian population is growing older and governments are cutting back their services. For those of you who don't bother to write a will, I hope this is one government department that will continue to have enough resources to process all of the paperwork for your family!

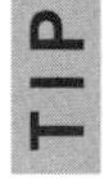

When you change from an RRSP to an RRIF, you must redo your beneficiary designation in writing as the previous designation does not automatically carry forward even if you have not changed financial institutions!

HIGHER COST OF ADMINISTERING YOUR ESTATE

The cost of administering an estate without a will is higher than the cost of administering a similar estate with a will. Additional costs may include:

- legal fees for your family to apply to the courts to have an administrator named
- the cost of posting security or a bond to ensure the assets in the estate are not mismanaged by the administrator; bonding is an expense not normally required for an executor who lives in the province where the will is probated or where a will states this is not necessary; this financial bonding may be obtained through an insurance company (for an annual premium)
- additional legal fees to settle other issues

Writing a proper will is a lot cheaper than the hundreds or thousands of dollars it could cost to settle an estate when there is no will. One lawyer I know will not even estimate the cost of settling an estate when there is no will until he knows the people involved, their issues, and the financial situation of the deceased.

ADDITIONAL INCOME TAXES PAYABLE

Most people merely resent the amount of income taxes they owe while they are alive, but they would be livid if they understood the potential tax bill on death. If you did not prepare a will, then you probably did not look at any estate planning and you could end up paying more taxes on death than necessary.

As discussed, if you have a spouse and children, your spouse does not automatically receive everything. The taxes on assets left to a spouse can be deferred. But any assets with capital gains left to your children in your will are considered "sold" by CRA, and without planning you could lose the ability to defer tax on these assets.

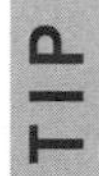

Sometimes, skipping a generation and leaving assets to your grandchildren in trust (such as for their education) can result in a lower overall family income tax bill, but this strategy and many others cannot be accomplished without a will.

LOST INVESTMENT OPPORTUNITIES

Without a will, no one has the legal authority to manage and renew your investments until an administrator is appointed by the courts. In one family, a brother died and a surviving sibling watched the value of shares owned by the deceased drop from $25 to $5 per share over five weeks. No one had the legal authority to step in and issue instructions to sell those shares before the price hit bottom. While there were other assets in the portfolio, only this investment had a significant drop in value. With 1,000 shares of this one stock in the portfolio, this was a loss of $20,000 because no one had the legal authority to issue a sell order or a stop-loss order. The deceased was only 33 and had not yet considered any estate planning.

Once appointed, the personal administrator may have limited investment powers. While there is nothing inherently wrong with these limits, if an investment needs to be sold when market conditions are less than favourable and special court approval needs to be obtained (more fees!), an opportunity may be missed. It also means your administrator cannot consider investments that might otherwise have fit into your investment strategy. With a will, you can give your executor the powers to manage your investments as they see fit.

APPOINTMENT OF GUARDIANS

A guardian is someone who looks after a child until that child reaches the age of majority. Legal documents refer to children as minors, but they are anything but a minor consideration. In fact, providing for children motivates many people to prepare their first will.

If you have children under the age of majority (which differs by province), and die without a spouse and a will, the courts will name a guardian for them. The person appointed by the courts may not be someone you would have wanted to assume this role for your children. However, the public trustee (also called the official guardian or children's lawyer) will consider the recommendations of your relatives.

UNDERAGE BENEFICIARIES

An inheritance paid to a child has to be held in trust for that child (unless the court instructs otherwise) until he or she reaches the age of majority even if you have a spouse. To protect the inheritance, the trustee may be required to report to the public trustee periodically and account for how money was spent and managed on behalf of the children—not something a parent normally has to do. If a large sum of money is involved, the trustee may also be required to post a performance bond for the money.

Alternatively, the assets might be administered by the public trustee of your province.

Minor beneficiaries are entitled to receive their share of the intestate estate when they reach the age of majority. Remember when you were 18? How would you feel about your children receiving a significant sum of money at that age? You may want to ensure that their day-to-day living and education requirements are provided for, but that they do not receive a large sum until they are older (and presumably more mature). Unfortunately, without a will the inheritance cannot be held longer, even if distributing it later better meets the children's needs.

NO PROVISION FOR JOINT DISASTER

Some couples assume that if they own their house and hold all their assets jointly, they do not require a will. But joint registration does not provide any protection if you and your spouse die together in a common disaster.

In some provinces, if spouses die in a common disaster without a will, it is assumed that each spouse predeceased the other. In other provinces, it is assumed that the older spouse is assumed to have predeceased the younger spouse. This could create the situation where all the property of the older spouse ends up in the hands of the family of the younger spouse, which may or may not be appropriate. It can also create additional costs and delays, since it may be necessary to settle one estate before the second one can be settled.

Q. If there is no will, do the courts have to get involved in settling the estate?

A. It depends on the circumstances and the types of assets held in the portfolio. If the value of the estate is small (less than about $20,000) and all the heirs agree, it may be possible to settle the estate without involving the courts or applying for probate. But this does not mean there will be no costs. If all the beneficiaries are competent adults (in the legal sense of the term) and are prepared to sign notarized documents and letters of indemnity, letters of administration may not be required. One small estate consisting of a small RRSP and a bank account involved beneficiaries who were all adults who lived in different provinces. They could not agree on the division of assets. Although the estate itself stayed out of the courts, the dispute ended up costing over $4,500 plus GST in legal fees, much more than the cost of preparing a will!

SUMMARY

The choice is yours. Plan your estate and prepare a will, or use the provincial plain vanilla "one size fits all" version. If your estate is distributed according to the intestate rules, it will likely face more legal fees, lengthy delays, and a higher tax bill, not to mention the additional aggravation to your surviving family. I'd rather have a will (and do!) that distributes my assets as I see fit, gives my executor some flexibility, is tax effective, does not require reporting to the government, and leaves any money for children under 18 to be managed by people who know what is important to me.

Now you know. You do have a choice.

chapter three

distributing your estate with a will

I went to the lawyer, signed my will, and got on the elevator to go home. The elevator got stuck between floors and I was sure that I was going to die then and there because my will had just been prepared. After what seemed like hours, but was really only minutes, the elevator doors opened and I crawled up to the nearest floor. My friend, who was waiting in a car, said I looked like I'd seen a ghost.

—M.

ARE YOU ONE OF THOSE PEOPLE who have put off preparing a will because you feel that writing down your instructions will shorten your life? Contrary to what you may think, writing a will does not result in a premature death! Yet many people find it difficult to think about preparing a will, let alone talk about it.

A will is the cornerstone document of an estate plan and has two main functions. The first function is to name or appoint an executor to administer your estate. The executor, executrix if female, is sometimes called a trustee, personal representative, personal administrator, or, in

Quebec, a liquidator. The second function is to document how the assets of the estate are to be distributed to your beneficiaries. Having a will generally makes settling your estate more straightforward and less expensive than if you die without a will. You are free to leave your assets and property to whomever you wish and exclude certain people from receiving any benefits, subject to family law in your province.

With a will, you can:

- appoint an executor of your choosing to administer and distribute your estate
- assign specific powers to your executor
- specify how you want your estate managed after your death
- decide who gets what
- indicate your choice of guardian for your children
- set up testamentary trusts for young children to hold and manage assets until they are older
- forgive debts owed by family members
- implement strategies to reduce income taxes that would not be possible without a will, and much more

A will is a signed legal document that can be revised and updated as often as necessary as long as you are mentally competent. The instructions in your will come into effect only on your death. Until then, they have no effect.

Q. I've prepared my will and have left my grand piano to my niece. If I move and don't have space for it, can I sell the piano without checking with her?

A. The instructions in your will do not take effect until your death. You are free to sell the piano at any time without your niece's permission. If you do not own the piano when the will takes effect, the instructions regarding the piano will just be ignored. You might also want to consider who you would want to receive the piano if your niece predeceases you.

The following are samples of estate distributions found in the simplest wills.

1. You have a spouse and children. You and your spouse have mirror wills—your will leaves everything to your spouse, and your spouse's will leaves everything to you. If your spouse is not alive at the time of your death, everything that passes into your estate is to be divided equally among your children. If the children are under 18, their education and living expenses will be paid for using money and assets held in the trust until they are 21 or older. Guardians are named in the will.
2. You have a spouse and no children. Your will leaves your estate to your spouse, with the condition that if your spouse predeceases you, your estate will be left to other individuals (they could be family members) or charities named.
3. You have no spouse or children. Your estate is left to individuals or charities of your choice. If any of the individuals named in your will are not alive at the time of your death, you have named an alternative individual or charity.

Even simple instructions may take seven or eight pages to express them in legal jargon! And not all wills are so simple. Depending on the situation, a will can be very lengthy and complicated.

You don't want to have a complicated will when a simple one will do. To paraphase Occam's razor, you don't want to make it more complicated than necessary.

Keep the instructions in your will as simple and straightforward as possible. Even though you might be tempted, don't try to rule your assets or your family "from the grave."

No one can foresee the future. So when planning a will, it's important to consider a number of "what if" life scenarios and ensure your will has the appropriate instructions. But you may also need to revise or prepare a new will down the road. "What ifs" might include:

- What if your spouse predeceases you?
- What if you and your spouse die together?
- What if you have more children?

- What if you and your partner have no plans to formalize your relationship?
- What if one of your children or other beneficiaries predeceases you?
- What if you have children or grandchildren who are under the age of majority at the time of your death?
- What if the main executor is unable to do the job when required?

Preparing a will often requires a fair amount of consideration to determine how you wish to have your estate handled and who will receive what. And a will is only part of an estate plan! Many people tell me they are surprised at the amount of time they spent on thinking about what they wanted to do and planning their estate. My *Estate Planning Workbook*, which can be ordered using the order form at the back of this book, can help you work through many of the points you need to consider. Often the hardest decision(s) are who to name as your executor(s) and guardian(s).

You can do just about anything you want in terms of your bequests, although there are some restrictions and provincial variations. If you are supporting a family member and you do not adequately provide for his or her support and maintenance, they (or if they are a minor, the provincial guardian on their behalf) can apply to the courts for continued support from your estate. In some provinces, spouses are entitled to special consideration. Failing to address these restrictions could overturn some of the provisions in your will.

In many families, one or two children might be considered more financially successful than the others. It may make perfect sense to you to leave the more successful adult child a smaller share of your estate because you want to help out the other adult child. You may want to help out the child who is currently less well off. However, while your children may understand your thought process, they may feel that you have favoured the child who received more. If you are thinking along these lines, remember that the financially successful child might not always be. He or she may suffer a major illness and become incapacitated, or have a child down the road who has special needs.

"Fair" may not always mean "equal." If you feel you need to help out one child more than the other, you might consider doing so in a way that is less public, such as life insurance or a gift outside the will.

On the other hand, if you are estranged from your adult son who does not require the inheritance, you could leave him nothing in your will. However, I suggest you consider carefully before doing this and discuss it with your lawyer. More than one estate has been held up for years, during which none of the beneficiaries received any benefits, because the estranged child did not feel fairly treated in the will.

Q. I do not want to leave my children anything. Can I leave them out of my will?

A. You can't write a will that says, "My spouse and children get nothing." If you try, provincial law may allow those who are financially dependent on you to challenge your will. And those who are left out may look at precedents in your province to see what has been deemed appropriate.

To prepare a will, you must be mentally competent and have reached the age of majority in your province. However, if you are under the age of majority, then you can prepare a will if you are married, a member of the armed forces, or a mariner.

At the time your will is prepared, lawyers and notaries usually make notes regarding your mental competency. This is done by confirming that you know the nature and extent of your assets, understand the legal implications of making a will, know the people or organizations that will benefit under the will, and understand your family situation. In most cases, someone in the advanced stages of Alzheimer's disease or another mentally debilitating condition may not be able to prepare or revise a will.

A lawyer or notary who has doubts about your competency may request that a doctor confirm that you are of sound mind at the time the will is drawn up. If he or she is unable to confirm that you are mentally competent, the lawyer will not be able to prepare your will.

A will that is successfully contested on grounds of incompetency would be ruled invalid. This could result in an intestate estate, or in the estate being settled by a previous will, if one exists.

If someone is mentally competent but death is imminent, it is possible for a lawyer to come to the bedside to document his or her instructions. It may be wise to allow the person to discuss his or her wishes privately with the lawyer to avoid accusations of undue influence from family members, business associates, or friends.

Although much of this book looks at estate planning from your own personal perspective, if you have parents who have not yet prepared their wills, I urge you to help them get to their lawyer. I am not suggesting that you should know the contents of their wills or their estate plan—it can be confidential until after death—but you would like them to have the opportunity to prepare their will and power of attorney documents for financial and health decisions.

WHO GETS WHAT

A person or an organization that benefits under a will is called a "beneficiary." Money or property that a person receives through the instructions in a will is sometimes referred to as a gift, a legacy, or a bequest.

Some people have goals that include building an estate so they can leave significant assets to their beneficiaries. Others feel no need to leave a large estate and intend that their beneficiaries will receive only whatever is left over if they don't "die broke." You get to determine what is appropriate for your situation and fits in with your beliefs.

Your will can deal with the assets and property you own, but it cannot deal with those assets that have other legal ways of being distributed on your death, such as:

- property held jointly with rights of survivorship (registered in more than one name)—not in Quebec.
- business assets that should be dealt with under a shareholders' agreement or buy-sell agreement.
- income from a trust, where the trust agreement states that the income stops on your death. For example, suppose you are receiving

income from a spousal trust that was set up in your late husband's will. The trust might state that on your death any remaining assets are to be distributed to the children from his first marriage.

- assets held in a trust. The trust will indicate how and when these assets are to be distributed.
- assets dealt with under a written marriage contract.

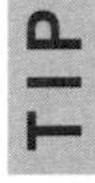

If you are concerned with how much to leave and when, some advisers suggest releasing money over a period of time, starting with relatively smaller amounts when the children are young adults and larger amounts as they get older in the belief that too much too soon can negatively affect an individual's career choices and motivation. Some people also believe that funds for education are key.

Are you a member of a loyalty program where you collect points or miles? Some can be left to your spouse or left in your will. Others could be lost forever.

Q. Our family is of Asian descent. According to tradition, my 80-year-old father has favoured his sons by leaving his estate to them and nothing to my sister, his only daughter. What can be done to ensure his daughter receives a part of the inheritance?

A. An individual can leave his estate to anyone he or she chooses, with a few exceptions. These include providing for a spouse or other dependent family member. However, many Canadians try to treat their children as fairly and equally as possible since doing otherwise without strong reasons can strain family relations for all the survivors. In B.C., some family members have applied to the courts to challenge the will under the *Wills Variations Act* for help in determining what is fair and reasonable even when no support was required.

If you suspect your will might be challenged, you could consider placing your assets in an inter vivos trust while you are alive (see Chapter 12) and having them distributed on your death according to the instructions in the trust agreement rather than your will. Sometimes, talking the situation through with a trusted person can help you determine what you feel in your heart you should do. Then talking to a professional can help you determine how to do it.

Q. I've been left out of my father's will. What can I do about it?

A. Before disputing what's in the will, consult a lawyer in your province. Disputing a will can be an expensive proposition, although there is a trend growing across the country to try to resolve estate issues through mediation. If you were financially dependent on your father, you may be able to make a claim against the estate for support.

Your children and grandchildren may be referred to as your "issue" in a will. In the event that one of your children predeceases you, consider how you would like your estate distributed. Options include leaving the bequest to their children (your grandchildren), allocating their portion to your other children, or naming an alternative beneficiary.

One option is to make the inheritance to your children "in equal shares per stirpes," sometimes called the grandchild clause. Per stirpes means that if a child predeceases you, the gift that would have been theirs would then pass to that child's children (your grandchildren).

A less common method to pass gifts on to the next generation is "in equal shares per capita." Per capita means that the inheritance would be divided equally among those children who are alive at the time of your death and could inadvertently cut some of your grandchildren out of their inheritance because of a technical wording. One couple I met had wills that had used the term "per capita" inadvertently. Oops.

EXAMPLE Let's look at the difference between per stirpes and per capita in a real-life situation.

You have two children who each have two children of their own.

Wording 1:

The will states that $100,000 is to be divided in equal shares "per stirpes." One of your children dies in a car crash before you. On your death, the $100,000 will be distributed as follows:

Child A	$50,000	
Child B	$50,000	is left to B's two children

Wording 2:

The will states that $100,000 is to be divided in equal shares "per capita." One of your children dies in a car crash before you. On your death, the $100,000 will be distributed as follows:

Child A	$100,000	
Child B	$ 0	B's children are not included in this distribution.

If you don't want B's surviving spouse to have access to the grandchildren's money, you could leave the money in a testamentary trust and select a suitable trustee to manage the money.

REDUCING THE COST TO DIE

In addition to who gets what, attention should be paid to the tax implications. How do you keep Canada Revenue Agency (CRA) from getting more than its fair share while adequately addressing the needs of your beneficiaries?

EXAMPLE Mr. Goderich has a wife, 62, who has never worked outside the house, and an adult son. He and his wife own their house jointly free and clear. His only other assets are a $300,000 life insurance policy and a $150,000 RRSP. In order to leave something to his son, he has named the beneficiaries as follows:

On the life insurance policy with a $300,000 death benefit, two-thirds of the death benefit would go to his spouse and one-third to his son.

Initial distribution:	wife	$200,000
	son	$100,000

On the $150,000 RRSP, two-thirds of the value would go to his spouse and one-third to his son.

Resulting distribution:	wife	$100,000	rolled over tax-free into her RRSP
	son	$50,000	initially receives (no withholding tax)

Net After Tax Distribution (option 1)

Total to wife: $300,000

Total to son:	$138,000	$138,000 *less* about $12,000 in tax to CRA on the RRSP since the estate did not have any cash
	$438,000	

If Mr. Goderich wants to leave his son about $150,000 with less tax due, he could designate his beneficiaries as follows:

On the $300,000 life insurance policy, designate that half of the death benefit go to the spouse, half to the son.

Resulting distribution:	wife	$150,000
	son	$150,000

On the $150,000 RRSP, 100% of benefit to spouse.

Resulting distribution:	wife	$150,000	rolled over tax-free into her RRSP

Net After Tax Distribution (option 2)

Total to wife:	$300,000	
Total to son:	$150,000	tax-free insurance death benefit
	$450,000	

The plan minimizes the financial taxes, helps his adult son with his education (his second master's) and hopefully won't leave Mrs. Goderich financially dependent on her son in the future.

Q. What happens if I name a beneficiary in my life insurance policy, but name someone else as the beneficiary of that life insurance policy in my will? Which beneficiary is valid?

A. If the beneficiary in the will was designated after the beneficiary on the life insurance policy, the beneficiary in the will should stand.

MAKING THE GIFT MORE TAX-EFFECTIVE

Rather than leaving all of your assets to your spouse, some income splitting between your spouse and your children could be arranged by setting up a family trust to reduce the overall family tax bill.

EXAMPLE Jack is leaving a $250,000 inheritance outright to his spouse, Sonna. Some of the money will be used to raise and educate his two children, 8 and 10. Sonna will be responsible for paying the income tax on any investment income earned unless some of the inheritance is left in a testamentary trust for the children set up in Jack's will.

Suppose the inheritance could be invested at 5% and earned $12,500 in interest income a year. If Sonna was in the 40% tax income bracket (because of her employment income), the annual tax bill on the family's inheritance would be approximately $5,000.

But what would happen to the family tax bill if the $100,000 was left outright to Sonna and the balance was to be held in a testamentary trust to pay for the children's expenses and education? The overall family tax bill could be lower since the children have little or no other income of their own.

Annual tax bill on inheritance income:

$5,000 income in Sonna's name	(40% tax bracket)	$2,000
$7,500 income earned in the trust		$1,650
Total		$3,650

Now the tax bill is less than if the inheritance was all left outright to Sonna. And if it made sense to leave the entire inheritance in the testamentary trust, even more tax could be saved.

If the income earned in the trust is paid out to the children or on behalf of the children who earn less than the personal exemption (just under $10,000), then the tax bill on the inheritance would be $0, saving the family even more each year.

Is it worth it? Well, there is a hassle factor related to filing an income tax return for the trust and administering the inheritance separately, and there may be trustee fees, but over the years the tax savings could certainly add up. The benefits can become quite creative for testamentary trusts in amounts between $200,000 to about $2 million because they are taxed on graduated rates.

WHAT IS FAIR?

When determining who gets what, there is also the issue of fairness. As I tell my children, fair does not necessarily mean equal. It depends on the individual situation. Just as you may wish to leave to family members specific items that have sentimental value to them, you may wish to leave them bequests of different amounts for certain reasons. There may be special circumstances, but you may want to be discreet because people are people.

But if it is your intention to have each of your children benefit equally from your estate, you need to consider how to manage this on an after-tax basis. People get tripped up trying to be *fair and equal* because they forget to consider the tax rules and that the value of their assets will change over time, due to the financial markets or their spending.

EXAMPLE Suppose you have an adult son and daughter whom you want to receive equal benefits from your estate. You have an RRSP worth $100,000 and GICs worth $100,000. You have named your son as the beneficiary of your RRSP and have left your daughter the residue of your estate in your will. If you were in the 40% marginal tax rate and had other income in the year of death, this is what could have happened. Your son received the full $100,000 of your RRSP since he was named beneficiary and the financial institution was not required to withhold tax; your daughter received the residue of the estate, and the GICs after the taxes had been paid.

	Amount Received by Beneficiary
RRSP left to son	$100,000
GICs left to daughter	$60,000 ($100,000 less $40,000 for the taxes due on the RRSP proceeds)

One way (but not the only way) to deal with this type of situation is to name your estate as the beneficiary of the RRSP (even though this could mean higher probate fees) and in your will leave your son and daughter each 50% of the residue of your estate. In the above example, if the beneficiary of the RRSP was your estate, your son and daughter each would receive about $80,000. Or in real life, share whatever was left.

FORGIVEABLE LOANS?

Has a family member ever borrowed money? Is there a loan outstanding that you want to forgive but still be fair?

Q. I loaned $12,000 to one of my adult sons and want to forgive the outstanding balance on my death. How can this be handled in my will?

A. First, I recommend you have your son sign a promissory note to keep the loan as businesslike as possible. File the note with your important papers. If it is your intention to have your children benefit equally from your estate, you can leave your children equal shares of your estate. After your death, your son with the loan would have his share reduced by the amount of the outstanding balance on the loan.

One man said that when his wife died, everything was left to him. However, his wife had loaned one of their daughters $30,000. When the mother died, the daughter took the unpaid balance as a gift. He was unable to raise the issue of repaying the loan with his daughter. However, five years later, the situation still bothers him. If only she'd said, "Dad, I'll continue making the payments to you now," or at least "Thank you."

Some loans are just that, a loan and that beneficiary's inheritance will be reduced by the outstanding amount of the loan after your death. Other loans that you might extend to a family member while you are alive might really be an advance of their inheritance. This can be clarified by a clause in the will regarding an ademption by advancement which can help ensure the end result is equitable. To simplify things after your death and to avoid family in-fighting, it's best to be very clear about formalizing the paperwork for the loan and what kind of loan you are making right up front, especially if you have more than one child.

Q. What happens if one of my beneficiaries cannot be located?

A. Your estate could be held in limbo. If this could be a potential problem, you might include a clause stating that a beneficiary would be presumed to have predeceased you if they cannot be located within 24 months.

YOUR EXECUTOR

"The qualifications to be a good beneficiary are different from the qualifications to be a good estate trustee." All too true. In some families, a family member can make a good estate executor and trustee. However, a corporate executor (such as a trust company) or a professional executor (such as a legal or accounting firm) may be appropriate where it is important to have an executor who can:

1. act impartially among—or on behalf of beneficiaries—such as where there are children from a first and a second marriage
2. deal with a large or complex estate that requires expertise in dealing with a certain area
3. do the job when there is no appropriate family member or
4. offer some sort of permanence for a trust that might last for many years.
5. you anticipate struggles for control of assets or a business
6. you do not know anyone who has the expertise to be your executor
7. there are assets in multiple jurisdictions, such as Canada and the U.S. or Canada and Mexico, or even assets in different provinces

One function of your will is to appoint an executor who is responsible for managing and distributing your assets according to the instructions in your will—ideally in a way that avoids potential conflicts of interest. The executor has a long list of duties related to the estate and wrapping up the deceased's personal affairs.

People used to consider it an honour to be asked to be an estate trustee or an executor for a friend or family member. Anyone who has ever acted as an executor will confirm that it is a job, and sometimes not a well paid job at that. An executor has to be prepared to write lots of letters and deal with lawyers, CRA, insurance companies, real estate agents, business valuators, former employers, creditors, accountants, beneficiaries, and other interested parties, as well as the deceased's professional advisers.

Responsibilities of the Executor

An executor's responsibilities include the following:

1. Arranging the funeral. Make sure that your family and executor are aware of specific requests or instructions you have regarding your funeral arrangements. You may want to write a letter to your executor stating your wishes. Although oral or written instructions regarding the funeral are not legally binding, your executor will normally follow your wishes. On the practical side, sometimes the instructions are found after the fact and your executor cannot carry them out!
2. Acting as trustee and managing the assets of the estate for the benefit of your beneficiaries. After your death, one of your executor's responsibilities is to locate your assets and property and transfer the ownership from your name to your estate. For example, the ownership of a brokerage account might be re-registered as "The Estate of Joan Smith." If required, your executor must probate the will (see Chapter 6). Ensure that your executor knows the location of your current will, personal inventory, and important papers. The more information you can provide your executor, the better he or she can ensure that all of your assets are found and handled properly.
3. Dealing with government benefit programs, such as CPP/QPP, and obtaining all benefits payable to the estate, such as from current and/or former employers.
4. Settling the bills of the estate, including all legitimate claims by creditors, the funeral bill, and other expenses.
5. Filing the final tax returns for the deceased and the estate on time and ensuring that any income tax owing is paid. Before all the assets of your estate can be distributed, your executor should obtain a clearance certificate from Canada Revenue Agency (CRA) to confirm that all income taxes have been paid.

6. Distributing assets and property to your beneficiaries according to the instructions in your will.

See Appendix 1 for a List of Duties for an Executor or Estate Trustee. Letting your executor know where he or she will find all your personal papers with key contacts, tax files, and financial statements will help them do the job.

Q. I've been named as a beneficiary in a will. When will I receive my inheritance?

A. You, like most beneficiaries, are interested in knowing the value of the inheritance you will receive and when you'll get it. To some degree, it depends on who the beneficiaries and executors are. Technically, the residue of the estate cannot be paid out until:

- all income taxes, funeral costs, debts, and the trustee's fees are paid.
- the clearance certificate has been received from CRA unless the executor wants to be personally liable for any income taxes and penalties that may be due.
- any family law requirements have been met.

One experienced individual told me he spent about 48 hours over six months working as the executor on one estate. There were no family conflicts, but the client's estate consisted of GICs (a large number of them, mind you) and her will included 42 specific bequests.

Family dynamics (should I say disputes?), outstanding financial issues, legal problems, and complex investments all add to the amount of time it takes to settle an estate.

Powers of the Executor

The executor gets his or her power from the will. If the extent of the executor's powers are not specified in a will, they are defined in your province's *Trustee Act*. The powers assigned in the will can be as broad and extensive as appropriate for your situation or as limited as you see fit. Additional powers could include:

- distribute assets, in kind or as is, to beneficiaries (legally called "in specie")
- sell assets and pay cash to beneficiaries
- purchase assets of the estate
- provide some funds to the family before the estate is completely settled
- make a contribution to a spousal RRSP
- authority to pay taxes before the assets of the estate are distributed; if there is income tax due, you may wish to indicate that the residue of your estate be responsible for paying these taxes
- make elections under the *Income Tax Act* that would be beneficial to your estate but are beyond the powers stated in the provincial *Trustee Act*
- decide if and when assets are to be sold
- invest as the executor sees fit. If your executor is a trust company, will you give them the power to invest in their own securities, such as a mortgage they arranged?
- decide which assets, if any, are to be held in a spousal trust
- borrow on behalf of the estate
- consult with or hire professionals, such as accountants, lawyers, professional trustees, or financial advisers, and pay them out of assets in the estate. These professional services can provide necessary advice to protect the interests of the beneficiaries. However, without clearly stating in the will that the executor has the power to hire and pay for these professional services, some beneficiaries may just see such expenses as reducing their inheritance. For example, what happens if five charities are to share the residue equally? If one charity requested/required audited records, but not the other four, would your executor have the authority to hire an accounting firm to prepare the accounts in the "required" format? Or even perhaps the experience to suggest that the other four charities do not demand this administrative requirement?

Sometimes executors are reluctant to hire professionals because they see it as spending the beneficiaries' money. For example, an executor might attempt to sell the house privately to save the estate the real estate commission. Unless the executor is familiar with the local real estate market, this might result only in a lower selling price for the house and no additional profits for the beneficiaries.

Appointing Your Executor

You are allowed to appoint more than one executor (co-executors) if you feel that better decisions would be made by two executors acting together or that the job is too complex for one person. You should also appoint a backup executor in case your first executor predeceases you.

The person you select should be someone you trust completely and who has the financial and business sense to manage and distribute your assets. Someone who has never completed an income tax return may not be the best choice. If your assets include a business, ideally that person should understand the business. It also makes sense to select someone who lives relatively close to where the estate needs to be administered. Also, consider the age and health of your executor; you are looking for someone who will be around when you—or rather your family—needs them.

Your executor may be your spouse, partner, other family member, a professional trustee, or a close friend. If your spouse is the only beneficiary of your estate, it often makes sense for the spouse or partner to be named as executor if he or she is able to manage the responsibilities. If "executor fees" are paid, they can be deducted as an expense on the trust tax return, but the person(s) receiving them would include them as taxable income. A spouse would not normally charge executor fees if he or she was receiving the entire estate, which does not need to be taxed as income. If you do not have a spouse or partner, you might appoint another family member or a close friend.

Your spouse might be entitled to make a claim against your estate under your province's family law. If your spouse is not your only beneficiary under your will, you might consider naming someone other than your spouse as your executor to eliminate the potential for conflict of interest between the role of executor and any spousal entitlement. And, better yet, set up your estate plan in accordance with your province's family laws.

If it is not appropriate to appoint your spouse, you might appoint your children as co-executors. (However, this is not advisable as a technique to try to bring your children closer together.) Before naming your adult children or anyone else as the executors of your estate, consider the following questions:

CONSIDERATIONS WHEN SELECTING AN EXECUTOR

Yes	*No*	*Unsure*	
❒	❒	❒	Are they capable of managing the financial responsibilities of the estate? Look at how they manage their own credit cards and financial affairs.
❒	❒	❒	Are they willing and able to accept the job?
❒	❒	❒	Do they have time to do the job?
❒	❒	❒	Can they handle the responsibilities fairly and objectively?
❒	❒	❒	Do they live in your province?
❒	❒	❒	Do they have the skills to manage investments prudently?
❒	❒	❒	Are the terms regarding compensation agreeable?
❒	❒	❒	Will they be likely to outlive you?
❒	❒	❒	If you are considering having co-executors, do they get along well enough to work together to make the necessary decisions?

If you've answered *No* or *Unsure* to any of these questions, carefully consider if you want to name your children as co-executors. In some cases, it might be better (and easier for everyone involved) to appoint one child as the executor and to leave a note for the other children explaining your reasoning.

It may not be fair to family members to have to deal with a complex estate.

If you are selecting a professional trustee through a financial institution, be sure to obtain independent legal advice from a lawyer not affiliated with that financial institution.

If the professional executor or trust officer handling the estate leaves or cannot continue to do the job for any other reason, the trust company will automatically assign someone else to administer the account.

If you decide to select a professional executor or trustee to manage your estate, here are some important questions to ask:

- What compensation arrangements are available?
- How many accounts does each trust officer handle?
- How many meetings will we have a year, and where?
- Are you experienced in dealing with situations similar to ours?
- What investment strategy/philosophy will be used?
- How does it work if we name a family member as co-executor?
- What types of information will be provided and how often?

Q. My spouse and I each have one child from our previous marriages and one from our own marriage. Whom should I appoint as executor?

A. There is no simple answer. Look at whether the children get along. Are you setting up a spousal trust? How are the assets to be distributed? The greater the family tensions, or the possible family tensions, the more useful a professional trustee may be.

Some people feel that appointing a family member to work with a professional executor might be a good compromise, believing the family member understands the situation and the professional can handle the administrative and legal requirements. If you decide on a co-executor arrangement with a professional executor, you can appoint the primary decision-maker or you could indicate that major decisions are joint and that the professional trustee is responsible for the administration.

Q. We've updated our wills and power of attorney documents. We have two sons in their forties. Our eldest lives in the same province we do and we've made him the executor of the estate. Have we made a mistake by not naming both of them?

A. If you name them for both roles they will both be "in the know." However, it is not always possible or practical to name all one's children to act together because they might not get along or they might live in different provinces where it is impractical for them to work together.

It seems that you are comfortable with your eldest acting as executor for the reason you stated and explain that you would like the other son to be involved in the process as much as possible so there is no misunderstanding or suspicion of the executor's actions—sort of an "open door" policy as much as is legally possible. There is no reason why the executor cannot share his files and actions on an ongoing basis with the other beneficiary. You could also speak to your youngest son and discuss your decision with him. If that is not practical, you may want to write him a letter that explains your reasons, and file it with the will. Have you treated them equally in the distribution of your assets? That's where it really matters!

People often neglect to ask the person, or persons, they have in mind as their executor if they would be willing and able to carry out the duties of the executor. (In the early 1990s, fewer than a third of Canadians who had written a will had discussed its contents with the executor they had named, according to a survey conducted by the Trust Companies Association of Canada.) Not much has changed.

Talk to the person or people you would like to name as executor(s), or have already named, to be sure that they are willing to assume the role. Review with them any special instructions contained in your will and tell them where they'll find what they need.

Q. I have a will that was written in B.C., but I want to appoint my brother who lives in Texas as the executor. Is this a good idea?

A. No. At a minimum, if your executor lives in Texas (or anywhere outside Canada for that matter), the courts may require bonding to be posted, and he or she may find it difficult to settle your estate due to the distance involved. There may also be issues related to the residency of the trust for tax purposes.

If you are asked and have never acted as an executor (and most people haven't), you may not be aware of the responsibilities of the job.

There's a list of the duties of an executor or estate trustee in Appendix I. You may be surprised at the amount of work that the job can entail and to find out that an executor who loses any of the estate's money can be held personally responsible. (If your spouse is the executor and the main beneficiary of your estate, this may not be an issue.)

Before you accept the role of the executor (provided you are still interested), you may want to ask for more details about the will to find out if:

- you will also be named as the guardian and/or trustee for any testamentary trusts for any minor children
- you will also be named as the trustee for any testamentary trusts set up in the will for spendthrift or mentally challenged children
- there are any family issues that could make settling the estate a headache
- you would be granted sufficient executor powers to seek outside legal and/or accounting advice if necessary
- if and how you will be compensated

Just in case your first choice for an executor predeceases you or is unable to do the job when required, you should name a backup or alternate executor. If you don't name an alternate, the estate could end up without an executor and have to go to court to get an administrator appointed, leaving no one to manage your estate until a court appointment.

Q. I was named as my friend's executor when she updated her will last year. And it's been a difficult week. I was diagnosed with ovarian cancer and my friend just passed away. I'm not going to be able carry out the duties as her executor. Now what?

A. First, don't feel guilty. Your first responsibility is to look after your own health. If she had good advice when she drew up her will, she will have named a backup in her will, so don't do any of the duties. The backup will be asked to step forward to carry out the duties of the executor.

SUMMARY

The contents of your will do not need to be disclosed to anyone (other than your lawyer) while you are still alive.

However, I recommend you tell your executor, spouse, and your family where your documents, accounts, and important papers are. While it is not necessary to tell them the details of your financial life, they should know where they can find what they will need to carry out their responsibilities.

In an ideal world, everyone would discuss with their executor and family how their assets are to be distributed, but it is difficult for families to be open, especially when it comes to finances and death. But if you are able to discuss your will and your wishes with your family, they may better understand and appreciate your decisions. At the very minimum, someone in your family and your executor should know your wishes regarding your funeral and organ donation, and where to find your will and your important documents. If the original will cannot be found, then the courts will normally assume you died intestate.

Q. Where should I keep my will?

A. In a safe place. Treat it as the important document that it is and make sure your executor knows where it is. You might leave your will

- with your lawyer (who would hope to assist your family with the administration of your estate)
- in a safety deposit box if someone has the authority to access the box after your death; otherwise the box may be sealed on death, making it difficult to access
- with your other important papers at home, or
- with a trust company if you decided you require a trust company as your professional executor

Keep a photocopy of your will so you can refer to it and review its contents at any time.

As we discussed in Chapter 1, your will is only one way you can distribute assets.

In the next chapter, we will look at the format of the will.

chapter four

the format of a will

Get black on white.
—Guy de Maupassant

A WILL IS A DOCUMENT MADE UP of a number of clauses, like paragraphs, that specify your instructions. Some wills are long, with pages and pages of instructions. Others are only a few pages. The shortest will I've seen was a military will that was just one page and contained only the bare minimum of instructions.

COMMON CLAUSES

Although the format varies from will to will, lawyer to lawyer, from notary to notary, and from province to province, a few common clauses are normally included. Each clause needs to be clear and precise so the instructions can be carried out when the time comes.

The sample wordings in this section are included to help you better understand the purpose of a clause or phrase when you read a will.

Identify the Testator

A will begins by identifying the person preparing the will by the name they use, their proper name, address, and sometimes occupation at the time the will is drafted. Each person requires his or her own will to document his or her own wishes. It is *not* a document that can be shared.

If the will is being prepared in contemplation of marriage and you want to ensure that the marriage does not revoke the will, you may want to state the will was prepared in contemplation of marriage and perhaps that the fiancé(e) will not benefit under the will if the marriage does not take place.

Revoke All Previous Wills

The first clause states that this will is your last will and testament and revokes any previous wills. This clause is included in almost every will as a precaution, even your very first will. If an earlier will happens to be found, only the instructions in the most recent will are followed.

There are situations where some people might have more than one will to reduce the cost of probate: one will for those assets that require probating and another will for those assets that don't. If a multiple will strategy was used, it would be important that this wording does not revoke the other will.

Appoint Your Executor and Trustee

Appointing an executor (executrix if female) and trustee is one of the two main purposes of a will. This clause names your executor(s) and gives him or her the powers you anticipate will be required to manage your estate. In addition to appointing an executor, your will should also name a backup or alternate executor in the event that the first executor is unable or unwilling to perform the duties when required.

Maybe you have been putting off preparing your will because you cannot decide who you can ask to be your executor. Some look to a spouse or other family member, a close friend, or a professional trustee for this important role.

You might have considered asking your financial adviser to be the executor since he or she already knows the details of your financial situation. Even if your financial adviser or planner is willing, he or she may not be able to accept the responsibility. Some firms restrict such arrangements because of the perceived conflict of interest. At other firms, he or she may be able to act as the executor, but may not be able to charge any commissions to the account.

Don't forget to ask anyone you are considering as your executor if he or she would be willing to do the job. It's better to to give them some basic details of your personal and financial situation right upfront so the person can make an informed decision. If he or she declines, it's better to find a replacement sooner rather than later.

If you are appointing more than one person to act together, you may want to consider how they will resolve any disputes that might come up, such as by majority vote.

In some wills, the executor is also named (sometimes by default) as the trustee for any testamentary trusts set up according to the instructions in the will, such as for young children or for a spouse.

Q. My father died a few months ago and my father's executor just died. Now who will settle his estate?

A. The first person asked to replace a named executor would be the backup named in a will. If there is no backup named in your father's will, the courts will look next to the executor's executor—that is, the person named in the executor's will—if the original executor had already taken out probate. Otherwise, your lawyer will ask the courts to appoint someone to take on the responsibilities.

Transfer Property to Estate Trustee

Your assets will be transferred to the estate and managed by the executor and trustee, and ultimately distributed according to your will.

Authorize Your Debts and Taxes to Be Paid

To ensure your executor has the legal authority to pay your debts out of your estate, including funeral bills and income taxes, there is normally a clause in the will to this effect. But if you do not authorize your debts to be paid, don't think you can avoid them; creditors would place claims on the estate to ensure they are paid, delaying the distribution of assets to beneficiaries.

Paying debts normally takes priority over the distribution of assets to beneficiaries, but you may want to offer instructions as to which assets are to be used. For example, if you have a business and a cottage and you want the business to stay intact, you could indicate that proceeds from the sale of the cottage are to be used first to pay the debts.

Specify Who Gets What

Next come clauses specifying who gets what, which may be in the form of a specific gift or bequest, or as part of the residue clause. These are the instructions beneficiaries are most interested in.

Make Any Specific Bequests

A specific bequest in a will gives the beneficiary something outright, such as "I leave my brother, Edward Scott, $10,000" or "I leave $5,000 to charity X." There are many types of bequests, each with a slightly different wording. For example, when you make a bequest of real estate, it is known as "devising a gift."

TYPE OF BEQUEST	SAMPLE WORDING
Gift of a specific sum of money	"I give A the sum of $___."
Gift of a specific asset	"I give B my collection of___."
Contingent gift (dependent on conditions)	"I give ___ to C only if my spouse does not survive me."

A will may contain many specific bequests, or none. If there are no specific bequests, the assets of the estate are distributed according to the residue clause in the will.

When making donations to charity in your will, do not leave the amount to the discretion of your executor. You might state that a specific asset or property be donated, or a specific amount, or use a formula to determine the amount, such as percentage of the residue of your estate. You should also indicate the names of the charities (and their successors).

You should also ensure your wishes can actually be carried out, and "what if" a situation is not as you thought it might be at the time of your death. One testator left $75,000 to his adult daughter to be deposited to her RRSP. His wish was to help with her retirement planning. However, this contribution could not be made because she had no RRSP contribution room when he died. His will did not have a backup plan, such as holding the money in trust or setting up a deferred annuity for her benefit—or even leaving the money to her outright. Instead, some of the money ended up being spent on legal fees.

Distribute the Residue

The residue is that part of the estate remaining after all taxes, debts, fees, and expenses are paid and specific bequests made. To ensure a will deals with all the deceased's assets and property, it should contain a residue clause. In some wills, the entire estate is distributed according to the residue clause. In others, the residue clause distributes only what has not otherwise been distributed.

The clause to distribute the residue might read, "I give A 30% of the residue of my estate and B 70% of the residue" or "I leave my spouse, C, 100% of the residue of my estate." If the residue clause is missing, part of the estate could end up being distributed according to the intestacy rules.

Powers of the Trustee

The estate trustee gets his or her authority and powers from the will. These powers can be as broad and discretionary as your executor needs to deal with your creditors and beneficiaries, and to protect, manage, and distribute the assets of the estate.

Compensating Your Executor

You can specify that your estate trustee can pay himself or herself income and/or capital out of the estate that is reasonable or according to a predetermined formula.

Your executor(s), whether they are family members or professionals, are entitled to receive compensation for their services out of the estate (before the residue is distributed). In Quebec, however, if the liquidator is also a beneficiary, he or she is able to receive compensation for these duties from the estate if it is specifically stated in the will. If some of your beneficiaries are acting as executors, you may want to ensure that they are compensated for the time and effort involved in the responsibilities of performing the executor's job.

If you do not stipulate an amount in your will, the fee amount is established by legislation in some provinces. Executor compensation appears to be around 3–5% of the value of the estate, but to some degree that depends on the time required to administer the estate. The courts have frowned on executors charging fees based solely on the value of the estate without any consideration given to the amount of time and expertise involved. If the amount of the executor fee was not outlined in the will and a beneficiary feels that the executor fees are excessive, he or she can object.

Trust companies have their own minimum fees for administering an estate. These minimums are based on the market value of assets passing through the will. In 2006, one trust company's trustee rate schedule was:

on first $250,000 of the estate	4.75% (with a minimum fee of $5,000)
on next $750,000	4%
on balance over $1 million	3%

If you are hiring a professional trustee, you can ask to see their standard executor fee schedule and perhaps negotiate fees that are appropriate for your estate. For example, a lower fee may be charged for administering a home passing through the estate, or where the trust company currently manages your accounts.

If the principal residence is passing through the will, the executor's fee on the house may be reduced by as much as 2.5% (subject to the minimum fee) especially if much of the value of the estate is concentrated in this one asset. The amount of time and expertise required by the executor needs to be considered.

Additional costs might include the cost to prepare the necessary tax returns and a fee for managing the assets if it is not included as part of the estate administration fee.

If these fees seem high, discuss with the professional trustee what services will be involved. These could include estate planning, preparing the will and a personal inventory, ongoing consultation, as well as administering the estate after death.

Professional trustees, of course, will want their compensation documented in the will.

Q. I expect my estate will be worth about $800,000. How much might a trust company charge to administer my estate?

A. Using the rate schedule on page 58, trustee fees would be approximately:

on first $250,000	$11,875
on next $550,000	$22,000
Total	$33,875

Some professional trustees (and now a few accounting firms) also offer a service to help the executor settle the estate without requiring the trust company to be named as an executor. This can help reduce the costs to the estate and assist the person named as the executor in dealing with the estate.

Funeral Wishes

You can include your funeral instructions in your will, which may not be located until days after your death.

However, the final responsibility for arranging your funeral lies with your executor. If your executor considers your instructions inappropriate, he or she can override your wishes.

ADDITIONAL CLAUSES

Depending on your wishes and family situation, a number of additional clauses can exist in a will. Some lawyers include these as standard clauses.

Appointing a Guardian for Minor Children

A guardian is someone who assumes the responsibility and custody for a child until that child reaches the age of majority. If you are a single parent, or in the event you and your spouse are killed in a common disaster, you should appoint a guardian for your children. And hopefully that person will never be called on to do the job.

The guardian you name in your will is often granted temporary guardianship of your children. It is assumed you are recommending that person. Although the court is not legally required to appoint the guardian you name, it generally does unless there is a valid reason not to. To obtain permanent legal custody, the guardian must apply to the courts. If your children are old enough to express their opinion, the courts may ask for their input before making a final decision.

If you have strong wishes as to who you would like to be appointed as guardian for your children, or who you would not want to be appointed, you may want to put it in writing and state your reasons. It could help the court make a decision in the best interests of your children.

Q. The guardian I appointed has died and now my will needs to be updated. Can I just write in the name of the new guardian?

A. No. Even though writing on a will does not invalidate the will, it does not update your will. Better to prepare a codicil to document the change and have it properly signed and witnessed.

Discuss your needs with the person you want to appoint as guardian to ensure that he or she is willing to take on this responsibility. If you have numerous children of various ages, you may want to consider if it is practical for them to stay together. You may also want to give the guardian a lump sum of money in your will as a token that you appreciate that he or she has taken on this role on your behalf. Raising one's own children is difficult; raising someone else's is noble.

Ask yourself these questions when you are selecting your children's guardian.

QUESTIONS TO CONSIDER WHEN SELECTING A GUARDIAN FOR YOUR CHILDREN

Yes	*No*	*Unsure*	
❒	❒	❒	Is the person someone your children would want to live with?
❒	❒	❒	Is the person willing to assume the responsibilities as the guardian of your children?
❒	❒	❒	Can the person afford to raise and support your children?
❒	❒	❒	Should this guardian also be named as the trustee for the children's inheritance?
❒	❒	❒	Does your will provide financial support for the children while they are in the guardian's care?

Any *No* or *Unsure* answers require special attention.

From time to time, check with the guardian or guardians appointed in your will to ensure they continue to be willing and able to take on the responsibility.

Managing Assets for Minor Children

Assets left to underage children should be held in trust until they reach the age of majority. If you have young children, you will need a clause naming a trustee to manage those assets on their behalf. If you don't, the public trustee is required to step in until the children reach the age of majority. If the children's guardian or surviving parent needs money for the children's benefit, a formal application has to be made to the public trustee. Government agencies have not been known for their quick responses to requests for funds.

If you do not want children (or grandchildren) to receive money or assets as early as age 18 or 19, you can have wording in the testamentary trust set up in your will to restrict payment until they are older and, presumably, more mature. Some parents restrict a lump-sum payment until the children reach 23 or 25, with access to the funds earlier for education expenses. (See Chapter 12 on trusts.)

Q. Can my children's guardian and the trustee of my children's money be the same person?

A. Yes. However, if a large amount of money is involved, there could be a perceived conflict of interest in managing the assets on behalf of the children's needs versus the guardian's own needs.

Common Disaster Clause

One of the "what ifs" to consider when writing a will is what happens if you and your spouse are killed in a joint disaster. Lawyers usually add a survivorship clause describing how your estate is to be distributed in the event that you and your spouse die simultaneously (this is usually defined as within a certain number of days of each other).

In some provinces, it is assumed the younger spouse outlives the older spouse. In other provinces, the distribution is based on who died last, unless your will states otherwise. If it is determined that your spouse survived you, then all your assets and your spouse's assets would go to your spouse's family; if you survived your spouse, all the assets would go to your family. To benefit both families equally in the event of a common disaster, you and your spouse could each document in your wills that half of the assets are to go to your family and half to your spouse's family. This clause could also eliminate the need to probate the same assets twice in a short time, saving probate taxes.

Alternatively, the will might state that your spouse must survive you by at least 30 days (or some other period of time) before that beneficiary can receive any benefit from the estate. Such wording also ensures probate does not have to be obtained twice in a very short period of time.

Another "what if" to consider is what if your entire immediate family dies in a car crash? Some people add a charitable bequest so the money goes to charity rather than distant relatives, in the event of this type of common disaster.

Investment Powers of the Executor

If your will does not specify your executor's powers relating to the investments in the estate, the executor's investment powers are defined by provincial trust legislation.

Some provinces have modernized their investment rules and require the trustee to meet the "prudent investor standard of care." Other provinces provide a list of allowed investments.

Prudent Investor Standard of Care

In provinces that have modernized their trustee acts, the executor is to follow the "prudent investor standard of care" when making investment decisions. That is, the level of care a prudent investor would take when managing money.

The investments must take into account factors including:

- general economic conditions
- the effect of inflation or deflation
- tax consequences of the investment strategy
- returns expected in terms of income and capital appreciation
- the purpose of any special asset in the trust
- the need for liquidity, income, and/or the preservation of capital

As an individual investor, you might have an investment policy statement with your investment adviser for your personal investment account, which outlines the above information.

List of Allowed Investments

Some testators prefer to follow the list of allowable investments, which includes:

- federal, provincial government, and municipal securities
- first mortgages for real estate in Canada
- guaranteed investment certificates of any trust company or bank
- bank deposits and term deposits in a credit union

- certain corporate bonds where the corporation has paid a dividend
- certain corporate shares (preferred and common) where the dividend payment meets the minimum requirement.

In some provinces, no corporate shares or corporate bonds are allowed.

Sometimes these investments are discussed in terms of restricted, or safe, investments versus unrestricted investments. The list of investments was designed to restrict an executor from taking unnecessary risks with the money held in trust. But safe doesn't mean the same things to all people, and in some cases it could mean settling for investments that produce lower returns. But if the assets are in the estate for only a short period of time, this may not be a major concern.

In today's world, you might want to give your executor a broader range of allowable investments, or unrestricted investment powers. If your executor has minimal investment experience, the more conservative route may work best unless the executor will be working with an experienced professional. But if your executor is comfortable dealing with money and you trust him or her not to speculate on some wild, get-rich-quick scheme, you may want to work within the prudent standard of care.

When in Quebec

In Quebec, the trustee may have simple administrative powers, the powers to perform what is necessary to preserve the property, or full administrative powers to not only preserve but to potentially increase the value of the assets in the trust.

The Quebec estate administrator can decide which investments to make, according to the "yield and anticipated capital gains as suggested by prevailing economic conditions," as stated in the *Quebec Civil Code*. The following are some of the investments the administrator can hold in Quebec:

- federal, provincial, and municipal government securities
- some corporate debt
- title in real estate

- no more than 5% of the trust can be held in the common and preferred shares of one company
- shares or units in a mutual fund or private trust, provided 60% of the portfolio consists of "presumed sound investments"

Mutual funds and pooled funds are not expressly mentioned in some provincial trustee legislation. If you want your executor or trustee to hold mutual or pooled funds in an estate, you may need to explicitly authorize the use of these in your will. If you have concerns about the risks of certain types of investments, you could indicate those types (such as investments in specialty areas such as India or gold) you might not want held in your estate.

In my own will, I want my executor and trustee to be able to follow an investment strategy that will provide the greatest benefit to my beneficiaries for both the short-term, as well as their long-term needs.

Alternate Beneficiary for Life Insurance

If you have life insurance, you may wish to include a clause in your will naming an alternate or contingent beneficiary for your policies just in case the primary beneficiary predeceases you. For example, in the event your spouse dies before you, you may want to name your children, a charity, or your estate as the alternate.

You can also appoint a backup or contingent beneficiary for your life insurance policy, and file it with your life insurance company. On your death, the life insurance policy would then be distributed outside your will.

The insurance proceeds can also be placed in a separate testamentary trust (often referred to as an insurance trust). Your lawyer will draft the insurance declaration with the details of this trust and confirm if you should register it with the insurance company.

Name a Beneficiary for RRSPs and RRIFs

In your will, you can name a beneficiary or multiple beneficiaries for your RRSP or RRIF overriding a beneficiary designated at a financial institution. In Quebec, your RRSP designations must be made in your will.

Q. Does naming any beneficiary on an RRSP or RRIF allow them to receive it without having to pay any tax?

A. Naming or designating a beneficiary helps to ensure the asset goes to the person you selected. If the beneficiary is your spouse or partner, the RRSP can be rolled over to them tax-free. While any other named beneficiary can receive the value of the RRSP or RRIF, naming a beneficiary does not eliminate the tax problem. If there is not enough money in the estate to pay the taxes from the RRSP/RRIF, the beneficiary is also (jointly and severally) responsible for those taxes.

Many people assume they should name their spouse or partner as the beneficiary of their RRSP or RRIF. This may very well be true, but not in all situations. Some people have capital losses or are planning on making charitable donations and may not need the tax sheltering available by rolling an RRSP or RRIF by naming a spouse. In these types of situations, it's definitely better to integrate your tax situation with your estate plan and 1) put some additional clauses in your will 2) update your will and beneficiary designations more frequently; or both.

Establishing Testamentary Trusts

Testamentary trusts can be set up after death according to instructions in the will. They can be used to manage assets for minor children and other beneficiaries, split income, or save some income tax. The will defines the powers of the trustee, how the testamentary trust is to be managed, and when the assets are distributed. (For a discussion of testamentary trusts, see Chapter 12.)

Helping Your Children Protect Their Inheritance

Let's assume the purpose of your estate plan is to preserve your assets for the succeeding generations in your family. In the event your son or daughter divorces, what can you do to ensure any inheritance will go to your grandchildren and not to your child's ex-spouse?

In most provinces, an inheritance is not considered family property—that is, assets and property divided on divorce. In Quebec, gifts and inheritances are excluded from the family patrimony. In Ontario, the will can include wording to exclude any growth or income resulting from an inheritance from being considered family property. Alternatively, you could set up a testamentary trust. (See Chapter 10 on family law and Chapter 12 on trusts.)

And don't forget, one way your adult children can protect their inheritance is to prepare their own wills.

The clearer the wording in your will, the more likely your estate can be settled and distributed smoothly and without delay.

HANDWRITTEN, SOFTWARE-BASED OR FORMAL WILLS

Wills can be handwritten (called a holograph will). They can also be completed using a preprinted form (in most provinces) or a software program. In addition, they can be drawn up by a lawyer (or a notary in Quebec and British Columbia).

In 1948, Cecil George Harris was working on his Saskatchewan farm when he was pinned under his tractor. Before he died, he scratched in the red fender of the tractor the words, "In case I die in this mess, I leave all to my wife," and signed it. The courts upheld this as a valid will. (If you'd like to see this fender will, you'll find it in Saskatoon, like I did, in the University of Saskatchewan Law Library.)

Where a holograph will is recognized, the entire will is written in your own handwriting and signed, at the end, by you. No witnesses are required. But because no witnesses are required, a holograph will could be contested on grounds of incompetency and charges of undue influence by another person. It could be necessary for your executor to prove the will is in your handwriting. Legal wording, clauses, and appointments routinely found in a formal will may be absent or incomplete, leaving a handwritten will open to interpretation and legal challenges.

Do-it-yourself forms and software programs are not recognized in all provinces. Caution is required to ensure the will is complete, reflects your wishes, and contains all the relevant clauses because they do not usually include planning tools such as spousal trusts. However, an estate plan is more than a will and having a will is not the same as having an overall review of your estate. Since this type of will is not written entirely in your own handwriting, formal witnessing is required.

A formal will is normally drawn up by a lawyer or notary who is providing you with legal advice. If a lawyer or notary is advising and preparing wills for you and your spouse or partner, he or she will expect that you both will be open and not keep any information secret from the other. If you need to keep any information confidential or secret, you will likely need to see your own lawyer.

When you pay a lawyer to prepare your will, he or she will meet with you, discuss your needs and take your instructions to prepare the will containing the appropriate clauses. You should be receiving personalized legal advice. He or she would then explain each paragraph of your will. You would then sign the will in front of the witnesses.

I always recommend a formal will to ensure that the wording and the provisions in the will are complete and valid. It is an unfortunate fact of life that our laws are getting more and more complicated. You do not want your will to be contested on a technical detail or have it, or parts of it, invalidated and any part of your estate distributed as if you had died without a will! A badly prepared will could lead to an expensive court dispute by your beneficiaries, which will cost more than preparing a formal will.

The more detailed your situation and complex the instructions in your will need to be, the more it will cost to prepare. But the cost of preparing the documents for an uncomplicated estate ranges from $500 and up plus HST/GST. If you are having a will prepared for yourself and your spouse at the same time, the fee would be about twice that. I hope *You Can't Take It With You* will help you make the most of the time you spend with a lawyer.

Q. What can I expect if I see a lawyer to prepare my will?

A. You can expect to meet with the lawyer to discuss your situation and requirements. To properly advise you, your lawyer will need to know your family situation, what you own, how the ownership is registered, where it is, how much it is worth, and how much it cost. The will is then drafted and revised if necessary. There will be a final meeting to review the wording of the will and to formally sign the will in front of the witnesses. As well, your power of attorney documents will be discussed and signed. The more complex your situation, the more time and expense involved.

SIGNING FORMALITIES

A formal will is signed and witnessed in the presence of two competent adults. The witnesses should not be anyone named as a beneficiary in the will or the spouse/partner of a beneficiary named in the will. Any gift made under the will to a beneficiary who witnessed the will is likely to be ignored since there is a concern they might have unduly influenced the testator.

If the person making the will is blind or cannot read, the person can still prepare and sign a will. The lawyer or notary will sign a special statement referring to the individual's limitations and that he or she appeared to have understood the document when it was explained.

Some lawyers will prepare an affidavit of execution at the time the will is signed, certifying that the witnessing of the will followed proper procedure. Then somewhere down the road, your executor will not have to locate the witnesses to confirm they witnessed the will being signed—saving time and expense.

In some provinces, such as British Columbia and Quebec, you can register your will and while not required, it can help locate it after your death. In British Columbia, you can file a will notice with the B.C. Vital Statistics Agency, which includes the date and location of the will. In Quebec, your notary can register the fact that your will exists in the Register of Wills of the Chambre des notaires.

KEEPING YOUR WILL UP TO DATE

Having a will is important. It is also important to keep your will current so your instructions are up to date. I've not seen any statistics that tell me how many wills are currently up to date, but from the wills I have seen, many do not reflect changes in family situations, changes in legislation, and even just what people want to have happen. The future does change.

I was stunned by a will I once saw. The individual had literally taken scissors and "cut" his financially dependent son out of his will. In fact, it was this father's exasperation with his son and his freeloading that had resulted in the act with the scissors. Now, I know what cutting someone out of your will means, but I had never seen it done so dramatically! Using scissors is not an appropriate way to change a will.

You can update or change the instructions in a will in one of two ways: 1) prepare an entirely new will or 2) amend your will using a "codicil." A codicil is a formal amendment that is attached to the will and requires the same number of witnesses as the will.

It used to be cheaper to prepare a codicil than an entirely new will, but ask your lawyer. You may be surprised to find that in some circumstances, there is not much of a cost difference.

To update your will, do not write on it. While it may seem simple, for example, to cross out one name and replace it with another, this can invalidate that clause in your will.

Q. How do I know if I should use a codicil or prepare a completely new will?

A. As a rule of thumb, you would want a new will if:

- a codicil might make your instructions complicated or unclear
- you've moved to a new province
- you're making major changes to the way your assets are to be distributed and you don't want to leave a paper trail of the history of the changes you have made to your original will and codicil(s)
- using a codicil might create some confusion or ambiguity

Once the new will is prepared, signed, and witnessed, old wills should be destroyed to ensure that your estate is not mistakenly settled with the wrong will. This has happened! In one instance, an executor had an original will and settled the estate on that basis, unaware that a newer will existed.

Don't destroy an old will until the replacement is signed and witnessed! If you die in between, you die intestate.

Reviewing your will periodically is not just an exercise in morbidity or a way to provide your lawyer with more fees. From time to time, review the contents of your will to ensure that it still documents your intentions and reflects current legislation, and that all named parties (executor, guardians, trustees) are still willing and able to perform those duties. Circumstances change. Family members come and go; you could marry, be widowed, divorce, start a family, or move, to name a few scenarios. Even the name of your charity of choice may have changed through a merger or closing.

SUMMARY

Preparing a formal will means you don't have to worry about scribbling a handwritten note and calling it a will just before you leave for a vacation or a business trip.

chapter five

giving away your estate now

A gift much expected is paid, not given.
—*George Herbert*

WE CAN'T ALL BE BILL GATES, Warren Buffett, Wolf and Joseph Lebovic, or Li Ka Shing and donate millions to philanthropy. We often overlook our own major donors in Canada, and I expect with the changes in the way charitable gifts are now taxed, we will see even more gifts. But large or small, the gifts we make while we are alive represent both our abilities and our value system. In Chapter 14, we'll be discussing charitable gifts.

In this chapter we'll be primarily considering gifts to family.

Family members often ask me if they should be concerned if their elderly parent or adult child might be behaving in a way that is too generous for their own good. They may ask me for a second opinion or to review a situation when someone might be considering giving away some assets to reduce probate tax and simplify settling their estate.

My view is that your first obligation is to be sure you have enough money for your own needs. No one should give away so much that he or she ends up living in poverty or becomes dependent on others.

You need to determine what you need and also set aside an additional cushion for your peace of mind.

Different people have different goals. Some want to leave as large an estate as possible; others have no such goals or, perhaps, want to leave only what is left over.

The strategies discussed in this chapter are not appropriate for everyone. Some may make sense for mature individuals who are sure they do not require all the assets they have accumulated, even if they live to be 100. Some of the gifting strategies are more appropriate if completed closer to the time of death.

As well, gifting assets should be done with professional advice to be sure you don't trip up over any income attribution rules or give away too much.

ADVANTAGES AND DISADVANTAGES TO GIFTING WHILE ALIVE

There can be some advantages to giving away some of your estate while you are alive.

- Probate taxes and fees may be lower.
- Executor fees, when based on the size of your estate, may be lower.
- Charitable gifts create non-refundable tax credits that can be used to reduce your current taxes now and for up to five subsequent tax years.
- Your future income taxes may be lower.
- Gifts made outside your will have privacy not offered by a probated will.
- Your family might even squabble less after your death if you have already exercised some of your wishes!
- You may take comfort from the feeling that you have put your affairs in order.
- You can (hopefully) see those people or charities appreciating your generosity.

You may want to discuss with the recipient any hopes you have for how the gift will be used. It is sad when I see someone disappointed because the person who received the gift did not use it exactly the way it was intended—sometimes just because of a misunderstanding—or because he or she didn't call a little more often. Sometimes they discovered that person's true nature after the gift was made or gave it to someone who was reckless with the gift.

It's not always easy for the person who receives the gift either. By accepting a gift, he or she may feel an obligation that is not the same as love.

There are four main disadvantages to giving assets away during your lifetime:

- You give up exclusive control over the asset or property, which may be a significant concern if it is a home, business, or cottage.
- If the "gift" has increased in value since you acquired it, Canada Revenue Agency (CRA) may consider that you have "sold" the asset at fair market value. This capital gain needs to be reported on your tax return in the year you made the gift and could increase your income tax that year (unless you gave the gift to your spouse).
- You may continue to be responsible for the taxes on any income earned on the asset under CRA's attribution rules.
- If you give away too much too soon, you may become financially dependent on others, such as your family or social assistance.

In some families, there may be a favourite son or a favourite daughter. And although a gift is not discussed with the other siblings, it would be a mistake for anyone to assume they are not aware of the gift. For example, in one family, one daughter suddenly had the funds to make a down payment on a house when only a month ago she had mentioned that there was no money available. Family members, especially siblings, are able to put two and two together and figure out what is going on. If there is a true need, people understand, but if it comes down to favouritism, that is another matter.

Now I'm not suggesting that you should or should not give away some of your money or assets. You must first assess your requirements for now and in the future.

To give assets, cash, or property, you must be mentally competent and give the gift without any strings attached. It is not considered a gift if you say, "I will give you $25,000 when you get married."

If there is any question of your mental competency at the time of the gift, the gift itself may be challenged—most likely by those who did not benefit from the gift. And, from a technical perspective, a gift is not complete until the ownership is legally changed, the item delivered, or the cheque is cashed—it just depends on the type of item that is being gifted.

So assuming it is appropriate in your situation, what do you give, and to whom? Maybe nothing at all. The choice is yours, with a few exceptions. You cannot give away your family home or property that belongs to your spouse without his or her consent. People have wanted to make gifts to family members, friends, or charity. You may be interested in helping your child or grandchild purchase a first home, start a business, pay for an education, or pay off some debts. In some situations, close family members become concerned when a family member makes a gift to someone he or she has known for only a short time or when they suspect he or she may be the victim of some sort of scam.

CRA has income attribution rules that might require you to pay the tax on any income earned by the gift, as if you still owned it! Table 5.1 summarizes the income attribution rules. Some types of income are exempt, depending on who receives the gift. These rules are in place so people continue to pay their "fair" share of income tax. Now this is not as bad as it sounds. Say you give your adult child some money for a down payment for his or her first house. There is no taxable income. However, suppose you give your 12-year-old grandchild $25,000 in Canada Savings Bonds. The effect of the attribution rules is that you would report the future interest on the bonds while you are alive until your grandchild was 18. However, after your death, the attribution rules no longer apply.

Table 5.1: Attribution Rules for Gifts to Immediate Family

GIFT GIVEN TO	TYPE OF INCOME EARNED	PERSON RESPONSIBLE FOR TAX ON INCOME
spouse*	Interest	You
	Dividend	You
	Capital gains	You
trust for a spouse	Interest	You
	Dividend	You
	Capital gains	You
child under 18**	Interest	You
	Dividend	You
	Capital gains	Child
grandchild under 18**	Interest	You
	Dividend	You
	Capital gains	Grandchild
child over 18**	Interest	Child
	Dividend	Child
	Capital gains	Child
grandchild over 18**	Interest	Grandchild
	Dividend	Grandchild
	Capital gains	Grandchild

* *includes common-law partner*

** *until child/grandchild turns 18*

GIVING AWAY PERSONAL POSSESSIONS

Some people mark all the personal items in their home with masking tape, such as on the bottom of each vase and piece of furniture, showing the name of the person who will ultimately receive it. Masking tape labels can and have been switched (sometimes by visiting young grandchildren who think it's a great game!) To ensure each item is given to the intended person, you could give it directly to the person while you are alive, include an itemized list in your will, or attach a letter to your will listing each item and who is to receive it. Some lawyers include a clause in the will stating that you are providing a letter or memorandum to assist your executor with distributing personal items. Then, if your plans change, you can update the letter or memorandum without having to redo your entire will.

Family members often squabble over items, however small, that they would have liked to have had or feel they should have had. Granted, it is hard to assess your children's true feelings, but it may be helpful to future family relationships if you note carefully who you want to have what. You might think, "If they are going to be so petty, then they deserve what follows." But if you understand that stress can bring out the worst in people, your planning may lead the way and perhaps help them get through it, with as much of the family relationships intact as possible.

Don't be surprised if some people are reluctant to accept a gift from you while you are alive. They may feel that it is premature to accept or even a bit morbid. They may not even be willing or as prepared as you are.

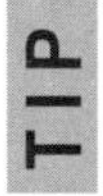

If you are offered a gift and are uncomfortable with accepting it, consider that this person may be putting his or her life in order and preparing to accept death. If you understand that the person really wants you to have the gift, perhaps you can accept it graciously.

GIVING TO YOUR ADULT CHILDREN

It's difficult for some adult children to get a solid footing in today's world. But I wonder if it's all that different now than for previous generations. Parents and grandparents can help out tax effectively. Here are a few ways.

If you give cash to an adult child, you may also have reduced your future income taxes because you will no longer earn income on that money. Your adult child will be responsible for reporting any future investment income and paying the related income tax.

EXAMPLE Bob has $100,000 that earns 4% or $4,000 in interest each year. Assuming he is in the 40% tax bracket, he would pay about $1,600 in tax.

Suppose Bob gives Sarah, his adult granddaughter, that $100,000. If she now earns $4,000 in interest a year, she (not Bob) is now paying the tax (because he no longer has the $100,000) at presumably a lower tax rate. Alternatively, if she put the $100,000 down for a home, any increase in value would not be taxable.

Does the young adult have RRSP contribution room? If they've been filing tax returns for their part-time jobs, they accumulate RRSP contribution room when they start to report earned income. If so, a cash gift could be contributed to an RRSP and provide years of tax-free growth on investments inside the registered plan. When appropriate, the receipt can be used to claim a tax deduction.

If you give an adult child or grandchild real estate (such as a cottage), mutual funds, stocks, or any asset other than cash, CRA assumes or deems that you sold the asset at fair market value, even if no money changed hands. If it has increased in value, there could be a taxable capital gain that you would be required to report on your income tax return in that year.

Be very careful about giving just to reduce income or probate taxes. I have seen a few people give to their children so generously that because of an unforeseen turn of events their spouses end up destitute. And just ask a lawyer. They have stories of people who put their cottage property into joint ownership with one or more of their children, only to have major problems down the road when a child later divorced or declared bankruptcy.

A Loan Versus an Outright Gift

Let's say you would like to give your adult grandchild money now rather than later. Maybe you want to help him or her purchase a home, but you are concerned about the stability of the marriage, or you just don't want to give the money outright. You could consider lending the money and securing the loan by taking back a mortgage on his or her house. This strategy would allow you to *both* help out the child and protect your estate. When the money is used to buy a principal residence, there is no income attribution, and you could forgive the loan at a future date if you want to.

However, if you made the loan in an attempt to split income among family members and the money was used to make investments, the income earned by those investments can be attributed back to you.

If your intention is to make a significant gift to your adult son or daughter and you can afford it, but you have concerns about what the future might hold, you could consider having a lawyer draw up a contract that would obligate your child to provide you with some financial support in the future if you require it.

GIFTS TO YOUNG CHILDREN

If a gift given to a minor child or grandchild earns capital gains income, that income is not attributed back to you and the child is responsible for reporting the investment income on his or her tax return at a (presumably) lower tax rate.

But even if you use an informal trust account to give money to a child or grandchild who is under 18, you are responsible for reporting any interest or dividends earned and paying income tax on them, earned under the attribution rules. But any income earned on the income from the gift (sometimes called second-tier income) is not attributed back to you, even if the gift originally earned interest or dividend income. This provides interesting tax planning opportunities.

EXAMPLE You gift your five-year-old granddaughter $10,000 to be invested in regular Canada Savings Bonds earning 3% in the first year. Under the attribution rules, you are responsible for the income tax due on the $300 of interest earned in year 1. But then you take the $300 interest and use it to purchase an additional $300 in CSBs in your granddaughter's name. In year 2, you are responsible for the income tax on the interest earned on the original $10,000, but your granddaughter is responsible for the tax on the interest earned on her $300 worth of CSBs. Assuming the interest rate was still 3% and she had no other income, this would save $3.60 in income tax.

Is it worth it? Remember it adds up over time. The amount saved will depend on the number of grandchildren you have and the money you have available. If you have the discipline to move the income each year to the separate account for the children (and maintain a proper paper trail), this is currently a legal way to lower your family's overall tax bill.

If you are in a high tax bracket and dislike paying income taxes, this technique may be easier than earning an equivalent amount of after-tax income! After all, lowering the family tax bill is one way to preserve your estate for the next generation.

A Registered Education Savings Plan (RESP) is also a tax-effective way to provide money for a child or grandchild to finance their post-secondary education. They can be set up for an individual or for a family. If there is more than one child in the family, consider setting up a family RESP rather than an individual RESP.

For any one beneficiary, the annual limit is $4,000 and the lifetime contribution limit is $42,000. The first $2,000 per child is eligible for a grant of 20% (up to $400 a year) for children living in Canada. The child requires a Social Insurance Number (SIN), which can be obtained through your local Human Resources Development Canada office.

Q. My father is now a resident of Florida. He wants to give my three children each $10,000 for their education. Does he have to pay income tax on the interest earned?

A. No. Attribution rules do not apply to gifts received from relatives who are not residents of Canada.

While RESP contributions are not tax deductible, the earnings in the plan grow tax-free. If the child or related beneficiary does not go on in their studies (and the range of eligible institutions and programs is broader than many people think and worth exploring as a method of gifting), the contributions can be withdrawn tax-free and up to $40,000 of the income can transferred to the RRSP of the contributor, provided he or she has unused RRSP contribution room. If the RESP has not been in place for 10 years, any amount that cannot be transferred to the contributor's RRSP is treated as regular taxable income in the year of the withdrawal and charged a 20% tax penalty.

Consider who should be named as the subscriber of an RESP for a grandchild. If the child(ren) do not want to continue their studies, you may no longer be eligible to have an RRSP (if you are over 69). In some families, if it is possible, consider gifting money to the child's parent to set up the RESP as the subscriber of the plan.

In addition to setting up an in-trust account for children, or using the Registered Education Savings Plan (RESP), you might also consider life insurance to save for their education. Some insurance companies have policies that are specifically designed to help save for education, with the added feature that if a parent or grandparent should die prematurely, the life insurance side of the policy would ensure the plan was paid in full.

SUMMARY

There can be some distinct advantages to giving away some of your assets while you are alive. But when I ask most clients why they saved the money they have, they admit it was for their own retirement. You owe it to yourself to make sure any gifts will not negatively affect your own financial security.

chapter six

probate

That that is is.
—William Shakespeare, Twelth Night

ON YOUR DEATH, YOUR EXECUTOR steps in to do the job and gets their authority from your will. Until then, your executor and estate trustee does not have any powers over your assets. If any decisions have to be made while you are alive and you are not able to make them for yourself, the person(s) named in your power of attorney documents have the authority to make them until your death.

And the executor's job is a job. He or she has to determine if your will must be probated—that is, if court certification or approval is required—to settle the estate and transfer the ownership of your assets. With a probated will, financial institutions can be certain that your executor has the legal authority to act on behalf of the estate. In other words, if a bank or trust company takes instructions from the executor (once probate has been obtained), the financial institution cannot be held responsible if the executor's instructions were wrong.

Until the will is probated, the assets of the estate are effectively "frozen." However, the executor can ask each financial institution what options he or she has that could help preserve the value of the accounts.

The executor will be dealing and corresponding with the Canada Revenue Agency (CRA), Minister of Revenue of Quebec (for Quebec residents), representatives from the Canada or Quebec Pension Plan, lawyers, former employers, accountants, creditors, business valuators, and other interested parties.

Probating the will is generally required if any third party requires court certification before it carries out any of the executor's instructions regarding the estate assets. These assets include:

- assets at a financial institution
- real estate registered at a land registry office
- shares in a public company, or when shares in a private company are sold to someone outside the company

Probate is also unavoidable if your executor needs to sue someone to settle the estate.

Probate involves submitting the original will with an accounting of the total value of the estate or, in some provinces, with an inventory of the assets in the estate and the completed application forms to the courts in the jurisdiction where you last lived.

If your executor, spouse, another family member, or lawyer knows the location of the will, it can usually be found quickly after your death. But occasionally a will is not located and read for weeks because no one knew where to find it.

Your lawyer might have the original will and invite the family in for a reading, but mostly this is a scene from a Hollywood movie.

If you live in a province that maintains a registry of wills, such as Quebec and B.C., the executor may be required to conduct a search for a notice regarding the location of the most recent will.

If the executor already has all of the assets in his or her possession, such as a spouse might, and does not need to deal with any third parties (such as financial institutions, a new company owner, or creditors), letters probate will not be required. This might occur where the assets of the estate are mostly cash on hand and some personal effects. In Quebec, probate is not required for a will that was prepared by a notary (under notary seal).

For small accounts, a financial institution may use its discretion and waive the requirement for probate if it knows the family and the assets are being transferred within the family. But rules and policies do change.

Q. My father died last week and we have the will in our possession. What should we do?

A. You may read the will and then ensure that the person named as the executor receives the original so he or she can carry out the responsibilities.

If you think finding someone else's assets might be a difficult task, consider those people who cannot even claim their own assets. As an example, the Curateur public du Quebec recently reported that it has more than $30 million of unclaimed investments that it would like to return to its rightful owners. (If you want to check their registry of unclaimed property, refer to www.curateur.gouv.qc.ca/cura/html/anglais/home.html.)

If the will and all the correct papers are in good order, the courts will give their seal of approval and issue the letters probate or grant of probate document within a few weeks. In Ontario, letters probate are now formally called "the certificate of appointment of estate trustee with a will."

Not all wills are confirmed as completely valid by the courts. Some wills contain provisions that are out of date or illegible, or it may not have been properly witnessed—all of which can be avoided. If the will is missing, the estate could be handled as if the deceased died without a will. However, if parts of the will are invalid or if certain provisions are missing, parts of (or perhaps all) the estate could be dealt with as if the deceased died intestate. For example, I saw one will that did not deal with the residue of an estate and the court was required to follow the intestacy laws for that portion of the estate.

The activities of the court are a matter of public record, including wills submitted for probate. It would be rare indeed if your lawyer were able to persuade the courts to seal a will file. The public and the media have access to the details in your will, including who is receiving what, and how much you owed and to whom. For those assets that flow through your will, this leaves your family, your business, and your beneficiaries no privacy. However, if your estate is unencumbered by mistresses, children born outside marriage, or questionable business dealings, this should not cause you any concern.

To obtain information about a will that is being probated, contact the office of the provincial government in the area where the deceased lived. This office may be called the Probate, Surrogate, or the Wills and Estate Court.

After the will has been confirmed through probate, your executor can begin to transfer the assets in accordance with the terms of the will. It may take six months to two years or more before your beneficiaries receive the bulk of their inheritance. Some property can be transferred immediately, and other property cannot be transferred until all of the expenses of the estate have been paid.

It may take an executor a few weeks to complete the application forms even if all the information is readily available. The application forms may require an itemized list of all the assets and property in the estate, including their market value, at the time of your death. Your executor may want to obtain assistance with the application forms, though they do not legally require a lawyer or notary.

Ask the financial institution, broker, or planner for a snapshot of the assets in the portfolio and their market value as of the date of death. The estate will need the details of the account, including the market value as of the date of death, the named beneficiaries, and any tax-related information.

The costs related to probating a will are referred to as a probate tax. As well, there are an increased number of administrative or verification fees.

PROVINCIAL PROBATE TAXES AND FEES

Related Fees

Verification or administration fees may be charged by the province for paperwork, photocopies, and searches related to the files. These fees can add up. Some people refer to them as "nuisance" fees. But there are other fees, such as the fee for an appointment of a guardian, and additional fees for a will that was probated in another provinces that needs to be resealed or approved for assets in another province that may affect your situation.

Probate Fees/Taxes

If you live in a province with a very low probate tax schedule or none at all, the rest of this chapter will likely be of interest to you primarily if you have relatives who live in different provinces who are concerned with the process and costs of probating their will. This chapter provides information on these issues, which you might have to discuss with them, or that you will need to know if you are asked to act as their executor.

Probate taxes, fees, or estate administration taxes range from nothing to the highest rate of 1.5% of the value of the estate's assets distributed through your will, even though the actual process is essentially the same in each province. When Canadians are planning to reduce the amount of probate they pay, this is the tax they are attempting to minimize.

The higher the value of your assets to be distributed through the will, the higher the amount of probate tax you would pay, although some provinces have a maximum. If just one asset in the estate requires the executor to apply for letters probate, then in some provinces, the value of all the assets flowing through the estate must be included in the calculation of the probate tax.

While some provinces refer to the cost to probate a will as a fee, there is some debate as to whether the cost is a fee or just another form of tax, especially in those provinces where there is no maximum. The amount of work required for the courts to probate a will (since most of the paperwork is completed by lawyers and not the government) is about the same whether an estate is worth $2 million or $200,000. However, the cost could be very different. Some people believe the cost to probate a will should be a flat fee, since the service is essentially the same regardless of the value of the estate.

In the fall of 1998, the Supreme Court of Canada declared that probate "fees" charged in Ontario were illegal because:

1. the probate service provided by the government is similar for large and small estates alike, so a "fee" based on the value of the estate looks and smells like a tax

2. taxes must be passed by government legislation, not through a regulation.

Table 6.1: History of Probate Fees in Ontario

May 1950 to May 11, 1960	$2.50 for each $1,000
May 12, 1960 to Aug. 31, 1966	$3.00 for each $1,000
Sept. 1, 1966 to June 7, 1992	$5.00 for each $1,000
After June 7, 1992	$5.00 for each $1,000 up to $50,000
	$15.00 for each $1,000 over $50,000

The province of Ontario quickly introduced an *Estate Administration Tax Act*, retroactive all the way back to 1950 so it did not have to refund any probate fees collected over the years. Now it's called what it really is—a tax.

Table 6.2: Probate Fees across Canada*

PROVINCE	RATE SCHEDULE	MAXIMUM
Alberta	$25 for the first $10,000 $100 on $10,001–$25,000 $200 on $25,001–$125,000 $300 on $125,001–$250,000 $400 over $250,000	$400
British Columbia	$0 for estates under $10,000 $208 on amount $10,000–$25,000 $208 plus $6 per $1,000 on $25,001–$50,000 Over $50,000: $14 per $1,000	none
Manitoba	$50 for first $10,000 Over $10,000: $50 plus $6 per $1,000	none
New Brunswick	$25 if less than $5,000 $50 on $5,001–$10,000 $75 on $10,001–15,000 $100 on $15,001–$20,000 Over $20,000: $5 per $1,000	none
Newfoundland	$75 for first $1,000 and $5 for each additional $1,000	none

PROVINCE	RATE SCHEDULE	MAXIMUM
Northwest Territories	$8 on the first $500 $15 on the next $501–$1,000 Over $1,000: $15 plus $3 per $1,000	none
Nova Scotia	$70 up to $10,000 $176 on next $10,001–$25,000 $293 on $25,001–$50,000 $820 on $50,001–$100,000 Over $100,000: $820 plus $13.85 per $1,000	none
Nunavut	$25 on the first $10,000 $100 on estates $10,001–$25,000 $200 on estates $25,001–$125,000 $300 on estates $125,001–$250,000 $400 on estates over $250,001	$400
Ontario	$5 per $1,000 on first $50,000 plus $15 per $1,000 over $50,000	none
Prince Edward Island	$50 up to $10,000 $100 on estates $10,001–$25,000 $200 on estates $25,001–$50,000 $400 on $50,001–$100,000 Over $100,000: $400 plus $4 per $1,000	none
Quebec	$0 for notarial will Nominal charge for holograph will	$0
Saskatchewan	$7 for first $1,000 and $7 for each additional $1,000	none
Yukon	$0 for estate under $25,000 $140 for estate over $25,000	$140

**Notes:*

The value of the estate—for probate purposes—is calculated according to the rules of each province. These rules may or may not allow deductions for items such as debts or property located outside the province.

Compiled from various sources believed to be accurate as of October 30, 2006. Fees are set by the provinces and are subject to change.

Using Table 6.2, an estate valued at $1 million would face probate taxes of $14,500 in Ontario. In New Brunswick, a $1 million estate would pay a probate tax bill of $5,000 and only $400 in Alberta. No wonder residents of Ontario, Nova Scotia, and British Columbia are upset!

Q. I live in Ontario and the costs to probate a will are lower in every other province. Can I have my will probated wherever I want?

A. Generally, your will is probated in the province where you lived when you died. If you have property in more than one province, your will may also have to be probated in that other jurisdiction. (This is called re-sealing.) Additional probate taxes are normally not charged, although an administration fee might be.

In most provinces, probate tax is calculated on the market value of your assets, not your net worth, and personal debts (other than mortgages on personal real estate) are not deducted before the fee is calculated. For example, if you have $300,000 of assets and property flowing through your estate and an unsecured line of credit for $100,000, the amount of probate tax would be based on $300,000, not $200,000.

But that's not all. If probate is required to transfer assets to your spouse on your death, fees could be due again on those same assets when they are transferred through your spouse's will to the next generation. Probate tax is not waived when assets are transferred from one spouse to the next. However, if the asset was held jointly with a spouse, probate tax would be charged on that asset only when the ownership passed through the will of the second spouse.

Probate tax cannot be deducted on the final income tax return.

Q. We paid probate tax on my husband's property when it was transferred to me on his death. Is probate tax due again on my death?

A. Yes, if those assets are distributed through the instructions in your will and any third party requires it.

STRATEGIES FOR REDUCING PROBATE TAX

Since probate tax is calculated on the value of the assets that flow through the will, the basic strategy to minimize these costs is to distribute as much of the estate assets outside the will as possible. These strategies can range from simple to ridiculously complex and may not work in all provinces.

Reducing probate tax should not be the primary focus of your estate plan. In fact, some of the "planning" strategies could end up costing more than the amount of probate tax they might save. Or the plan could involve a strategy that you might not otherwise consider putting in place. For example, although it might save probate taxes, you may not want to make your son a joint owner of your house! Registering property and assets jointly with married children could expose your assets to their marital or creditor problems.

But why would you want to pay any additional tax if you don't have to? Some strategies for reducing probate costs are relatively easy to implement and maintain, such as naming a beneficiary on your life insurance or pension plan.

Before implementing any technique, you should estimate the value of the assets that will flow through your will, the amount of probate tax and discuss it with your professional advisers. You should also calculate the potential cost (initial as well as ongoing costs) of implementing any technique as well as the potential savings. These costs could include re-registration of ownership, income taxes, legal fees, ongoing administration fees, land transfer tax (if the property has a mortgage), and maybe GST.

If you focus too much on reducing your probate tax bill, you could do something complex and expensive such as create an immediate tax problem and perhaps lose control of the asset.

Let's look at how taking steps to transfer assets outside your estate can affect the value of your estate for probate purposes for most provinces.

Example: Value of Estate Flowing through the Will

Before Planning for Probate	
Marital home (registered in one name)	$200,000
Life insurance payable to estate	$100,000
Stocks and bonds in your name	$250,000
RRSP payable to estate	$ 30,000
Total value of estate for probate	$580,000

After Planning for Probate	
Marital home (owned jointly with spouse)	0
Life insurance payable to spouse	0
Stocks and bonds owned jointly with spouse	0
RRSP (spouse named as beneficiary)	0
Total value of estate for probate	0

If some probate tax must be paid, ensure that there will be enough cash on hand, or assets that could be sold, to pay them. Sometimes insurance is suggested as a way to provide enough funds to cover probate and final income taxes. But you must first determine if the taxes and your overall objectives warrant purchasing a life insurance policy.

If just one financial institution requires probate, there may be an alternative to probating the will (and probate tax). The financial institution may accept a suitable security arrangement, such as a probate bond (like an insurance premium) or a letter of indemnity, to ensure it will not be held financially responsible if it follows the executor's directions.

Designate Beneficiaries

On Your Life Insurance

If you do not designate a beneficiary, or designate your "estate" as the beneficiary for your life insurance, the death benefit value will be distributed according to the instructions in your will and probate will be calculated on the value of the insurance.

The simplest, cheapest, and most practical way to reduce or avoid the cost of probate is to name a beneficiary on your insurance policy so it can be paid directly to the designated beneficiary.

While this seems simple enough, there are some additional items to consider. For example:

- If the life insurance death benefit is to help the estate pay the final income tax bill, it may be appropriate for it to be paid to the "estate," even though probate may be levied.
- If you want to keep the death benefit out of the estate, you may also want to name a backup or contingent beneficiary.

On Your RRSP/RRIF

If you don't designate a beneficiary, or designate your "estate" as the beneficiary for your pension plans, RRSP, and RRIFs, their value will be distributed according to the instructions in your will and probate will be calculated on the market value of those assets at the time of your death.

The simplest, cheapest, and most practical way to reduce or avoid the cost of probate is to name a beneficiary on your RRSP or RRIF so these assets are distributed outside your will.

While this seems simple enough, naming a beneficiary on your RRSP who is not your spouse could end up with an inequitable distribution of your estate that could cost your estate more in court costs than it potentially saved in probate tax.

For example, suppose you have an adult son and daughter and an RRSP worth $200,000 and a non-registered investment account also worth $200,000. Your initial plan is to name your daughter as the beneficiary on your RRSP (this could reduce some probate costs) and leave your son the other account through your will. However, the RRSP would be paid directly to your daughter and your executor would be required to pay the taxes dues on the RRSP out of the estate. This would leave about $120,000 for your son (assuming a marginal tax rate of 40%). If your goal was to leave them an equal share, you would get a fairer result if the RRSP was paid into the "estate." Then after all the debts and taxes had been paid, your son and daughter could each receive 50% of the residue. This would be equal and fair even if it means some additional probate costs!

There is some debate about whether naming beneficiaries on RRSPs and RRIFs held with banks and trust companies will avoid probate, since financial institutions can insist on probate to protect themselves before releasing funds. One reason is because an RRSP beneficiary designated in the will can override a beneficiary designated at a financial institution if the will was prepared more recently.

My survey of banks and trust companies indicated they were more concerned if the value of the RRSP or RRIF was over $30,000. Ask your financial institution about its policy. It might pay out the proceeds without probate if you post a bond or if it receives a letter from the estate's lawyer indemnifying the institution in the event the executor's instructions were incorrect. Regardless, if you name your spouse or partner as the beneficiary on RRSPs and RRIFs, practice is to pass these assets to your spouse without including their value in the calculation of probate tax.

Keep your beneficiary designations up to date since these assets are distributed according to the last beneficiary on record. If your spouse is your beneficiary, consider adding an alternate beneficiary to cover the possibility that you both die at the same time.

Joint Ownership of Assets with Rights of Survivorship

Registering assets, such as the family home, shares, bonds, or mutual funds as joint tenants, or joint tenants with rights of survivorship, is another technique used to reduce the cost of probate, but it is not available in Quebec. On financial statements, you may see the term "JTWROS" after both your names. One firm used the term "JT TEN" due to the way they coded the accounts on their computer system. The same firm coded Tenants in Common as "TEN COM." Plain language is increasingly used in most firms.

If you are unclear how your account has been legally registered, ask the firm in writing. You may have to ask to have your request forwarded to their legal department for clarification.

When property is registered as joint tenants with rights of survivorship, the deceased's interest in the asset is automatically passed to the surviving owner. The transfer is not handled by the will. The assets stay out of the estate and are not included in the calculation of probate. Suppose you and your spouse are the joint owners of a bank account registered with rights of survivorship. If your spouse predeceases you, the bank account is transferred to you. No probate is needed to transfer ownership, only proper proof of death.

Some professionals have always held their home in their spouse's name because of potential liability. If protection from this potential liability is still important, then it would not be a good idea to transfer the home into joint ownership.

You still need a will, even if you own all your assets and property jointly or if you live in an area where joint ownership is not an option. Joint ownership does not distribute the assets if everyone on title dies in a common disaster.

However, an asset registered as tenants in common is treated differently. It does not automatically transfer to the other registered owner. On death, the deceased's share is transferred according to the instructions in his or her will.

Q. Can I register my RRSP jointly?

A. No. RRSPs and RRIFs cannot be registered jointly. See Chapter 8 for details on naming beneficiaries for registered plans.

While it can often make good sense for spouses or common-law partners to own assets jointly, it can be full of problems if it is with anyone else. It can cause inequitable distributions of an estate after-tax; it could inadvertently write grandchildren out of their inheritance. I do not recommend joint ownership just to avoid probate costs. It also has to make good common sense.

Although it is relatively easy to change the registered ownership of assets, you should consider the disadvantages of joint ownership.

- You lose exclusive control of the asset and potentially the freedom to do what you want with it.
- If the other person named files for bankruptcy, creditors could seize the asset.
- If the asset is real estate, you require the consent of the joint owner to sell it.
- If the asset is a bank account, the joint owner could deplete the account without your consent (such as a spouse leaving the marriage).
- If one person becomes mentally incompetent, the provincial public guardian could step in and freeze half the assets.
- If the property is classified as a matrimonial home (house or cottage), the property could be affected as part of a divorce settlement.
- If you go through a separation, you could end up with a temporary restraining order on the assets that are registered JTWROS.
- CRA will consider that you "sold" a portion of the asset to that individual at fair market value (unless it was to a spouse) and create a tax liability. If there was profit from the "sale," even if it was only on paper, income taxes could be due that year.
- If the joint registration is done in name only (solely to avoid probate tax) and is not a true transfer of ownership and the rights of ownership, technically it may not be enough to keep the asset out of the probate fee calculation.
- There is the potential for challenges by other family members who are not named on the joint ownership if it is not clear the joint tenancy is being used in name only (to avoid probate if that is not documented) for convenience, or if it was an actual gift.
- It does not deal with potential situations. For example, if your child happens to predecease you, do you want anything special done with what would have been his or her share? This wish could be dealt with in your will, but not through joint ownership.

Q. I have a portfolio of mutual funds and stocks that are registered in only my name. To reduce probate tax, I want to register these investments jointly with my adult son. Will there be any costs involved?

A. Probably. CRA will consider there to have been a sale, or a "deemed disposition," of the assets in your portfolio. If there is a capital gain (profit) from "selling" 50% of the portfolio to your son, you are responsible for the income tax on that gain unless it was in name only. In addition, there may be commission or transfer fees to change the account registration and/or re-register the certificates.

Two things to keep in mind: RRSPs and RRIFs cannot be owned jointly. And in Quebec, there is no joint tenancy with automatic right of survivorship.

Real Estate

Real estate that is registered in joint tenancy does not pass through a will and does not require probating.

Q. Should I register my house jointly with my daughter? My husband died last year.

A. That depends. You would be giving up the ability to completely control the house. If you want to sell the house, you will need your daughter's written consent. If your daughter is married and is living in the house with her husband and her marriage breaks up, it gets even more complex. If she is registered as a joint owner of "your" house, the house could be considered the matrimonial home (which has special status depending on provincial family law). To avoid this situation, it is sometimes suggested that the spouse-in-law sign a single-purpose marriage contract (even if they've already been married for a number of years) agreeing not to claim any interest in the home. Although good in theory, this may not be a practical step unless all parties agree and understand the legal, personal, and financial implications.

After considering the disadvantages of joint ownership, you may decide you would prefer to pay the probate tax, rather than add another name to the ownership.

If there is a mortgage on the property, the lender generally must approve the addition of the second owner. If the name being added is your spouse, this is usually a formality. There may be legal costs to re-register the ownership.

If you originally registered your home or cottage in your spouse's name to protect the house from any professional liability, or because under old laws each spouse used to be able to have a principal residence, review your situation and determine whether it still makes sense to keep the house in one name only. A house worth $500,000 registered jointly could save your estate up to $7,500 in probate tax in Ontario, less in other provinces. However, if you still want the protection, keep the house in your spouse's name.

If you are asked to be added as a joint name, say, to your mother's house, consider if this strategy is in your best interest or in your mother's best interest.

- If you already own a principal residence, your share of your mother's property could be considered an investment property and you may have to pay income tax on any profits earned on your share when it is eventually sold. This tax bill could be much greater than any probate tax that might be saved.
- If you do not have your own home and live in your mother's house, you could lose the ability to participate in some of the government programs for first-time home buyers, such as the RRSP loan program because technically you would be an owner.

Other Assets

To change the registration on investment accounts, you would request the issuer to add the second name with a right of survivorship. For guaranteed investment certificates, the ownership normally can be changed at renewal. For mutual funds or stocks, the investments might need to be sold and repurchased under the new names, which may trigger taxable capital gains. Consult with your adviser before proceeding. On money market and bank accounts, ownership can be changed without triggering capital gains.

For example, Steve had $500,000 in money market mutual funds. As part of his estate plan, he re-registered these funds jointly with his spouse, Sheila, for two reasons:

1. to ensure she would have access to "their" money if he died suddenly, and
2. to reduce probate tax.

No fees were charged to re-register the ownership of these funds, and there was no taxable capital gain. Although Steve is still responsible for reporting the annual income from these funds, this paperwork will save his estate about $7,500 in probate tax (Ontario) and give Sheila quick access to the money.

Gifts

If you give away cash or other assets during your lifetime, there will be no probate tax. The basic premise is simple. If you don't own the asset when you die, it is not included in the probate tax calculation. However, I would never recommend giving away assets just to save any type of tax. Your priority is to take care of your needs today, and your future needs and those of your spouse or partner.

Watch out, though. A gift of non-cash assets may be deemed to be a "sale" with a potential taxable profit in the eyes of CRA and fall under the attribution rules. For example, if you give your adult daughter $12,000 in cash, neither you or your daughter would have to pay tax on the gift. But suppose you gave your adult daughter $12,000 of Bank of Nova Scotia shares that cost $2,000 when you bought them. CRA would deem that you had sold them, even though they were a gift. You would be required to pay income tax on the taxable portion of the gift ($12,000-$2,000=$10,000 for a taxable profit of $5,000) in the year you made it.

It may also be possible for your representative to make appropriate gifts on your deathbed, using your enduring power of attorney for finances. This type of gift is known as *donatio mortis causa*. These gifts could have some practical benefits, including simplifying the administration of your estate and reducing the cost of probate by keeping the value of the gifts outside your estate.

Canada Savings Bonds

Canada Savings Bonds can be registered jointly when purchased or when existing bonds mature. If the bonds are registered jointly with rights of survivorship, the Bank of Canada will re-register them in the name of the surviving owner after receiving proof of death.

However, the Canada Savings Bonds web site www.csb.gc.ca outlines how bonds can be transferred or redeemed under various circumstances, including when:

1) there was a will and letters probate have been issued
2) there was a will but no letters probate have been requested
3) the deceased died without a will

Q. Does every will need to be probated?

A. No. If the will and the estate are simple, there is no law requiring the will to be probated.

Multiple Wills

Rather than preparing just one will, some lawyers may suggest preparing two wills to reduce probate tax (referred to as a multiple wills strategy).

There are two variations on the use of multiple wills.

1. If you have some assets that require probate and some that do not, two wills would be prepared, one to deal with the assets that do not require probate (such as shares in a private corporation) and one to deal with those assets that will require probate. After death,

probate would be calculated only on the assets flowing through the second will.

2. If an individual holds some assets in one province with either a high probate tax rate or no maximum and other assets in another province with a much lower (and cheaper) probate tax schedule, he or she might consider multiple wills. Two wills are prepared, one for the assets in each province.

In some provinces, the use of multiple wills is not an effective planning strategy. For example, probate tax is calculated on assets passed "by a will or wills" in Nova Scotia, effectively calculating probate on both wills.

Multiple wills should be drawn up only with the advice of a lawyer. You need to ensure that the second will does not revoke the first will.

Testamentary Trusts

Probate tax is charged each time the ownership of assets is transferred through a will. For example, if you leave a $250,000 stock portfolio to your spouse in your will, probate will be charged on those stocks. When your spouse dies and those stocks are distributed according to his or her will, probate tax would be charged a second time on that same stock portfolio before it is transferred to the next generation. To avoid paying probate the second time, some people consider holding the stock portfolio in a spousal testamentary trust set up in the deceased's will if it fits in with the overall plan. Then, on the death of the second spouse, the stocks would be distributed to the children according to the instructions of the trust agreement where probate is not required, rather than your spouse's will.

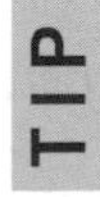

Some wills contain a joint disaster clause that is sometimes referred to as a 30-day survival clause. The clause might say something like, if your spouse does not outlive you for more than 30 days, other beneficiaries (say, your children) will receive your spouse's inheritance. If triggered, this clause can save time and the cost of probate because the assets go directly in trust for your children, rather than going to your spouse's estate and then to your children.

Inter Vivos Trusts

Another method sometimes used to reduce the cost of probate is to transfer assets to a living trust while you are alive. These assets would not require probate because technically they are not your property at the time of death. These assets would be transferred to your beneficiaries according to the instructions in the trust agreement, rather than through your will. To make this technique worth the bother, the potential amount of probate that could be saved should be significant enough to offset the costs of setting up the trust and the ongoing trust expenses. (See Chapter 12 for a discussion of trusts.)

Alter Ego Trusts or Joint Spousal Trusts

Normally, when assets are transferred into a trust while you are alive, they are deemed to have been disposed or sold and any profits are taxed in that year. However, under the rules of the alter ego trust, if you are 65 or older, you could transfer your personal assets into this type of trust, on a tax-free rollover basis, for your exclusive personal use while you are alive without triggering a deemed disposition and an immediate tax bill. You could receive income and capital from the trust and would be responsible for paying tax for all the income earned on the assets in the trust annually at your personal tax rate (almost as if it was still held in your own name). On your death, the assets would be distributed to your beneficiaries according to the trust agreement, not your will, reducing the cost of probate. Any remaining profits are taxed at that time.

A joint spousal trust is similar to the alter ego trust, except that both you and your spouse can receive income and capital from the trust and defer the final tax bill on any remaining profits until the death of the last surviving spouse.

However, you cannot transfer these assets to a testamentary trust, which can create income-splitting opportunities for a surviving spouse or partner, or your children. These income-splitting opportunities could save more income tax on an annual basis than the probate tax that might be saved. Of course, it all depends on the particular situation.

Converting Personal Debt to Secured or Corporate Debt

If you don't have any debts, or don't intend to have any future debts, or your only debt is a personal mortgage, this section does not apply to you.

Except for a personal mortgage (in most provinces), personal debts cannot be deducted from the value of your assets before probate costs are calculated. So if, at the time of your death, you have assets valued at $100,000 and personal liabilities (such as credit cards or an unsecured line of credit) of $40,000, probate would be calculated on the assets valued at $100,000, not on $60,000. But debts held in a personal corporation or holding company could be deducted before probate is calculated.

If you live in a province where there is no maximum on the probate tax charged (such as Ontario) and you have a fair-sized unsecured line of credit, you might consider replacing the unsecured line of credit with a personal mortgage or just paying it off. Would it be worthwhile? You would need to consider the costs involved, including the legal fees to register the mortgage. You could then compare those costs to the potential reduction in probate tax in your province.

Personal debts	$400,000	
Personal assets		$1,050,000
Value of corporation		800,000
Total estate for probate		$1,850,000
Probate tax payable (using Ontario's schedule):		
0.5% on first $50,000 =		$ 250
1.5% on $1,800,000 =		27,500
Total probate taxes		$27,750

If you have a corporation or a holding company and personal debt, you may want to rearrange your affairs so that the corporation holds the debt, or hold the debt as a personal mortgage.

Personal assets		$1,050,000
Assets of corporation	$800,000	
Corporate debt	– 400,000	
Net value of corporation		400,000
Total estate for probate		$1,450,000
Probate taxes payable:		
0.5% on first $50,000 =		$ 250
1.5% on $1,400,000 =		21,000
Total probate taxes		$21,250

To determine whether it makes sense as part of your overall business objectives and from the cost-benefit side, calculate the costs of setting up the corporation (if it does not already exist), continuing administration fees, and refinancing, as well as the cost of probate in your province.

SUMMARY

Probating a will is a process that is required when an executor needs to provide proof to financial institutions that he or she has the authority to act on behalf of the estate.

This chapter has described some of the strategies that can be used to reduce the cost of probating a will. Any strategy can have advantages and disadvantages and you do not want to implement a strategy that would cost you more than the probate tax you might save.

I think that it is best to consider the strategies to reduce probate taxes in the following order:

1. First, estimate the amount of probate tax/fees that might be due.
2. Estimate the financial cost of implementing any technique that you might be considering.
3. What are the implications of using the strategy?
4. Would implementing any strategy make your estate unduly complex or cause a major problem?

If you live in a province with a high probate tax schedule, you might be interested in implementing strategies to save a few dollars. But don't let the tail (in this case, probate costs) wag the dog!

chapter seven

power of attorney for finances

My mother was smart. She signed a power of attorney before she entered the hospital so that I was able to pay her bills and renegotiate her rent. I don't know how our family would have managed without that power of attorney. I've seen how important the document can be, so I prepared the documents so that my sons can help me out if it ever becomes necessary.

—*M.*

SO FAR, WE HAVE PRIMARILY DISCUSSED putting a plan in place that would take effect on your death. However, for you to have a complete set of estate planning documents, you also require documents that will speak for you if you are alive but unable to speak for yourself. I refer to these documents as your pre-estate documents (since we traditionally refer to your will as your estate document). In this chapter, we will deal with the document in which you (sometimes referred to as the donor) can appoint someone to make ongoing decisions on your behalf: to manage your business or your investment portfolio, as well as day-to-day financial matters. In Chapter 15, we discuss the document in which you can give someone the legal authority to make decisions related to personal and health care.

What if you are in a car accident and in a coma for weeks? Or are incapacitated by a stroke? Or out of the country for an extended time? Or dealing with a severely debilitating condition? Your bills still have to be paid.

These types of situations can happen at any time. They do not just happen with age. Things happen. You do not have to have oodles of assets or to be elderly to put documents in place to make sure you have appointed a representative to make financial decisions on your behalf in the event you cannot. Your will speaks for you only after your death.

My adult children have always thought it was weird (their words, not mine) that I thought these documents were important. After all, when they were 18 and 19, they didn't really understand why I insisted they have these documents in place.

With a properly prepared pre-estate document for finances, you can give the person(s) of your choice the legal authority to make decisions and manage your financial affairs on your behalf while you are alive. Preparing this document allows you to choose who will look after your finances if you are temporarily or permanently unable to.

The authority you give your attorney or representative is valid only while you are alive—it stops on your death. After death, the instructions in your will come into effect, appointing your executor to look after your estate.

When you write or update your will, your lawyer or notary will also recommend that you prepare your power of attorney, which is a separate document. Often, the person named as the attorney in your power of attorney document and the executor named in your will are the same. I know they are in my documents. But the person(s) named gets his or her authority from different documents and different situations—one document allows the person to manage my finances while I am alive, and the other document allows the person to wrap up my affairs after my death.

Like many people, you may believe that your spouse or adult child can automatically look after your financial affairs if you become incapacitated due to an accident or illness. This is not true. Without a signed power of attorney naming them, your family has no immediate legal rights to control your finances, including paying your bills and managing your assets—at least, not without obtaining court approval.

If you are asked if you would be willing and able to take on the responsibilities of a power of attorney for finances and are not sure what might be involved, refer to Appendix II for a List of Duties for your Representative When Making Financial Decisions on Your Behalf.

Even having a bank account where you have a joint owner may not give that other person an automatic right to manage that account on your behalf should you become mentally incompetent.

Joint ownership does not replace the need for an enduring power of attorney or a representative agreement for finances. The public trustee has been known to freeze a mentally incompetent individual's share of the bank account to protect them.

Q. I've signed a power of attorney at my bank. Do I need another one?

A. The power of attorney at the bank covers only specific assets at that bank. If you have other assets, the bank form is not enough! If the attorney you've appointed at the bank is not the same person you've appointed as your general power of attorney, you might want to document that in your general power of attorney to prevent confusion. Be sure to check the wording of the power of attorney to make sure it does not invalidate your general power of attorney document.

These documents are referred to by a number of different names across the country, including a power of attorney for personal property, a power of attorney for financial decisions, representative, proxies, or just a power of attorney. See Table 7.1 for the term used for your substitute decision maker for finances in your province.

Table 7.1: Who's Who for Property?

	Name of Decision Maker	Name of Document
Alberta	attorney	Enduring Power of Attorney
British Columbia	representative	Representative Agreement for Property or Finances
Manitoba	attorney	Springing Power of Attorney
New Brunswick	attorney	Power of Attorney
Newfoundland	attorney	Enduring Power of Attorney
Northwest Territories	attorney	Power of Attorney
Nova Scotia	attorney	Enduring Power of Attorney
Nunavat	attorney	Power of Attorney
Ontario	attorney for property	Continuing Power of Attorney for Property
PEI	attorney	Power of Attorney
Quebec	mandatary	Mandate Given in Anticipation of Incapacity
Saskatchewan	attorney	Enduring Power of Attorney
Yukon	attorney	Enduring Power of Attorney

In Quebec, a Mandate Given in Anticipation of Incapacity allows you, the mandator to name another person or trust company as your mandatary to make decisions on your behalf should you become mentally incompetent. You can use one document to name your mandate for finances, personal care, and to document your wishes regarding organ donations and your living will. Before the mandate becomes effective, your mandatary or power of attorney must apply for certification of your incapacity. The application to the courts may require a psychological and medical assessment of your incompetency.

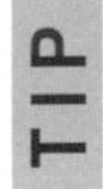

If you are acting as the power of attorney for financial matters, see Appendix II for a list of duties and keep a journal logging everything you do in the role, including copies of all letters, faxes, email, etc., and the date and time of all correspondence, noting the topic, who was spoken to, what was discussed, the decisions that were made, and the next step.

OFFICE OF THE PROVINCIAL GUARDIAN AND TRUSTEE

If you do not formally appoint someone to act on your behalf to protect your interests, a government office—the Office of the Public Guardian and Trustee—will step in to protect your rights and look after your affairs.

It is a misconception that the government is waiting to take over whenever possible. One Office of the Public Guardian and Trustee describes itself as the "decision-maker of last resort." In the event you become mentally incapacitated and do not have a power of attorney in place, the *Substitute Decisions Act* (Ontario) allows a family member to apply to the public trustee to be appointed as your attorney, committee, or representative. To protect its own liability, the public trustee assesses all applications and may require even close family members to file a management plan for the assets and monitor their decisions, and to post a bond (like a premium for an insurance policy) or other security for the assets and monitor their decisions.

The court can waive the requirement, perhaps when the guardian is a family member and the assets are family assets. My personal feeling is that I would not like to expose my family to whatever potential decision might be made at the discretion of a court official. Since this is something we don't normally want our spouses or partner to have to do, it is usually best to appoint a power of attorney in advance to save your family the added stress.

In some cases, the public trustee will manage your assets and property and may make decisions that are different from those your family members or friends might make. The public trustee is permitted to take possession of your bank accounts, bonds, and all other assets without consulting your family—regardless of how ethical and supportive your family is—to protect your interests. If you have family or friends that you believe would protect your interests, then you can prepare a power of attorney for finances giving them the authority to make these decisions on your behalf.

Q. Does my power of attorney need to be a lawyer?

A. No. The "attorney" is just the term for the responsibility. Your "attorney" could be a spouse, relative, or trusted friend and you are not required to have one. If necessary, the government will step in until someone can be appointed.

WHAT MIGHT BE IN YOUR POWER OF ATTORNEY FOR FINANCES

The statements required in an actual pre-estate document for financial matters vary from province to province.

Your lawyer will be able to ensure that your document meets all of the requirements of your province. For example, in Manitoba, you must specifically state that you are giving your attorney powers under the *Homestead Act* if you want your attorney to be able to deal with the family home. In Ontario, if you are preparing an enduring power of attorney, the document should refer to the *Mental Health Act*.

Appointing Your Power of Attorney

The person named as your attorney must be able to make good financial decisions. He or she has the following responsibilities:

- to act in your best interest (not their own) and in good faith
- to avoid conflicts of interest
- to exercise good judgment on your behalf

- to maintain records
- to consult with you wherever possible

The person should be someone you trust unconditionally who also has the ability to do the job. Look at how the person manages his or her own financial affairs. Is that how you want your affairs handled?

Typically, people name their spouse, a trusted family member, or a close friend. If you choose not to name your spouse, or name someone to act jointly with your spouse, be sure to discuss with your spouse whom you have named and why. Your spouse could become extremely frustrated with the day-to-day management of the family's financial affairs if he or she is required to report to a third person.

Naming the wrong person to act as your attorney or representative could lead to major abuses of this power. Your lawyer may ask you if you can really trust that person. You'll have to use your best judgment. And don't forget to ask that person if he or she would be willing to act on your behalf before you name him or her in your document.

Trust companies and lawyers can also be appointed as a power of attorney (or a backup). When your situation is complex or when you do not have a family member who is willing or able to be appointed, a professional may be suitable for you.

We've talked about naming backup executors and backup guardians. You also need to appoint a backup or substitute attorney in case your first choice is unable or unwilling to act when required. Select your backup with the same care you made for your main choice.

You may need or want to appoint more than one person to make decisions on your behalf. If so, do you want them to act together when making decisions to keep a check on each other and reduce the possibility of abuse? Or do you want to authorize them to act separately for convenience, which in legal terms would be "jointly and severally"? Or do you want them to report their activities on an annual basis to a family committee? In British Columbia, an individual drawing up their representative agreement can select to have a monitor to oversee the activities of the representative or the power of attorney. Personally, for vulnerable people, I think this is a step in the right direction.

Q. My father has just died after a long illness. My brother was his attorney at the bank. We think that there should be more money left, but it seems to be all gone. What can we do?

A. Unfortunately, financial power of attorney documents open the door for both mismanagement and abuse by the person named as the attorney which may not be discovered until after death. If you can prove fraud, you could consider laying charges.

Your attorney is not required to make exactly the same decisions that you might have made if you were able. However, you can assist your attorney by providing written instructions in advance stating how you would like your assets or property to be handled should you become incapacitated, especially if there may be major decisions to be made. (It's one thing to lose your mental abilities forever; it's another thing to be in a coma for six months and wake up to find that decisions have been made that you have to live with.)

You may also give your attorney the right to see your will so that he or she can manage your affairs in a way that reflects your overall intentions. Although such written instructions do provide some guidance, they are not legally binding on your attorney.

Authority Given to the Financial Power of Attorney

This is a powerful document and it gives someone else the power to make any decision you would legally be able to make (except decisions related to estate planning, such as preparing a will).

Not all power of attorney documents are pre-estate documents. Some have limited powers; others are more general.

A limited power of attorney may place limits regarding the time frame or types of transactions. For example, this type of document might be helpful if you were selling your house and planning to be out of the country, or need help with banking or dealing with your CPP/QPP cheques because you find it difficult to get out.

A general power of attorney might give your attorney the power to do all financial acts on your behalf, such as paying your bills, arranging a mortgage, selling your investments, or taking money out of your accounts.

In Quebec, unless you specifically state that you are giving your mandatary full administrative powers, it is assumed that you have given only simple administrative powers. Simple administrative powers are powers that include acts and decisions considered necessary to preserve your property, such as making mortgage payments, completing your income tax return, and dealing with your bank accounts. Investment powers are limited to investments that are presumed to be sound, such as bank deposits, shares, bonds, and investment certificates. With full administrative powers, your mandatary has powers that would also allow him or her to sell property without requiring the permission of the courts.

If you have specific instructions for how your assets are to be administered, or if your estate is large and you want the protection of the *Trustee Act* of your province, you might consider transferring your assets to a living trust rather than being administered under a pre-estate document. The trust document would formally specify what you want done and the person(s) you appoint to carry them out, and would require its own tax reporting.

Some Limitations People Have Used

Some people have incorporated limitations into their powers of attorney in an attempt to reduce abuses. Limitations place restrictions on your attorney and have been used in an attempt to safeguard assets, but they can also keep your attorney from acting quickly, which can sometimes be very important. For example, if you state your attorney cannot act unless you are declared mentally incompetent, your attorney will need to have independent doctors document that fact. But you might also want your attorney to be able to act for you if you are physically unable to get out, but mentally competent. Without proper legal advice, it's an easy mistake to make.

The following is not a list of recommended limitations. However, you may want to discuss some of these ideas with your lawyer or notary to determine if they might be appropriate for your situation.

- Have a third party, such as your lawyer, hold the power of attorney documents with written instructions as to when the forms should be released to the named power of attorney.
- Place limits on the attorney's powers by specifying for what it can and cannot be used, and under what conditions.
- Select more than one person to act jointly as co-attorneys so that one person does not have all the control or the responsibility. "Jointly" means they must act together; "jointly and severally" means they can act together or independently. But consider if this is practical. If your two daughters live 1,000 kilometres apart, there will be some delay when their signatures are required.
- Require the attorney or mandatary to prepare an inventory of financial assets and property for periodic review by a third person, or in British Columbia, a monitor.
- Document that the power of attorney cannot be used unless you are declared mentally incompetent. Some lawyers like this; others do not. It could make it difficult to determine when your attorney has the legal authority to act, and it restricts your attorney from acting for you when the problem is not related to mental competency. It could also create additional headaches depending on your situation. For example, the financial institution you are dealing with may want a copy of the medical certificate that declares you are mentally incompetent along with the power of attorney document.

How Will Incapacity Be Determined?

When do you want the attorney to have the power to act? Immediately? Only when one or two doctors declare that you are mentally incompetent? Once you have been declared as such, will it be assumed that you will always be mentally incompetent?

Some people specify in their documents that two doctors must declare when they are mentally incompetent. One spouse was surprised when she noticed this in her husband's document while they were in my office and was very concerned as to how she would fulfill this requirement. In this particular situation, he said that it didn't matter which doctors made the declaration if he was in the hospital. But all this was news to his wife. But now that they have had a chance to discuss it, they both understand the purpose of the wording and what to do in the event of a medical crisis. This was a reminder of how important it is that people discuss their wishes and instructions with each other—and how they will actually work when the time comes.

Continuing and Enduring Powers

In some provinces, a power of attorney document is revoked by mental incapacity. But this is when you would need this document the most. So to get around this, some lawyers include wording that states the document will endure or continue if you become mentally incompetent. ("Endure" is just another word for continue.) Wording similar to "survives my subsequent incapacity" under your province's act may be necessary to prevent your pre-estate document for finances from being cancelled if you become mentally incompetent. In Quebec, the document must state it "is in contemplation of incapacity."

If your power of attorney document was prepared a number of years ago, you should have it reviewed to ensure that it has the most recent powers that are available. You want your documents to speak for you when you might need it the most.

Powers to Manage Property

Your document will likely contain a clause that states that your attorney can do anything that you can legally do, except make a will, and may have to make some or all of the following decisions on your behalf, including:

- decisions regarding your investment and RRSP/RRIF portfolios
- paying for the costs necessary for your support and care
- paying for costs necessary for the support, education, and care of your dependants
- giving consent on your behalf regarding any property where you have rights under your province's family or matrimonial laws

- signing contracts and other legal documents on your behalf
- collecting debts owed to you
- hiring professionals to assist in the management of your property and fulfill your financial obligations
- managing and/or selling real estate
- managing and making decisions related to your business
- mediating or arbitrating disputes on your behalf
- reviewing the instructions in your will to understand your long-term instructions
- acting as your legal representative with the Canada Revenue Agency

Powers should not be assigned lightly. A full power of attorney gives your attorney the legal authority to do almost anything that you can do, including withdrawing money from your bank account, buying or selling real estate, making gifts to charity, lending money, and transferring securities. Because this is such a powerful document, it is open to abuse. Police have seen many abuses of powers of attorney by family members, as well as business associates. To reduce the risk of fraud, exploitation, and/or mismanagement, choose the person carefully and consider building some limitations into the powers of attorney.

A power of attorney can be given powers as extensive or as limited as you see fit. For example, you could give your attorney the authority to make gifts to family members or charity.

Someone who is concerned that the attorney may not be acting in the individual's best interest can apply to the courts for review.

Consent to Deal with a Matrimonial Property

If you are declared mentally incompetent and did not name a financial power of attorney with the appropriate powers, your spouse may have to obtain court approval to sell the family home, obtain a secured line of credit, or perhaps even renew a mortgage. Family or matrimonial property law may require the signature of both spouses for any transaction involving the home, even if only one spouse is named on the title of the property.

Compensating a Power of Attorney

In some provinces, your attorney is entitled to compensation according to a set fee schedule, or compensation you specify in your document.

The person acting as your attorney is also entitled to be reimbursed for all reasonable expenses related to looking after your affairs, including postage, mileage for going to the bank, and parking.

When a spouse acts as the attorney, he or she does not normally request compensation. However, since the services of a power of attorney or mandatary may be required for many years, consider compensating even close family members for their services.

Q. Who decides if I am not capable of managing my own affairs?

A. Sometimes the decision is easy, such as if you are in a coma after a car accident. If you become a resident of a psychiatric facility, your physician might decide. There is a review process if someone's capacity is in question. But generally, you are assumed to be able to make your own decisions unless there is good reason to believe you are not.

If You Live in British Columbia

The *B.C. Representation Agreement Act* (similar to Ontario's *Substitute Decisions Act*) enables B.C. residents to prepare representation agreements in order to name the person(s) of their choice to represent them for matters related to their 1) financial affairs and 2) personal and health care.

They also have the option of naming a monitor who will oversee the actions of their named representative to determine if he or she is complying with their duties.

If you are asked to act as a representative for financial matters, and are unsure what your responsibilities and duties might be, refer to the list of duties in Appendix II. Some representatives act on behalf of others on a long-term basis, and while they do not have the same legal authority as an executor (that authority comes only from the wording of a will after death), you will notice that there are some practical similarities.

PREPARING A POWER OF ATTORNEY FOR FINANCES

To prepare a power of attorney for finances, you must have attained the age of majority in your province and be mentally competent. In some provinces, do-it-yourself kits are available, but be forewarned: Some lawyers have suggested that these kits leave room for people to make errors.

Some provinces have kits online. Others recommend that you see a lawyer or notary. Ontario residents can obtain power of attorney kits from the Office of the Public Trustee by calling the Office of the Public Trustee at (416) 314-2800 or 1-800-366-0335 or online at: www.attorneygeneral.jus.gov.on.ca/english/family/pgt/

If you have a continuing power of attorney, and you are later asked to sign a power of attorney at your bank or trust company, be sure it has wording to the effect that says, "I am not revoking any previous power of attorney documents. I want multiple power of attorney documents."

It currently costs more than $100 to prepare a power of attorney through a lawyer if you package it with preparing a will, although in some provinces it is not required that you see a lawyer to prepare the document. Nevertheless, wherever you are, I recommend you talk to a lawyer or notary to ensure that your document will be acceptable to your financial institutions.

If you have property in other provinces or states, you should also determine if you require an attorney document in those locations.

Signing and Witnessing the Document

Power of attorney documents must be properly witnessed to reduce the potential for abuse. In Ontario, a power of attorney document requires two witnesses who are not your spouse, child, or others who have certain relationships with you. In Quebec, your notary or lawyer will certify that you understood the mandate document at the time it was prepared.

In provinces where you are not required to consult with a lawyer when preparing your document, it may still be in your best interest to do so.

Q. My mother is 85 and refuses to give my brother and me a power of attorney. What can we do?

A. Nothing. It is her right not to prepare a power of attorney. However, someone must manage her financial affairs if she is unable to. Many people prefer to choose an individual rather than leaving any decisions that might need to be made on their behalf to a government agency. Your mother may feel that she does not trust you enough, or feel that an independent body such as the public trustee is appropriate for her situation. No one is required to sign a power of attorney. It should be done only if a person feels it is in his or her best interests for both the short and long term.

Reviewing a Power of Attorney

A power of attorney document does not expire. Periodically, you should review this document to ensure that it still meets your requirements and that the person named is still willing to act on your behalf.

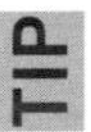

Review your pre-estate documents when you review your will.

Revoking a Power of Attorney

A power of attorney document is revoked:

- by your death; after death, your executor is given the authority to manage your affairs.
- by mental incapacity unless the power of attorney document contains the correct legal wording so that it will survive a mental incapacity.
- by the death of the person named as the attorney unless you have named a backup.
- by formal, witnessed revocation in some provinces.
- by delivering a letter to the person named as the attorney stating that the power of attorney has been revoked as long as you are mentally able. You should also notify any people that the attorney

may have dealt with on your behalf and inform them that the power of attorney has been revoked. This might include your bank, your financial adviser, and your mortgage company. It is also recommended that you obtain the original power of attorney document.

A power of attorney or mandatary can also be revoked by the provincial public trustee or public curator (in Quebec) if they are deemed to have been acting inappropriately.

Q. Should I set my assets up in a trust or an alter ego trust rather than using a power of attorney?

A. If your financial situation is particularly complex or you are concerned about the potential of abuse, a trust might be more appropriate than a power of attorney document, since the trust document specifies your instructions regarding your assets. Otherwise, a power of attorney for finances names a representative to make financial decisions on your behalf should you become mentally incapacitated.

SUMMARY

Everyone 18 or over with a bank account or any assets should have a power of attorney document for finances that appoints someone they trust to step in and act for them if they are not able to.

This document ensures that a representative of your choice—and not some official in a government office—will make decisions on your behalf.

With careful planning, you decide who decides.

chapter eight

death and taxes

Nothing can be said to be certain, except death and taxes.
—Ben Franklin

DEATH TAXES, INHERITANCE TAXES, succession duties, estate taxes—they all have more or less the same meaning to Canadians, and they're nothing new. George Gooderham, president of the Bank of Toronto and son of the founder of the distilling firm Gooderham and Worts, died in 1905. The succession duties on his estate were more than enough to eliminate the entire debt of the province of Ontario!

All estate taxes were eliminated in the early 1970s. Even so, our government is waiting to collect. Your registered plans (RRSP, RRIFs, etc.) are treated as if they have been cashed out and any assets with profits are deemed to have been sold on your death unless they are left to your spouse or partner. Canada Revenue Agency (CRA) wants us to pay up on death! Just imagine how much tax could be collected from all the RRSPs and RRIFs if we didn't build spending into our retirement plans.

One of the responsibilities of the executor (or an administrator if there is no will), or a liquidator (in Quebec), includes reporting to CRA and:

- filing the final income tax return (called the terminal return) for all income earned in that year, up to the date of death

- filing any outstanding tax returns from previous years
- paying taxes owing out of the estate before distributing assets to the beneficiaries

Q. How much income tax will be due on my death?

A. The amount depends on many factors, including the types of assets you owned, their value, your profits and losses, which beneficiaries will ultimately receive them, any charitable gifts you are making, and your other sources of income in that year.

While it's been said that up to half of the value of RRSPs or RRIFs could be taxed away, that is not true for most people. The amount of tax will depend on your marginal tax rate and you do not reach the top rate unless your income in the year of death is over $100,000. If you live in Alberta, the top rate at the time of writing was about 39%; in other provinces, it was closer to 50%.

But if your RRSP was worth $100,000 and you had no other income in the year of death, you would not be paying $50,000 in tax because we have a graduated tax system. For example, on the first $40,000 of your RRSP, you would pay less than $7,000 in tax—nowhere near 50%! It is possible to roll these registered plans over to your spouse or partner, and make arrangements to leave them to minor or dependent children. This can defer the tax bill and address family concerns.

Other assets, such as investments that have increased in value, are deemed to have been sold at death so that a market value can be determined, even if no sale took place. The capital gain or loss is then reported on your final tax return unless they were transferred to your spouse or partner.

Although we don't have anything called a "death tax," the Canada Revenue Agency (CRA) wants to collect undeclared capital gains before the asset is transferred to a beneficiary who is not your partner!

Understanding the way the tax rules apply on death can help you plan your estate. However, as with any planning, I don't believe that the tax rules should drive what you do. Rather, you should determine what your main objectives are and then, if you can, do so in a way that may reduce or even eliminate the tax bill due without complicating or compromising those main objectives. After all, if you can minimize the amount of tax, there will be more of your estate for your beneficiaries—unless you really want the government to be one of those beneficiaries.

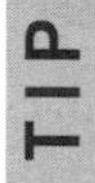

In your will, you can provide your executors with discretionary powers to make elections under the *Income Tax Act* in the best interest of your estate and all your beneficiaries. They may then be able to make some elections according to the most recent budget changes to reduce your final tax bill.

Here are some areas that can affect your final tax bill.

PRINCIPAL RESIDENCE

Your home is exempt from capital gains under the principal residence exemption, plus immediately adjacent land up to ½ hectare, unless the taxpayer can establish that the additional land was necessary for the use and enjoyment of the home. If you had continued to live in the house until death, no increase in value up to the date of death is taxable.

While you are limited to one principal residence, the exemption is available on a number of properties you might live in, even if it is for a short period of time. Some people choose to use their principal residence exemption on their home or their cottage—whichever offers them the greatest tax benefit.

If the market value of the principal residence increases from the date of death to the time it is transferred or sold out of the estate, this portion of the profit during this time is taxable.

Q. How do I figure out how much tax will be due after my death? My estate is worth $1,000,000 as follows:

House	*$300,000 (cost $150,000)*
GICs, T-Bills	*$100,000*
RRSP	*$300,000*

Investment account of Canadian stocks and mutual funds, now worth $300,000 that originally cost $100,000.

Are the taxes really going to eat up 40% of my estate?

A. The tax an estate pays depends on the types of assets, their costs, and values at the time of death. Since these assets could be left to your spouse with no immediate tax bill, I'm going to assume that you are interested in the taxes that could be due if your spouse predeceases you (before your estate passes to the next generation).

First, the good news. Your house is your principal residence, so it will pass into your estate without attracting any tax. Your GICs and T-bills face minimal tax—any taxes due would be based on the interest earned in the year.

Now the bad news. If your marginal tax rate is 40%, the tax on your RRSP would be about $120,000. Your investment account has $200,000 of capital gains ($300,000 – $100,000) for another $40,000 in tax.

Based on today's values and tax rules, your tax bill would be about $160,000, or 16% of $1,000,000. In your particular situation, this is a long way from 40%.

TRANSFERS TO A SPOUSE OR PARTNER

The simplest way for couples to defer the taxes on death according to the *Income Tax Act* is to name a spouse or partner of the same or opposite sex as the beneficiary on registered plans, such as RRSPs or RRIFs, and to leave him or her all other assets that have increased in value.

These assets, when left to a spouse or partner outright or through a trust, receive favourable tax treatment. Non-registered assets can be transferred at the deceased's original cost and the tax on any capital gains deferred until your spouse dies.

Of course, on the death of your spouse, his or her executor must include any capital gains on those assets on the final tax return as if they had been sold on the date of death. Remember that tax bills don't go away. Sometimes they are just deferred until another day. (Also, see "Registered Plans" later in this chapter.)

It is sometimes advantageous as part of long-range tax planning (and to keep more for the next generation) to declare some or all of the profits or withdrawals on the final tax return and elect to *not* roll all the assets over to the spouse at the original cost. Here are a couple of situations where it might make sense to transfer some or all of the assets to the spouse at a higher cost rather than to just transfer them at the original cost:

- when the deceased is not paying much in the way of tax in the year of death, perhaps because their taxable income is low
- to use up a non-refundable tax credit from a charitable donation
- when the deceased has unused capital losses
- when the deceased is using up the balance of the 1994 $100,000 capital gain exemption
- to claim any eligible capital gain exemptions
- to use up the deceased's personal tax credits

When there is any opportunity to transfer the assets at a value that is higher than the original cost without triggering any additional tax, it saves a tax bill in the future. When your surviving spouse or partner decides to sell any of these assets or is deemed to have sold the assets (such as on his or her own death), tax would be due only on the profits that had not previously been declared.

EXAMPLE At death, Paul had capital gains of $300,000 and losses of $50,000. His executor consulted with an accountant, who advised that $250,000 of the capital gains be rolled over tax-free to Paul's wife, Linda, and that $50,000 of capital gains be declared to offset the capital loss. The net result on Paul's final tax return was the same as if the executor had rolled over the entire $300,000 at the original cost base.

But the real tax benefit came when Linda died two months later. We'll assume that the actual value of the assets had not changed. But since Linda's final tax return had no rollover option (it would have if she had quickly remarried), the capital gains must now be included on her final tax return (all but the $50,000, which had been previously declared).

ASSETS NOT LEFT TO A SPOUSE (NOT INCLUDING YOUR RRSP/RRIF)

Assets and property you owned (and do not leave to your spouse) are considered or deemed to have been sold by Canada Revenue Agency (CRA) at fair market value at the time of death even though no actual sale takes place. This is called a deemed disposition. If these assets are deemed to have been sold at a profit, the resulting capital gain could mean a substantial tax bill.

Some people believe everything they own has to be sold, but this is not true. Assets and property do not have to be *actually* sold unless it is necessary to raise cash to pay taxes or other liabilities. In fact, even assets in the estate can be distributed without being sold.

Capital gains did not exist in Canada before 1972, so taxable profits are based on the increase in value from December 31, 1971 (called valuation day or V-day), or the day the asset was acquired, if later. If the asset is real estate but not a principal residence, the rules are more complicated.

Do you have a relative in another country who will be leaving you assets or cash? If they have a properly worded will that keeps the inheritance out of Canada, you might pay less in future income taxes than if it was left to you outright.

TAX IMPLICATIONS WHEN MAKING BEQUESTS IN YOUR WILL

I always believe that it is important to first consider what your intentions are. It is also important to consider how the tax rules will affect the way you might structure your estate plan. I've seen more than one estate plan that was set up that did not do the job intended. Fortunately, we had the time to make sure the plan was revised before it was too late.

Suppose your intention is to leave some assets to your spouse and other assets to another family member who was important in your life. You could leave your spouse/partner the assets with the taxable capital gains and the other family member assets that would not create a tax bill so that little or no tax would be due immediately on death. This itself is an important tax planning tool, but in reality you need to also consider when your spouse would need cash from those assets and what would be left after taxes would be due over time. But here is an example that looks at this at one point in time.

EXAMPLE You have a portfolio of mutual funds that cost $25,000 in 1996. These investments have done well and now have a market value of $225,000. You are reviewing your estate plan and are considering leaving this portfolio to either your spouse or your brother. Look at the difference in the tax treatment.

Mutual fund portfolio left to	*Spouse*	*Brother*
Value of deemed disposition	$25,000	$225,000
Adjusted cost base	$25,000	$ 25,000
Resulting capital gain on death	0	$200,000
Taxable capital gain (50%) on final return	0	$100,000
Taxes due on final return (assuming 40% tax rate)	0	$ 40,000

Left to your brother, about $40,000 in tax would be due on the profits that would be paid out of the estate, leaving less for the other beneficiaries, including your spouse. Left to your spouse, the taxes on this portfolio could be deferred until your spouse sold the investments—perhaps to create income she might need—or deferred until her death.

CAPITAL GAINS AND LOSSES

A calculation of the profits for each asset that has any untaxed capital gains has to be included on the final tax return. For tax purposes, these are deemed to have been sold, even though no actual sale may have taken place.

Fifty percent of *all* deemed capital gains (net of capital losses), except those qualifying for the $500,000 capital gains exemption, must be reported as taxable income, creating a higher tax liability and a bigger problem for people who wish to preserve assets or the value of their estate. It would be a shame if your family had to sell a business or cottage that you wanted to keep in the family just to pay your final tax bill. A forced sale is never desirable, and is even worse if the market value is down.

Over the years, the taxable amount of capital gains has increased and decreased. In 1987, the first $100,000 of capital gains was exempt from tax and only 50% of the capital gains over $100,000 was taxed. Later, the inclusion rate was increased to 75%. Then in late 2000, the taxable amount of capital gains was lowered back down to 50%.

In my opinion, the elimination of the $100,000 capital gains exemption was a form of estate tax—for some Canadians, death was the only time they ever claimed any of the capital gains exemption.

The $500,000 capital gains exemption (less amounts already used under the $100,000 exemption) still exists for qualified small business corporation shares and qualified farm property.

Capital losses (the opposite of a profit) can be deducted against capital gains and other income on the final tax return. Any net capital loss not used on the final tax return can be carried back for up to three years to reduce any taxable capital gains in those years.

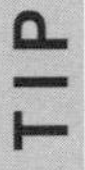

Use it or lose it! Before rolling assets over at their cost base to a surviving spouse or common-law partner, the executor should consider taking full advantage of any capital losses you had. Be sure your personal records indicate the amount of any unused capital losses and that you report these to CRA annually.

If the deemed disposition is for depreciable capital property (such as a building, equipment, or machinery), a terminal loss or recapture of the depreciation may be created, which needs to be reported on the final tax return of the deceased.

Q. *My widowed father died in November 2006 when the stock market was still relatively high. His stock portfolio was valued at $500,000. Since his cost was $100,000, there was a taxable capital gain of $200,000 (50% of $400,000). In the 40% tax bracket, his estate would have to pay about $80,000 in tax.*

But when it was time to distribute the estate to his children, the stocks had fallen in value to $400,000. Do we still have to pay all that tax?

A. There is an exception that can be used when the value of an asset falls. If the executor sells the portfolio in the first year of the estate, the loss can be applied to the deceased's final tax return. In your case, the loss of $100,000 could be applied to your father's final tax return, reducing the overall tax bill. But don't forget to consult your accountant and factor in the costs of selling the assets.

Income Taxes Due from Capital Gains

To estimate just how much income tax would be due from capital gains on your final tax return, I'd first take a snapshot of your current situation. List all your assets not left to your spouse, their cost base for CRA purposes, and their current market value. Then calculate the undeclared profits on each asset since 1972 by subtracting the cost from the market value and unused capital losses. What's 25% of that? That approximates the amount of tax due on capital gains at death. For a more exact figure, see your adviser. Since the value of your assets will change over time, the tax estimate should be recalculated periodically.

EXAMPLE In 1983, Georges bought 1,000 shares at $10 each. When Georges died, these shares were worth $50 each and were left to his daughter in his will.

The income taxes due on these shares would be calculated as follows:

Fair market value of shares at time of death	$50,000
Cost	$10,000
Capital gain (profit)	$40,000
50% of capital gain (taxable portion)	$20,000
Taxes payable (assuming 40% tax rate)	$8,000

The tax is calculated the same way it would be if Georges had sold the shares through his broker while alive.

If you sell an asset that has significant capital gains while you are alive, you may end up paying alternate minimum tax. Alternate minimum tax is a tax calculation designed to ensure that people with large amounts of preferential tax deductions, such as capital gains, pay at least a minimum amount of tax on the profit. If the tax based on the alternate minimum tax calculation is greater than the tax calculated on the regular tax return, the greater amount is due. There is some good news, though. Alternate minimum tax does not apply to the final tax return.

If you give your home to your children while you are alive and they do not live in it, they will not be able to use the principal residence exemption, and any increase in value from the time of the gift to the time they sell it would be taxed. But if you left them your home in your will (assuming you had continued to live in it), any increase in value would not be taxed because it would be eligible for the principal residence exemption.

REGISTERED PLANS: RRSPS AND RRIFS

Money contributed to a registered retirement savings plan creates tax deductions for the contributor (except overcontributions). That money grows—hopefully—in the RRSP or RRIF on a tax-deferred basis. When the annuitant of an RRSP or RRIF dies, the government wants to get back some of that income tax (and maybe even a little more!). Some people forget that they received a tax deduction when they made their contributions and are incensed when they have to pay tax when the money is withdrawn.

RRSPs or RRIFs not left to a spouse or partner are considered to have been cashed in and are taxed, with few exceptions.

Although the rules of RRSPs and RRIFs are slightly different, there are a number of similarities. When you die, your registered plan dies as well. An RRSP can be transferred to a surviving spouse or partner's RRSP tax-free—it is actually rolled over with a "refund of premiums" on your tax return. An RRIF can be transferred to a surviving spouse or partner's own registered plan, or arrangements can be made so the RRIF payments continue to be paid if he or she was designated as the surviving annuitant.

When the designated beneficiary is not a spouse or partner, the value of the plan is normally paid to the named beneficiary. If no beneficiary is named, the money is paid to the estate.

When no beneficiary is named, or when the beneficiary is not a spouse or partner, the amount of tax due will be calculated on the final tax return. The amount of the RRSP/RRIF is added to the final tax return and included in the calculation of the final tax bill.

The tax will be paid out of the estate. If the estate does not have enough money to pay the tax on the RRSP/RRIF, the *Income Tax Act* states that the beneficiary and the estate are "jointly and severally" liable for the tax on the RRSP/RRIF. So, if the estate does not have enough money to pay the tax bill related to the registered plan, the beneficiary can be held responsible for those taxes.

The *Income Tax Act* does not specify that withholding tax is required on death. The executor can request that withholding tax not be withheld, if it is appropriate for the estate.

Naming Your Beneficiary

Who you name or designate as the beneficiary of your registered plan affects the final tax bill so it is important to keep your beneficiary designation up to date, especially if you divorce or remarry.

Some financial institutions will not let you name multiple beneficiaries for your RRSP/RRIF because a multiple beneficiary designation may not tell them what should be done if one of your beneficiaries predeceases you. For example, if you wanted to name your adult children as your beneficiaries because you do not have a spouse, what would you want to be done if one of your children predeceases you? Should their share be reallocated to the surviving beneficiaries, or become part of your estate? Financial institutions want to avoid any unnecessary legal hassles and without clear beneficiary instructions, they might have to obtain written consent from everyone who could have a claim to the RRSP proceeds, or the deceased child's share could become part of your estate. In Quebec, you should designate your beneficiary in your will.

If an RRSP is with an insurance company, insurance legislation can help and might have reallocated the deceased child's share amount to the other children named as beneficiaries. Again, you need to confirm that what might happen is what you want to have happen.

A Spouse or Partner

When a spouse or common-law partner is the named beneficiary, RRSP or RRIF assets can be passed to them—rolled over as a refund of premiums—with no immediate tax due.

If you are separated or divorced, do not assume that your beneficiary designations on your life insurance, group pension, RRSPs, or RRIFs will change automatically. Review and update your beneficiary designations if necessary.

Final Contribution to a Spousal RRSP after Death

If the deceased had unused RRSP contribution room and is survived by a spouse or partner (same or opposite sex) who is under 70, the executor or personal representative may elect to make a final contribution to a spousal RRSP and receive a receipt that can be used on the final income tax return. This final contribution must be made in the year of death or by the following March 1, or the opportunity is lost forever.

EXAMPLE John died November 30, 2006, and was survived by his wife. When he died, he had $10,000 of unused RRSP contribution room. His executor elected to contribute $10,000 to a spousal RRSP on February 1, 2007. Since John was in the 40% tax bracket, this saved about $4,000 on his final income tax return.

When your spouse is your sole beneficiary under your will, your executor (who may be your spouse) may decide to make this election based on your overall financial situation, not just the potential tax savings.

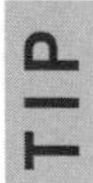

If your spouse is not your sole beneficiary under your will, you may want to state that your executor has the discretion to contribute to a spousal RRSP. Since a spousal RRSP contribution would reduce the amount other family members may be expecting to receive under the will and they might perceive a spousal RRSP contribution as being unfair to them (some people!), explicitly stating that your executor has the authority to make this contribution could help defuse any potential conflict.

RRSP

When your spouse or common-law partner is the named beneficiary, the assets in the RRSP can be transferred to his or her own registered plan (or a new plan if your spouse did not have one). The transfer is done through what CRA calls a refund of premiums, where the amount of the deceased's RRSP is included in the beneficiary's income and offset by an RRSP tax receipt for the same amount. This allows the registered funds to continue their tax-deferred status without affecting the spouse's own RRSP contribution limit.

Of course, your spouse has the option of making a withdrawal from the registered plan at any time and paying tax on the amount withdrawn. However, it is often better to transfer the full amount of the RRSP or RRIF and leave it intact until it is needed. Once money is withdrawn, it cannot be put back.

If you have a home buyer's loan inside your RRSP, the outstanding balance will need to be included as income on the final income tax return—unless your spouse is named as your RRSP beneficiary and took out a home buyer's loan when you did.

If you withdrew money under the Life Long Learning program, any outstanding balance will need to be included as income on the final income tax return.

EXAMPLE Barb and Manuel borrowed $15,000 each from their RRSPs under the home buyer's loan program to help them purchase their first house. They each named the other as the RRSP beneficiary. Five years later, when Barb died, she had $10,000 remaining on the loan. Manuel, her executor, had two options.

1. He could add the $10,000 RRSP loan balance to Barb's final income tax return (and roll the rest of the RRSP over to himself), or
2. He could roll Barb's whole RRSP, including the loan balance, over to his own RRSP. His RRSP loan balance will now be $20,000, since he also had $10,000 outstanding. He will continue to repay a minimum of $2,000 per year for the next 10 years.

RRIF

When your spouse or partner is the beneficiary or the "successor annuitant" on a RRIF, he or she can become the annuitant of the RRIF and continue to receive the RRIF payments without having to transfer the RRIF to a new account. If this is not appropriate at the time, the RRIF can be transferred to the surviving spouse's own RRIF.

If the surviving spouse is under 70 and does not require the annual income from the deceased's RRIF, the RRIF can be converted back to an RRSP. This would provide an additional tax shelter for the investment income until the surviving spouse turned 69 or required money from the RRSP.

A Dependent Child or Grandchild

If you name a minor child or grandchild—who was financially dependent on you at the time of your death—as the beneficiary of your RRSP/RRIF, the registered funds can be used to purchase an income-producing term-certain annuity that matures when the child is 18, even if you have a spouse or common-law partner.

The income from the annuity amount could be spread over several years, resulting in a lower tax bill. For example, if your RRSP was valued at $60,000 and your grandchild was 15, about $20,000 would be taxed annually for three years at the child's tax rate, rather than $60,000 on the deceased's final tax return.

This could be a useful joint disaster planning tool, or method to get money to the child for the future, which might be used, say, for his or her education.

If you have more than one child, you may have to name multiple beneficiaries in your will, since some financial institutions do not allow you to name multiple beneficiaries on an RRSP/RRIF.

If your spouse predeceased you and you do not have a young child or grandchild to name as the beneficiary, the entire amount is taxable in the year of death on the final tax return.

If you have a disabled adult child or grandchild who was financially dependent, you may be able to roll your RRSP or RRIF over tax-free to him or her (no longer only if the child is a minor), based on the federal government's income dependency threshold. Of course, the tax planning always needs to be weighed with the practical planning needs of the adult child.

Lifetime Benefit Trust

Changes to the Lifetime Benefit Trust and the Qualified Trust Annuity have been proposed. Currently, money can be transferred from an RRSP to an annuity for an infirm dependant child or grandchild for a term annuity to age 90. The changes broaden them to allow the money to be transferred from an RRSP to a trust to last until age 90.

Only the child or grandchild of the deceased would be eligible to receive any income and capital out of the trust.

What if you are survived by a spouse, but did not name him or her as the beneficiary on the registered plan? If your spouse receives the proceeds under the will, he or she, and the executor, can jointly elect to have the RRSP proceeds transferred to his or her own RRSP as a refund of premiums to minimize the tax bill.

The Estate

If no beneficiary designation is made, the money in an RRSP or RRIF is cashed and paid to the estate. The full value of the registered plan at the time of death is added as income, on top of any other income you had that year, to the final income tax return, and the market value of the plan would be included in the probate calculation.

If you do not have a spouse, partner, or children under 18, it is sometimes effective to name your estate as the beneficiary, particularly if the estate will need the money to pay bills—if you expect no other significant income in the year of death. (If only we could time this accurately!)

Q. I am a 65-year-old widower with an RRSP worth $100,000. My annual income is $45,000. I don't want my estate to have to pay a huge tax bill on my RRSP when I die. Should I think about taking the money out of my RRSP now?

A. If you withdraw the entire amount from your RRSP now, you will pay tax on the full amount. If you leave it in the plan, your estate will pay tax on the full amount. But if *you* need some funds, consider withdrawing modest amounts now if it will not increase your annual tax bills significantly, but first check if this might affect any government benefits you receive.

Someone Else

Careful tax planning is required when the beneficiary on your RRSP or RRIF is not a spouse, partner, or financially dependent child or grandchild. When a beneficiary is one where no tax rollover or deferral is available, the value of the RRSP/RRIF on the date of death is treated as if it was cashed out.

Most financial institutions will pay the entire RRSP/RRIF proceeds to the named beneficiary, without withholding tax up to 30%. The estate is responsible for settling the tax on the final tax return, which reduces the value of the estate for other beneficiaries named in the will.

EXAMPLE Susan is widowed and has three adult children. To be fair, she wanted to leave each child an equal amount on her death and when she considered just three of her assets, she planned to distribute them as follows:

- To her eldest, $300,000 in cash through her will.
- To her middle child, her home worth $300,000 through a bequest her will.
- To her youngest, her RRSP worth $300,000 through the RRSP beneficiary designation.

But on Susan's death, this is a highly simplified version of what happened:

- Her middle child received the house (no tax due because it had been Susan's principal residence).
- Her youngest child received $300,000 from the RRSP.
- The eldest child received approximately $180,000 (the $300,000 cash less the taxes paid out of the estate on the value of the RRSP).

The result did not reflect Susan's wishes. She did not consider the tax implications of her estate and how the calculation would affect the distribution. All she wanted was for each of her daughters to receive an equal share. If she'd known, she would have organized her affairs differently so each would have received an equal share on an after-tax basis.

Q. I have a lot of strip bonds and stocks in my self-directed RRIF. My children are the named beneficiaries (my husband died two years ago). These are good-quality investments. Do they need to be turned into cash before they are given to the beneficiaries?

A. Not necessarily. If the money in the registered plans is not needed to pay your estate's final taxes, your executor can request the financial institution to transfer the assets "in kind" into a personal investment brokerage account for each adult child.

An estate may face substantial taxes on assets and registered plans that are not left to a spouse. And if you do owe the CRA, they like cash and on time. A good question to ask yourself is, "Will my estate have ready access to enough money to pay the tax bill?" To preserve the assets in your estate, you may need to name your spouse as your beneficiary, or transfer assets with no capital gains to other beneficiaries or have enough liquidity (cash or assets that you are willing to sell) to pay the tax. If you do not expect to have enough cash and want to keep assets in the family, you might want to consider life insurance or rethink your estate plan.

If an estate does not have enough cash or assets that can be sold to pay the tax bill, CRA has the authority to go to those who might have received gifts prior to your death to find assets to pay the tax. Or the executor can be personally liable for the tax if he or she distributes the assets before paying the taxes.

Q. My only asset is my RRSP worth $100,000. I've named my sister as the beneficiary. Have I just beat the taxman?

A. No. If there is not enough money in an estate to pay the tax bill that results from the transfer of a registered plan, the *Income Tax Act* holds the estate and the beneficiary "jointly and severally" liable for the tax on that plan. That means that CRA is legally entitled to "ask" the beneficiary to pay these taxes. Since you named your sister as the beneficiary, the financial institution could pay $100,000 directly to your sister unless your executor requests that withholding tax be deducted. The executor and CRA would approach your sister to collect the additional tax. Let's hope she wouldn't spend it all!

Charitable Donations

If you're miffed and still think that your RRSP/RRIF might be taxed away at 40% or more and thinking of leaving it all to charity, you can name the charity as the beneficiary of your RRSP or RRIF. On your death, the value of the registered plan is transferred to the charity and the charity will issue a tax receipt. The proceeds of the registered plan are reported on your final tax return as if it was cashed in and your executor will claim the non-refundable tax credit on your final tax return to reduce the tax bill.

Charitable gifts are often called planned gifts because you want to make sure you make the most of the tax-saving opportunities available to you.

See Chapter 14 for more details.

FARM PROPERTY

A family farm that was used mainly used for farming on a regular and ongoing basis by the deceased, the deceased's spouse, or common-law partner may be transferred to children (including land, a farm partnership, qualified fishing property and shares in a family farm corporation) to be passed to the next generation without triggering a taxable capital gain.

A qualified farm property in Canada is eligible for a special rollover and can be transferred at an amount equal to its adjusted cost base, provided all the conditions set out in the *Income Tax Act* are met.

Your executor may elect to make the transfer at an amount somewhere between the adjusted cost base and the fair market value to make the most of all other items being reporting on the final tax return, such as any capital gains exemptions, capital losses, and charitable donations.

It might also be eligible for the $500,000 capital gains exemption available for qualified business corporations.

The next generation includes children (including adopted children), stepchildren (the child of the deceased's spouse or common-law partner), grandchildren, or great-grandchildren who are residents of Canada, or a person who, while under 19, was wholly dependent on the deceased for support and in his or her custody and control and was a resident of Canada. A spouse or common-law partner of these children are also included.

EXAMPLE Chris bought a farm for $25,000 many years ago. At the time of his death, the fair market value of the farm was $425,000.

The executor of Chris's estate can elect to transfer the farm to Ron, Chris's grandson, using:

- the rollover provision at a zero cost base, or
- at the fair market value of $425,000 and use the capital gains exemption for qualified farm property for the $400,000 profit

Either option would result in no tax due to the estate. But proper estate planning and using the capital gains exemption would save Ron some income tax if he later sold the farm at a profit.

U.S. ESTATE TAXES

If you are an American living in Canada, or a Canadian married to an American, or a Canadian who owns property in the United States, you may be required to pay U.S. estate taxes based on your total wealth.

A Canadian who owns property in the U.S. is called a "non-resident alien." (It has a really friendly ring to it, doesn't it?) A non-resident alien could face estate tax on the market value of the U.S. property at the time of death. Property includes, but is not limited to, real estate, such as the condominium in Florida, jointly held property, U.S. stocks, and U.S. mutual funds.

While Canadians pay tax on any profits they have earned on their assets and property up to the date of death (that they have not yet settled up with CRA), these Canadians are also required to file U.S. estate taxes based on their total wealth.

The Canada–United States Tax Convention provides Canadians with some relief from double taxation (and they may not be subject to U.S. estate tax) if a large percentage of their assets (including life insurance proceeds) are held in the United States and their worldwide estate for the year in question is valued at less than the following:

2007	$2,000,000
2008	$2,000,000
2009	$3,500,000
2010	no longer applicable, since taxes fully repealed
2011	$1,000,000 return to 2002 level if not extended

If a very small percentage of the estate's assets are held in the United States, there will be little tax relief.

The unified tax credit—a U.S. tax credit that applies to federal estate and gift taxes which have been integrated into one unified (but not simple) tax system—is based on the following formula:

$$\text{unified tax credit} \times \frac{\text{value of assets in the U.S.}}{\text{value of worldwide assets}}$$

Table 9.1: Unified Tax Credit and Highest Estate Tax Rates

YEAR	UNIFIED CREDIT	HIGHEST ESTATE TAX RATES
2007	$ 780,800	45%
2008	$ 780,800	45%
2009	$1,455,800	45%
2010	n/a	n/a
2011	$345,800*	55%

*If not extended

Estimating Your U.S. Tax Bill

The U.S. currently has a plan in place that is gradually lowering estate and gift taxes that will ultimately eliminate them in 2010. And it also dropped the top estate tax rate to 45% in 2007. However, this tax change includes a "sunset" provision that could, in 2011, restore the estate and gift tax rates and rules to pre-2002 levels or resurrect them in some form. This complicates estate planning for Canadians who hold significant U.S. assets.

We'll have to see what their politicians do. If the U.S. government has no need for money, they could leave it alone. However, if the government needs money—and they really do need money—then perhaps they may restore some version of the earlier rules.

Strategies to Deal with a Potential U.S. Estate Tax Bill

Non-resident aliens have used a number of techniques to reduce their U.S. estate taxes, including:

- Making small, regular gifts of U.S. property (although this is not practical if your only U.S. asset is a condo worth $300,000).
- Selling property prior to death. If you don't use that condo as much as you used to, or perhaps you've been diagnosed with a terminal illness, you might sell the property while you are alive and bring those dollars to Canada. If you do not own U.S. property at the time of your death, your estate will not pay U.S. estate taxes on it.
- Holding U.S. investments inside a Canadian corporation. Some advisers recommend holding U.S. investments (but not personal real estate) inside a Canadian corporation, where the objective of the corporation is to hold personal-use property. The U.S. government may change its rules at any time and determine that assets held this way are not really corporate assets, limiting the effectiveness of this strategy.
- Leaving property to your Canadian spouse, since the current treaty provides an additional spousal credit.
- Reducing the value of your estate so it is worth less than U.S. $1.2 million. Note that this is affected by the value of the Canadian dollar relative to the U.S. dollar.
- Buying additional life insurance to offset the tax due. But before proceeding, request a cost-benefit analysis projecting the tax bill and the cost of the life insurance premiums.

If your estate needs to write a cheque (or should I say check?) to the Internal Revenue Service, the IRS likes to be paid in U.S. dollars. The currency exchange rate at the time the cheque is written will affect the amount left over for your beneficiaries. If the amount owed is U.S. $100,000 and your estate's liquid assets are in Canadian dollars, the executor would need to buy U.S. dollars to pay the bill. When the Canadian dollar is at 65 cents, the bill would end up costing the estate about $153,800 Canadian. When the Canadian dollar is 88 cents, the bill would be about $112,360 Canadian.

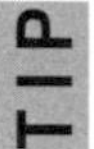

Expatriate Americans can explore renouncing U.S. citizenship and give up their U.S. assets if they wish to avoid U.S. estate tax.

Canadians who are married to a U.S. citizen, have dual citizenship, or hold a green card have additional estate planning considerations and should consult an accountant who specializes in U.S. tax and estate planning for Canadians.

If you own property outside Canada or the U.S., you may have an added complexity to your estate planning. Consult with your adviser to determine if you might owe tax in that country.

SUMMARY

Annual tax planning is normally concerned with deferring taxes for as long as possible.

Estate planning—and related tax planning—recognizes the day will come when you must finally settle up with Canada Revenue Agency. Some estate planning strategies include reporting income sooner rather than later, especially if there is an opportunity to do so when your marginal tax rate is lower than it might be in the year of death. Another strategy to deal with the tax bill is to ensure that you have enough cash or assets to deal with the inevitable. Some people consider purchasing life insurance to pay the taxes to maximize the value of their estate for their beneficiaries (insurance does not eliminate the tax bill); others decide to pay their taxes out of their estate when the time comes.

By understanding the potential impact the tax rules will have on your estate, you and your adviser can build an estate plan that ensures you and your estate pay no more tax than necessary.

chapter nine

filing the final income tax returns

The art of taxation consists in so plucking the goose as to get the most feathers with the least hissing.
—*Jean Baptiste Colbert*

DEATH IS ONE WAY TO HAVE YOUR NAME permanently removed from Canada Revenue Agency's annual mailing list! But before that can happen, your legal representative (your executor, administrator, or liquidator) is responsible for recreating your tax life, filing your final tax return and any returns from any previous years that may not have been filed correctly, and ensuring your taxes are all paid up.

The final income tax return is similar in many ways to the tax return you file every year—in fact you can often use the same T1 General Income Tax and Benefit Return—with a few notable differences in reporting. This return includes all your income in the year of death, up to and including the date of death.

The executor also has to ensure that the deceased's tax filings with CRA are up to date. If the executor discovers the deceased had not filed past returns, perhaps due to illness prior to death, it may be possible to apply under the fairness package for relief. However, if the executor discovers that the deceased had not complied with his or her tax obligations, such as perhaps failing to report income, the executor may want to explore making a voluntary disclosure. Minimum tax does not apply in the year of death.

Canada Revenue Agency (CRA) wants you to settle up with them for any deferred taxes on:

- your registered plans (RRSP, RRIF, LRSP, LIF, etc.). You are considered to have received an amount equal to the fair market value of the plan immediately before death and this is included in your taxable income. Exemptions are available for a designated spouse or partner.
- all capital property you owned as of the date of death. This requires a calculation for each asset that could result in an unrealized capital gain or loss. A capital gain results when proceeds of the "sale" are more than its adjusted cost base. These assets are deemed to have been sold, even though no actual sale may have taken place unless these assets are left to a spouse or a common-law partner.

The executor should be able to get a statement of the value of registered plans (RRSP, RRIF, LIF, etc.) and investment accounts as of the date of death.

Even if the deceased's tax returns are up to date, the executor should review them to ensure that they are accurate. A number of people fail to claim credits they would have been eligible for. As executor you could go back and amend prior returns. These credits could include caregiver credit, disability tax credits, and medical expenses just to name a few.

You can obtain a tax guide prepared by Canada Revenue Agency (CRA) called *Preparing Returns for Deceased Persons*, which is available online at www.cra.gc.ca.

I've selected some of the more commonly encountered rules for discussion here that we have not already discussed in other chapters.

DUE DATES—OR SHOULD I SAY *DEAD*LINES?

The due date for the final return and any tax due depends on the date of death. Generally, if death occurs between January 1 and October 31, the final return is due by April 30 of the following year. If death occurs between November 1 and December 31, the final return is due six months after the date of death.

In some circumstances, the executor may be entitled to an extension if the deceased or their spouse was running a business, or where a spousal trust is handling some of the debts of the estate.

Q. I'm the executor of my brother's estate, but I can't seem to find much information about his last tax return. How do I get what I need?

A. You can contact CRA for his information. You'll need to send them a copy of his death certificate, his social insurance number, and a copy of the will that indicates you are his legal representative.

If the final return is filed late, Canada Revenue Agency (CRA) charges a late-filing penalty *plus* interest on the balance owing and the penalty. In 2006, the penalty was 5% of any balance owing, plus an additional 1% of the balance owing for each full month that the return is late, to a maximum of 12 months. If any other returns were filed late in the last three years, the penalty could be even higher. The *Preparing Returns for Deceased Persons* guide states that, "even if you cannot pay the full amount owing by the due date, you can avoid this penalty by filing the return on time."

If your executor has to file the return late for reasons that were beyond his or her control, a letter can be sent to CRA with the return, explaining why the return was filed late, requesting that the interest and penalty be cancelled.

While CRA is not in the banking business, in addition to the penalties and interest above, they will charge compound daily interest on the unpaid amount from the day after its due date to the date you actually pay it.

If there is limited cash available in the estate, your executor could elect to pay the income tax resulting from the deemed disposition over time, rather than be forced to sell that capital asset, such as real estate, at a poor time in the market. If CRA approves an "instalment plan" arrangement to pay off the taxes owing, the estate will have to come up with the cash for each instalment and will be charged interest until it is paid in full.

Executors responsible for determining whether to sell or to pay by instalments may want to obtain the opinion of a certified real estate appraiser or other professional to ensure that they have acted in the best interest of the beneficiaries.

Paying by instalment could also delay the distribution of the estate because the executor may choose to wait until the tax clearance certificate is received from the CRA before fully settling the estate to ensure that the executor will no longer be responsible for any of the deceased's tax liabilities.

Q. I am a widower and own a building worth $1 million. Since there is $800,000 capital gains on this building, will my estate be required to sell the building immediately to pay the income taxes due?

A. I'll assume that the building is your only significant asset. It could be sold immediately if the price was right and there was a willing buyer. Alternatively, you could give your executor the power to hold the property in the estate until market conditions are right and pay the income tax by instalments. Your executor would do a cost-benefit analysis of the different scenarios, calculating the amount of income tax plus interest and penalties that would be due by instalments, and assess the market conditions for real estate in the area. After looking at the numbers, some executors may decide to sell the property sooner rather than later, to wrap up the estate.

FINAL RETURNS

Up to four tax returns *may* be filed for the deceased: the final return, which must be filed for every deceased taxpayer, and up to three optional returns, depending on the types of income the deceased received.

All the deceased's income, including CPP/QPP, can be included on the final return, and an executor is not required to submit optional returns. However, an employee may receive up to $10,000 of death benefits (which in some cases can include sick leave payments) from an employer that are not taxable.

But if optional returns apply (and they do not apply to everyone), certain tax credits and deductions—including the basic personal amount, age amount, spouse/common-law partner amount, and others—can be claimed more than once, certain types of income can be split between returns (i.e., your executor does not have to report it all on one return), reducing the overall amount of tax that might be due.

There are three types of optional returns.

A Return for Rights or Things

Rights and things are amounts due to the deceased at the time of death that had not been paid, including:

- vacation pay, salary, or commissions earned
- Old Age Security benefits that were due and payable before the date of death
- investment income earned, such as a dividend that was declared before death, or interest from a matured bond coupon that had not been cashed.

Interest earned on a bank deposit, where the interest had not been posted to the account, is not considered a right or thing.

Alternatively, the income from rights and things on assets transferred to a beneficiary within one year of the date of death can be reported on that beneficiary's tax return if the income of the beneficiary is very low.

A Return for a Sole Proprietor or Partner

If the deceased earned business income from a partnership or sole proprietorship with a year-end that was not December 31, the executor can file an optional return for income earned from the last business year-end to the date of death. Again, the income on the optional return may fall into a lower tax bracket, resulting in some tax savings.

EXAMPLE Lynn's consulting practice has a year-end of January 31. If Lynn died on April 30, 2007, her executor could choose between filing:

- one final tax return: reporting 15 months of income from February 2, 2006 to April 30, 2007, or
- two tax returns: a final return reporting 12 months of income for the period ending January 31, 2007, and an optional return reporting the business income for three months from February 1, 2007 to April 30, 2007.

A Return for Income from a Testamentary Trust

If the deceased had been receiving income from a testamentary trust (a trust set up in someone else's will) with a year-end that was not December 31, the executor can file an optional return for the trust income received to the date of death, rather than reporting the income on the final tax return. Again, reporting this income on a separate return may result in less tax. This is not the same as the return filed by the estate.

TAX RETURNS FOR THE ESTATE AND TESTAMENTARY TRUST

Your legal representative is responsible for filing the final income tax return and any optional returns that may be appropriate. Your legal representative may also have to file a T3 Trust Income Tax and Information Return to report the income earned annually on any assets held in the estate from the date of death until the assets are all distributed, with a few exceptions.

However, it may not be necessary to file a T3 return in every situation, such as when the estate can be distributed immediately after death, or if the estate didn't earn any income before the assets were distributed to the beneficiaries.

Q. My husband's estate existed for only a few months and everything was left to me. The estate earned $8,000 of interest income. Do I need to file a separate tax return for the estate?

A. No, you have the option of simply adding the income from your husband's estate to your own income tax return. However, if you have income of your own, you may be able to save some income tax by filing a separate tax return for the income earned during the "estate" period. For example, if you reported the interest income on your own tax return and you were in the 40% tax bracket, about $3,200 would be due on the interest income. If the $8,000 interest were reported on a separate tax return for the estate period, very little tax would be due.

It makes it worth filling out another government form for the estate, doesn't it? But an estate cannot exist just for income splitting. To hold the assets in trust for a beneficiary for a longer time, the will would need to establish a testamentary trust.

You can request a tax clearance certificate after you have paid amounts owing and received assessment notices for all the deceased's tax returns. Then you can complete form TX19 Asking for a Clearance Certificate.

If the executor is named as the trustee for testamentary trusts established under the will, he or she will file separate income tax returns for these trusts. (See Chapter 12 on trusts.)

chapter ten

family law and your estate plan

There is nothing like staying at home
for real comfort.
—*Jane Austen*

ALL PROVINCES HAVE LEGISLATION related to family law (family patrimony in Quebec) that deal with how assets will be divided in the event of separation and divorce. In some provinces, this legislation includes the death of a spouse and grants a surviving spouse no less than they would have received had they divorced. In general, this entitles the spouse to half of the assets, and the increase in value, accumulated during the marriage in many provinces.

So what's a family today? It may be a single parent raising children, a married couple growing old together, a couple living together. Grandparents, parents, and children living in the same home. For you, it's whatever works. However, what is considered a "family" in terms of your financial and legal estate responsibilities may be somewhat different.

The one thing I know for sure is that when it comes to protecting yourself, your partner, and any children you have, don't *assume* you are protected unless you are legally married or, in certain provinces, have taken steps to formalize your relationship in such a way that you know gives you rights on the death of your partner or the powers to act in the event of the incapacity of your partner.

Just because you may declare yourselves to be a common-law couple when you file your tax returns, it does not mean that you have spousal rights. It is important to have the appropriate documents in place so your estate will be distributed the way you wish, otherwise you could have limited or no legal rights. These documents might include a cohabitation agreement (or specific agreement set up by your province), documents that name you as the beneficiary, or a will and power of attorney documents in place. For example, according to a case in Nova Scotia where a couple had lived together for about 10 years but not married and had then separated (Walsh and Bona), the court determined that the decision to marry or not was intensely personal and did not grant the common-law partner spousal support.

The courts are not quick to make assumptions regarding relationships. However, now in Nova Scotia, it is possible to register a Domestic Partnership Declaration. In Alberta, it is possible to create a legal relationship referred to as an Adult Interdependent Partner (AIP) that, once registered, recognizes and acknowledges your partner with certain rights.

What follows is not a legal summary of what exists across the country. It provides a few examples of the changes that are occurring.

If you have a family—however you define it—*do not* leave it to the standard provincial regulations. It is important for you to consult with a lawyer or notary in your province to put your estate planning documents in place to ensure you leave your family secure.

SUPPORT AND MAINTENANCE

Although you might not believe this, you can't do whatever you want or write whoever you want out of your will. Each province has its own family laws to protect the rights of a spouse and dependants. Your legal and financial obligations remain your obligations after death and affect your freedom to distribute your assets. Lawyers refer to this as the "restriction on testamentary freedom." A dependant is a person who relied on you for financial support immediately before your death and usually includes a spouse (who also has spousal rights) and dependent children. In PEI and Ontario, a common-law partner's parents and grandparents are included in the definition.

If your will fails to provide adequate support and maintenance for your dependants, your dependants (or your dependant's guardian) can apply to the courts to obtain an order against the estate for continued support. The legislation for support is found in such acts as the *Family Relief Act* (Alberta), the *Dependants Relief Act* (Manitoba), the *Wills Variation Act* (B.C.), the *Dependants of a Deceased Person Relief Act* (PEI), and the *Succession Law Reform Act* (Ontario). Although the name and the wording of the act varies from province to province, the intent does not. In each province, the courts have the authority to order the estate to provide support to the dependants of the deceased (known as the testator). To give you an idea of how broad this wording is, here is part of the clause from the *Testator's Family Maintenance Act* of Nova Scotia:

> *Where a testator dies without having made adequate provision in his will for the proper maintenance and support of a dependant, a judge, on application by or on behalf of the dependant, has powers, in his discretion and taking into consideration all relevant circumstances of the case, to order whatever provisions the judge deems adequate to be made out of the estate of the testator for the proper maintenance and support of the dependant, where the dependant means widow or widower or child.*
>
> *If a dependant contracts out his right to apply under this act, the promise is not binding on the dependant.*

And just how long would support be required? If you have children in school, are you required to provide them with support until they are 18? Until they complete any post-secondary education? It's important to consider all your obligations and intentions so the instructions in your will are not overturned.

The order for maintenance and support may be made from income or capital in the estate and could be paid out as:

- a monthly or annual amount for a limited or an indefinite time, or until a specific age or event, such as marriage
- a lump sum to be held in trust
- property to be held in trust for the dependant for a limited or indefinite time
- possession of specified property for life or a specified time
- any other way the court considers appropriate
- if an order is granted, it overrides the instructions in your will and can restrict the distribution of the estate

Additional obligations may be found in a marriage contract or separation agreement.

Under Alberta's *Family Law Act*, if you have been a sperm donor and have not have had any relationship with the mother or the child, you do not acquire any parental or guardianship rights.

MARRIAGE AND REMARRIAGE

If you are contemplating marriage or have recently married, your will needs to be reviewed. (Or prepared if you do not have one.)

Marriage and remarriage automatically revoke a will (except in Quebec) unless, in most provinces, the will specifically states that it was drawn up "in contemplation of marriage." If you do not write a new will after marriage and then you die, you more or less die intestate unless your spouse elects to accept the old will. But how likely is that if your new spouse is not named in the will? If you don't prepare a new will, expect to die intestate!

If you remarry and have children from a previous marriage, you may want to make special plans to provide for them. A simple mirror will (where spouses leave everything to each other, and when both are deceased, leave everything to the children) could leave children from the first marriage dependent on the wording in your new spouse's will, which is not desirable or ideal for some families.

And if you have a new spouse, you can take advantage of the tax-deferred rollover on an RRSP or RRIF by naming him or her as beneficiary.

COMMON-LAW RELATIONSHIPS

Under the federal *Income Tax Act*, common-law partners (of the same or opposite sex) have the same rights, as well as responsibilities and restrictions, as married couples. Property, RRSPs, and RRIFs can be transferred to a common-law partner and the income tax deferred until the death of the surviving partner.

But it is not so when it comes to rights regarding estate planning. The rights of common-law partners across the country vary; some partners in some provinces are treated like a spouse for an intestate estate; when it comes to property rights, some common-law partners may prepare a cohabitation agreement; in other provinces, property rights are extended automatically to unmarried spouses who have lived together for a number of years with or without a child. It's up to you and your partner to clearly document your plan and use the documents available to you.

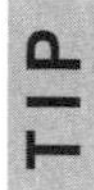

To protect a common-law partner (or yourself) and children, you could:

- own property jointly, outside of Quebec
- prepare your wills naming each other as executor
- name each other as beneficiary in your wills, on life insurance, pension plans, and RRSPs and RRIFs
- name each other in your power of attorney documents or mandate
- prepare a cohabitation agreement regarding property and support or your province's official agreement regarding your relationship in the event of separation and death
- obtain advice from a lawyer or a notary in your province

For example, in Nova Scotia, same-sex couples can register a Domestic Partnership Declaration. In Alberta, they can create a legal relationship referred to as an Adult Interdependent Partner (AIP). In Ontario, it is legal for two people of the same sex to marry. However, in many other provinces, common-law couples are not automatically recognized as having property rights on death or when the relationship breaks down. Put your own estate plan in place.

Same-sex partners have recently been granted rights by the courts that will affect their estate planning. While it is not entirely clear exactly what the changes will be and when they will come into effect, it seems reasonable at this time to expect that:

- pension benefits will be extended to all members of public and private pension plans if they name their partner as their beneficiary and spouse
- CPP survivor benefits will be extended to same-sex couples.

However, at the time of writing, the possible free vote in the House of Commons was put on hold.

Q. My partner and I are in a same-sex marriage. Are we protected under family law?

A. In Ontario, a recent court ruling gave married same-sex couples support obligations, but elsewhere same-sex relationships may have little or no protection. Married couples still need to put an estate plan in place.

SEPARATION

Separation does not automatically affect the instructions in your will nor any of your beneficiary designations. As long as you are legally married, you cannot write your spouse out of your will unless you have a marriage contract or separation agreement stating otherwise.

However, if you prepare a separation agreement, you likely will want to write a new will. If you are supporting your children, you will want to ensure you have adequately provided for them even after your death to reduce the likelihood that your estate would be challenged.

In addition to determining if you should re-register any assets held jointly, you should review and update:

- your will and power of attorney documents

- the beneficiaries named for your RRSPs, RRIFs, pension, insurance, and annuities

While your separation and divorce agreements may have wording regarding revoking your beneficiary designations, this in itself is not enough to actually change the beneficiary designation unless it specifically identifies the insurance contract, pension plan, or other affected contract. It is recommended that you approach each financial institution and change the beneficiary designation so they do not need to see the details of your separation agreement.

DIVORCE

If you were divorced and providing spousal or child support through a divorce agreement, your estate may be required to continue support payment after death. Some agreements state that support ends with death. Other agreements might require you to maintain adequate insurance coverage to provide funds to continue dependant support after your death. Some agreements may not state anything. Failing to meet your obligations could override the instructions in your will and complicate settling your estate.

A will prepared prior to the divorce is not automatically revoked, but a couple of provisions in that will are affected:

- Any asset or bequest left to your now ex-spouse is revoked.
- Your ex-spouse cannot act as executor, so your estate would have to apply to the courts to have an executor appointed.

On divorce, review your will. Chances are your intentions have changed. In my opinion, you should write and sign a new will at the same time as the separation or divorce agreement is written and signed. If child-support payments are required according to the divorce agreement, make sure that you have adequately provided for the support to continue after your death. And if you wish to name your ex in your new will, you'll need wording to the effect that this is what you want even though you are divorced.

Also review the beneficiary designations on your pension plans, life insurance, RRSPs, or RRIFs. Revise them as appropriate, and keep them up to date.

MOVING

Family law is provincial. Estate planning is governed mainly by provincial legislation, and the rules vary from province to province.

If you have moved to another province, review your will in light of that province's laws. If you move, review your estate plan to ensure it reflects the family legislation of your new province.

MATRIMONIAL PROPERTY

Some provinces have laws that protect a spouse's right to a just and equitable distribution of property (including the matrimonial home) on death. In other words, the spouse cannot be written out of the will, or receive less than would have been received on divorce. These rights could override the distribution in your will.

The executor can be held personally liable for any loss to the spouse if he or she fails to address a spouse's right to property on death.

The impact of these laws must be considered when preparing a will. Otherwise the will can be overridden. Later in this chapter we will discuss how the laws work in Ontario.

The executor of an estate could face personal liability if he or she fails to inform the surviving spouse of the right to receive an equalization payment. This could create a potential conflict for an executor who has the responsibility both to make decisions in the best interests of the surviving spouse and to follow the deceased's instructions.

MARRIAGE CONTRACTS

In most provinces, to protect the assets brought into a marriage, or to formalize their oral agreements and understandings, couples could prepare a marriage contract or a pre-nuptial agreement.

Before signing any contract, answer these questions:

Yes	*No*	*Unsure*	
❐	❐	❐	Do you know your legal rights related to family law?
❐	❐	❐	Do you understand how this contract will affect you personally and financially today and in the future?
❐	❐	❐	Have you received independent legal advice?

FAMILY LAW FOR ONTARIO RESIDENTS

Neglecting family law in Ontario can create unnecessary stress on family relationships, delay the settling of an estate, and result in outcomes that were not intended. Regardless of when or where your will was written, if you die while you are a legal resident in Ontario, its family laws are applied to your estate.

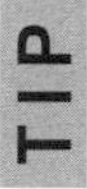

If your province's family laws do not reflect your family or business needs, consider putting your intentions in writing. Suppose you are marrying for a second time and you want to protect your business for your children. Set up your estate so that your instructions will be followed through a properly prepared will, marriage contract, or a living trust arrangement.

Ontario family law states that property and assets acquired during a marriage are to be shared equally if the marriage breaks down; death is included as a form of marriage breakdown. The surviving spouse has the legal right to elect to receive the inheritance as stated in the will or, if left less than 50% of the net family property, to apply to the courts within six months (unless extended by the courts for special circumstances) to receive an equalization payment based on property held the day before death "as if they had separated." If an election is not made within six months, the spouse is assumed to have accepted the terms of the will.

Some spouses are reluctant to elect the entitlement even if it would be to their benefit. Making an election does not draw into question the state of the marriage. Rather, it reflects poor planning on the part of the deceased.

Q. I live in Ontario. My wife will receive a generous annual income from my estate. Is this enough?

A. Under the *Ontario Family Law Act*, a spouse may elect to take either the terms of the will or to receive a net equalization payment. Your wife would determine if she is better off accepting the terms of the will or electing for the equalization payment. If she prefers to receive an outright lump sum rather than an annual income (however generous), she can so elect. If an equalization payment is elected, it takes priority over the instructions in the will.

The Net Equalization Payment

If your spouse does not receive everything under your will, he or she should weigh the value of the benefits that would be received under the will against the value of an equalization payment. Independent financial advice is recommended. To calculate the amount of an equalization payment, the value of net family property is calculated, in general terms, as the value of all property the day before the date of death

less the value of property brought into the marriage, but not including the matrimonial home (the home and cottage used by you and your spouse)

less the value of gifts or inheritances received during the marriage unless the money was used to pay off a matrimonial home

less any income received from a gift or inheritance if there were written instructions from the donor to exclude it from net family property

EXAMPLE On Marsha's death, the family's assets and liabilities are:

Tom	*Marsha*	
$250,000	$250,000	jointly held home
	$200,000	investment real estate
	$400,000	business where children are employed

	($100,000)	(less value of business at the time of marriage)
0	0	less liabilities
$250,000	$750,000	family property held

In Marsha's will, investment real estate valued at $200,000 is left to Tom and her business is left to the children. The house was held jointly.

Calculation of net equalization payment:
($750,000 – $250,000) ÷ 2 = $250,000

Tom could elect to receive the equalization payment, which is $50,000 more than he would get under the terms of the will. Since the estate does not have sufficient cash to pay Tom the $50,000, his election could force the sale of the business, or he could become a reluctant partner in the business with the children.

The value of all property owned by either spouse the day before the date of death is included in the equalization payment, not including the proceeds of any life insurance owned by the deceased. Fortunately, Marsha's $500,000 life insurance policy covers his needs and is greater than the net equalization payment—solving the potential issue.

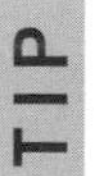

If you are not planning to leave everything to your spouse, project the value of an equalization payment, and take any necessary steps so that your spouse does not need to make a claim.

In Tom and Marsha's case, Marsha might want to protect her business for the children and ensure her husband does not change his mind. In addition to wills, they could prepare a marriage or single-purpose contract to formalize their agreement so that the understanding is not left to the goodwill of the surviving spouse. Such a contract can be signed at any time during a marriage. Each spouse should obtain independent legal and financial advice to ensure he or she is not being coerced into "giving away" something, and make it more difficult to challenge the agreement later. You must also consider how realistic it is to expect your spouse to sign a marriage contract after you have been married for 20 years!

EXAMPLE André's will leaves his wife, Lise, property and assets valued at $150,000. The net family property calculation at death indicates that Lise had $50,000 of net family property in her name and André had $450,000 in his name. Under Ontario family law, Lise is entitled to half of the net family property ($450,000 – $50,000) ÷ 2 = $200,000.

Since André's will leaves Lise assets and property valued at $150,000, Lise would be better off to make an election to receive the equalization payment of $200,000.

IN QUEBEC

Regardless of where the marriage took place, the laws of Quebec apply if the family lived in Quebec at the time the death occurred.

In Quebec, a spouse also has an interest in the family patrimony, the family assets, which consist of the following (less any debts), regardless of the legal ownership of the property or asset:

- the family residence and furnishings
- vehicles used by the family
- benefits that have accrued from a pension plan or RRSP during the marriage

SUMMARY

Legislation related to estate planning, succession law, trusts, taxation, probate, and family law changes periodically.

I have discussed what can be complex issues in just a few pages. Professionals can best help you assess the impact of such changes on your estate plan. Be sure to discuss with your lawyer how family law in your province affects your estate plan.

chapter eleven

life insurance

Whoever created the name "life insurance"
had to be the sales genius of all time.
—Robert Half

WHO KNOWS WHAT THE FUTURE HOLDS? When you buy life insurance (and pay premiums), a life insurance company agrees to pay tax-free cash on your death to your beneficiary. Insurance is often referred to as risk management: the risk you are managing is the financial impact your death would have on your dependants.

Simple Definition of Life Insurance:
You pay. You die. Insurance company pays.

Before you buy life insurance, the need you must identify is whether or not you—or actually your dependants—really need it. Most people either need it, or they don't. In reality, life insurance is purchased for many more reasons than just managing the financial impact your death would have on your spouse or dependants. Others may also stand to lose out financially on your death if some of that value is not replaced through life insurance, such as your business partner.

The need for life insurance can be very personal—it's not all about dealing with a tax bill. For example, one couple I know was discussing whether or not they should consider purchasing some additional life insurance. He stated that he did not think insurance was a good investment, but this was not the issue we were trying to discuss. This particular woman was turning 65 and her retirement income would be about 50% of her pre-retirement income. While they had savings, part of their retirement plan included an inheritance that could still be years from being received. His plan was to continue to work as a professional (he was 63 and in relatively good health) to enable them to stay in their house—a key priority for her—until it all fell into place. However, if anything happened to him, before they received the inheritance, they would have a shortfall. Purchasing life insurance would literally buy them some time to figure out how they might rearrange their finances. It would also take some of the financial pressures off the husband, and perhaps increase the quality of their life and their financial security.

When discussing insurance, I recommend you consider insurance in two parts: Part 1: Does your family need additional financial protection in the event something should happen to you? And Part 2: What is the best way to cover that?

COMMON USES FOR INSURANCE IN ESTATE PLANNING

There are a number of estate planning uses for life insurance. These include, but are not limited to the following:

- Create an "instant" estate so your family can be raised, educated, and supported. If you are divorced, you might be legally required to have life insurance to cover any support payment responsibilities that continue after your death.
- Provide financial security for your surviving spouse. The first point might be focused on younger families, but families of all ages may want to ensure their surviving spouse or partner has an estate or sufficient monthly income so they can mature or age with dignity. Your financial adviser can help you estimate the income that is available (from sources such as a survivor pension, CPP/QPP benefits, and/or OAS benefits) and expenses, and ways to provide you and your spouse with financial security.

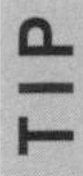

While you are employed, you may have group life insurance based on your salary. But when you retire, that group coverage often drops to $5,000 or less. Since life insurance gets more expensive as you get older, it's important to pay attention to the amount of coverage you might need before you retire (and before you need it).

- Pay off liabilities, such as the mortgage, car loan, or credit card debts. Suppose you and your partner can afford the mortgage payment as long as you are both working, but you don't want your partner to have to sell the house if you die prematurely.
- Settle the expenses of your estate (including probate taxes, legal fees, and U.S. estate tax) so no assets have to be sold.
- Offset taxes owed to Canada Revenue Agency (CRA) on taxable capital gains and the taxes on the RRSP/RRIF when it is left to someone other than a spouse or partner so the estate assets remain intact (see Chapter 8).
- Pay for your funeral.
- Provide cash so your business partner can afford to buy out your share of the business.
- Make a more generous gift to charity than you might otherwise be able to afford.
- Use the tax deferral features of life insurance.
- Replace some or all of the value of the estate you might want to spend or give away during your lifetime.
- Accomplish succession planning for privately held corporations and partnerships.
- Equalize benefits among family members. For example, if you want to leave the cottage or business to one family member, you might leave others life insurance.
- Maximize the amount you leave for your beneficiaries.

Q. *I'm 66 years old, in good health, and a widow. How can I reduce the taxes CRA wants to collect on my death?*

A. The tax rules are not in your favour, but you should first estimate what the tax bill might be. Here are a few ideas that might help you reduce that final bill:

- If the size of the inheritance you leave is important, you could purchase life insurance. The life insurance proceeds could provide cash to pay the taxes due to CRA, leaving a larger estate.
- Compare your current marginal tax rate with the marginal tax rate you might face on death. If you are currently in a lower tax rate, you could consider withdrawing some funds from your RRSP/RRIF or crystalize some capital gains while you are alive.
- Consider giving away some of your estate so you won't own as much when you die.
- Make some charitable donations to help offset some of the taxes due.

BUYING LIFE INSURANCE

You want to have *enough* life insurance—and to make sure it goes to the *right* place. Once you've decided (or your partner has helped you decide) you need life insurance, you also have to determine how much, which company, the type of policy, and what features or options the policy should have.

How Much?

The amount of life insurance you require depends on many factors, including:

- your situation (the number and needs of your dependants and business partners)
- how much insurance you currently have
- your current income
- your current assets and debts as well as a projection of the future value of your assets and debts
- executor fees and probate taxes
- income taxes due on death
- any education you want to fund

- other sources of income your survivors may have
- some assumptions about the future, such as rates of returns and tax rates

When you look at buying a new vehicle, you have a sense of what your family needs. If you have three children and the dog, you know a sports car will not be appropriate no matter how much you really want it!

If you have young children, you might ask yourself a series of questions and think about what your family's situation would be if you were hit by a bus tomorrow. Would your survivors have enough money to pay the bills, finish their education, or just have enough money to live on? Will there be enough money to create the income they require? Discuss this with your spouse; it might give you a better sense of whether there is a need for life insurance.

If you are looking at purchasing life insurance to maximize the value of your estate, or to offset the tax bill, or to maximize a charitable gift or for a business need, your financial adviser can help you with the questions and potential solutions for your situation.

If you are looking at life insurance to protect your family, or to protect your spouse/partner, the following worksheet looks at the assets you currently own, your expenses, the monthly income needed in the future, and ultimately how much money (in this case, life insurance) you would require and have invested to produce the amount of income needed.

As a general rule of thumb, the more assets you have already accumulated, the less life insurance you need. The amount of life insurance you require depends on your situation (the number and needs of your dependants and business partners). The calculation considers the amount of insurance you currently have in place, the assets you have, your debts, executor and probate fees, income taxes due on death, education funding, other sources of income your survivors may have, and some assumptions about the future.

Traditionally, the husband would have been insured, so that if anything happened to him, the insurance would be paid out to the spouse. In today's world, I believe both partners should ensure they have sufficient life insurance coverage, particularly if there are debts and children. I recommend you do a calculation for yourself, as well as one for your spouse/partner.

Do you have a retirement plan that provides monthly pension benefits during your lifetime with a survivor benefit for your spouse on your death? Consider that, when you die, your pension will drop to the amount of that survivor benefit.

LIFE INSURANCE WORKSHEET

You can use this worksheet to estimate the amount of life insurance coverage that you and your spouse or common-law partner might need.

This calculation is only an estimate of the amount you might need from a personal perspective. It does not include any insurance that might be required for any business interests.

Step 1:

List the capital you expect will be available after your death that is currently in your name.

The value of assets in your name only
(GICs, bank accounts, investments, etc.) $__________

Assets where "estate" is the beneficiary

The value of your RRSP/RRIF +__________

The death benefit or commuted value of your pension plan +__________

The death benefit of insurance you have (include group insurance) less any policy loans +__________

The commuted value of annuity payments within guaranteed period + __________

The death benefit from CPP/QPP (maximum $2,500) +__________

Other assets registered in your name only that would likely be sold on your death +__________

Step 2:

List the value of capital your spouse/partner will receive on your death.

Assets registered jointly with your spouse +__________

Assets where your spouse/partner is the beneficiary

The value of your RRSP/RRIF +__________

The death benefit or commuted value of your pension plan +__________

The commuted value of annuity payments within guarantee period +__________

The death benefit from insurance you have +__________

Total amount of capital available from steps 1 and 2 = $__________

Step 3:

Deduct the liabilities and expenses that will need to be paid on your death.

Uninsured debts to be paid in full (mortgage, loans, credit cards, etc.) – $__________

Canadian income taxes due on death – __________

U.S. estate taxes due on death – __________

Probate taxes/fees – __________

Executor fees – __________

Funeral costs – __________

Legal and other professional fees – __________

Other final expenses – __________

Net amount of capital available $__________*

*Amounts in steps 1 and 2 less amounts in Step 3

Step 4:

Deduct any amounts that might be required for special purposes, including the amount needed to establish an emergency fund, pay for your children's education, or make gifts to other family members or to charity.

Present value of amount needed to fund your children's education	– $__________
Estimate amount needed for emergency fund (minimum of three months' expenses)	– __________
Special bequests and gifts, including gifts to charity	– __________
Other purpose: __________________	– __________
Other purpose: __________________	– __________
Capital available/shortfall after lump sums spent	= $________ **

** If this amount is negative, you have a shortfall of capital for your final expenses and/or your lump-sum items that could be funded by life insurance. However, you may also need additional insurance after you complete Step 5.

This is before estimating the annual income your dependants may need after your death.

Step 5:

Estimate the annual income your dependants might need after your death to support their current lifestyle. This involves estimating your family's expenses and the sources of income they would have available to determine if additional capital might be needed to generate additional income.

Current annual expenses:

Accommodation (rent, property taxes, condo fees, etc.)	$__________

Utility costs ____________
Property insurance ____________
Communication
(phone, cable, Internet, etc.) ____________
Recreational property ____________
Transportation
(car, public transit, taxis, etc.) ____________
Food (groceries, dining out) ____________
Clothing ____________
Personal care ____________
Health care
(drugs, dental, alternative, etc.) ____________
Vacations ____________
Entertainment ____________
Alcohol and cigarettes ____________
Clubs/associations ____________
Gifts ____________
Allowance for children ____________
Pets ____________
Child care
(daycare, babysitting, summer camp, etc.) ____________
Charitable donations ____________
Income taxes ____________
Other ____________
Other ____________
Other ____________
Current annual expenses (G) = $____________

Estimate the annual income your dependants will have available after your death.

Spouse's employment income $____________

Survivor pension income	______________
Spouse's investment income	______________
Spouse's income from RRIF/annuity	______________
Survivor CPP/QPP income	______________
GST rebate/Universal child care	______________
Dependent survivor CPP/QPP income	______________
Other sources of income:	______________
Anticipated annual income	(H) = $______________

Calculate the annual income surplus/shortfall

Annual income surplus/shortfall	(H) – (G) $____________*

* If these amounts are negative, you may want to eliminate the shortfall by purchasing additional life insurance to protect your family's lifestyle or by revisiting any bequests to charities or beneficiaries who are not dependants in order to leave more for your dependants.

The next step is to estimate the amount of capital or life insurance—the death benefit—you may require to fund the annual income shortfall (if any from Step 5) by answering the following question:

> *If a death benefit were invested at today's rates, how much would be required to generate the additional income required (G – H) each year?*

You also need to factor in inflation, a rate of return that could realistically be expected, the number of years the income would be required, and the tax rate of the person receiving the income. The higher the rate of return you could reasonably expect to earn, the less life insurance required. However, when rates of return are low, more life insurance may be required.

Of course, this would only be an estimate of the amount you might need. For a more accurate estimate, you would also need to consider the rate of inflation, the rate of return that could be realistically expected, the number of years the income might be required, and the tax rate of the person receiving the income.

To estimate the amount of capital required, divide the income you need by the rate of return currently offered on five-year GICs:

- If GICs are currently earning 5%, divide the annual income needed by .05.
- If GICs are currently earning 4%, divide the annual income needed by .04.

Of course, if you believed you could make more in the market or were prepared to purchase an annuity in the future with the death benefit proceeds, you could consider purchasing less insurance. And the type of insurance you purchase will affect the cost.

EXAMPLE Suppose your young family would need an additional $20,000 a year (not including inflation) for the rest of their lives if you were to die within the next 12 months. If it was reasonable to be able to earn an average of 5% a year, the amount of capital, or life insurance, needed might be estimated as follows:

$20,000 ÷ .05 = $400,000

If you already have accumulated some capital, you could deduct this amount from the $400,000, and consider purchasing less life insurance.

Now this is a simplistic example. It's also been said a person should consider having insurance equal to 5–10 times their income, but that makes for a very wide range.

If you based your life insurance needs on a calculation done when interest rates were 7% (when your money could double every decade), I recommend you re-do this calculation, based on today's interest rates and your family's income needs. When interest rates fall, it takes more capital to maintain an income level, and more life insurance to provide that capital.

While there is no way to know what the rate of return might be in the future or how many years the income might be required, this is a starting point for discussion with your adviser. If you anticipate the capital might be invested in a mix of fixed income investments and stocks, you might use a higher projected rate of return to reflect the possible longer-term rate of return. However, overestimating the potential rate of return could mean your family ends up with too little income.

TOO MUCH OR TOO LITTLE?

The amount of insurance you need when you're 40 is likely quite different from the amount you need at 60. If you require less insurance than you currently have, the first thing to do is review your current policy. There are many ways to reduce your coverage:

- The existing policy may have a base policy and a rider. Sometimes the rider has a different period than the base policy and may fit in with your needs.
- Take out a new policy for a smaller amount. (Watch out, though. A new policy could be more expensive because you are older or your medical health has changed.)
- Change an existing policy to a paid-up status (if it has a cash value).
- Cancel it if you do not need the insurance at all.
- Donate it to charity.

There are pros and cons to these options, so discuss them with your adviser to ensure that you don't face any adverse tax consequences and to determine what's most appropriate for you.

Q. How often should I review my insurance?

A. Insurance policies often just sit in a file somewhere gathering dust. Your insurance policies are important documents. I think that they should be filed where you file your important papers and your family and your executor should know where they can find them.

As your family situation changes, or if you change your employer and your group coverage, or if the value of your investments changes, the amount or type of insurance you need may also change. Do you have too much? Is your insurance coverage sufficient? Like applying for a loan at the bank, the time to obtain it is before you require it. Be sure to review your insurance coverage every few years and whenever there is a significant change in your situation.

PURCHASING LIFE INSURANCE

In order to buy life insurance, you need to make an application. The life insurance company will assess your application, your medical history, and other factors. If the insurance company accepts your application, it will issue a life insurance policy contract. The company will assess your potential risk and may assign you to a particular risk group, which may be different than the medical risk your doctor has discussed with you.

However, the insurance company looks at your medical history based on its financial experience, and its priority is to reduce its potential financial risks. The actual reality of your personal health is between you and your doctor.

You have the right to examine a policy issued to ensure it will provide the protection you require. As with any contract, be sure to read the insurance policy and ask for an explanation of anything you do not understand.

The financial stability of the insurance company, the features of the policy, the guarantees, and the cost are important considerations when selecting an insurer and a particular policy.

Q. Are there any guarantees that a life insurance company will pay up?

A. Under Canadian law, the insurance company has financial obligations to its policyholders. Insurance policies specify which situations are not covered (excluded) by the contract, such as suicide within two years of purchasing the policy. But if an insurance company goes bankrupt, Assuris (formerly CommCorp) fully protects up to $200,000 of life insurance death benefit coverage per person at any one insurance company. For more information, you can contact their consumer assistance centre at info@assuris.ca or 1-800-268-8099 (in the Toronto area, call 416-777-2344). Their Web site is www.assuris.ca.

If you need more than $200,000 of life insurance coverage, you may want to consider splitting the amount between two or more companies to maximize the Assuris coverage. The more companies you use, the higher your total premium will be (because each company charges a policy fee), but this can help to ensure the coverage will be there when it is needed.

What Kind?

A number of insurance products are on the market, some of which make more sense in some situations than others. Life insurance can be broadly classified as temporary or permanent, with many policies being combinations and variations of these broad classifications. The name on a policy does not always indicate the type of coverage.

There are all sorts of life insurance policies. When buying life insurance, you are trying to match your needs with an appropriate type of policy, to get value for the coverage you need without paying for features you do not require.

Q. What is the best type of life insurance?

A. There is no simple answer. You want to ensure you purchase sufficient coverage with a quality insurer at a competitive price.

The cost of life insurance—the annual premium—is based on such factors as your age, sex, the amount of insurance applied for, the type of policy, special features, such as cost of living indexing and guarantees, your health, whether you are a smoker, your hobbies (such as flying), the policy definitions, and the insurance company's pricing structure and assumptions about mortality rates. (The mortality rate is the company's calculation of the probability of death at any given age.)

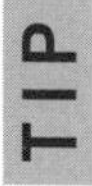

If you were renovating your house, you would get more than one quote or put the job out to tender. To be a good consumer of life insurance, I recommend you obtain more than one quote for the coverage you require. (But don't delay too long. You don't want to expire before you get your life insurance in place.) Because product names and policy features vary from one insurance company to the next, compare the coverage based on the features you require. If the policy has features you don't require, you might be paying extra.

Term

The two most common estate-planning uses for term insurance are: 1) to create an instant estate for a family, and 2) to eliminate significant debts, such as a mortgage.

Term insurance (sometimes referred to as temporary insurance) pays a specific death benefit for a particular period of coverage (the term). It often provides the highest death benefit for the lowest premium, so you can get the maximum amount of insurance for the dollars spent. Term insurance is often referred to as pure insurance because there is no savings or investment component.

The price of term insurance increases each time the term of the policy expires. Each time the term is up, the insured is older and the probability of dying is higher—and so are the premiums. The premiums for a one-year term policy increase every year. Premiums for a 10-year term policy increase every 10 years.

Many contracts guarantee the premiums at each renewal. "Guaranteed premiums" guarantee the premium cost at any given age in the policy contract for the life of the policy. For example, a 10-year guaranteed renewable term policy guarantees the premiums and that you have the ability to renew the insurance without producing evidence of good health every 10 years until the expiry age of the policy. With this type of coverage, the insurance company cannot refuse to insure you under this policy regardless of your health in the future, as long as you meet the premium obligations.

Read your life insurance policy periodically or have it reviewed by your insurance adviser. Why? It may include some valuable provisions. As an example, some term insurance policies include an automatic continuation provision, which might automatically allow you to buy a new policy using the same health and risk class as when you purchased the original policy, without evidence of insurability. While in some instances, a new policy may be cheaper, this provision may be useful for some to consider before a term policy expires.

Suppose you would like to continue to have insurance, but would like a policy that last longer than age 69 or so. But in the last couple of years you had been diagnosed with an illness that would make you ineligible for a new policy. Or even if you could get a new policy, the premiums would be much higher because of the state of your health (and not just because you are older). If you were not aware that you had this feature in your policy, you might overlook an opportunity for life insurance.

Term to 100

A term to 100 insurance policy guarantees that the annual premium cost will remain the same until age 100. As an added bonus, if you live past 100, the premiums stop, but coverage continues. (This does not apply to all policies, so check your contract.)

Term policies are available where the premiums stay level to other ages. For example, the coverage (and the premiums) for a term to 75 policy ends at age 75. However, if you lived to be 79, the policy would have expired at age 75 and your beneficiary would not be entitled to any death benefit. With life expectancy increasing for both men and women, if funds are required, it is important to select a policy that will stay in force as long as coverage is required.

Although a term to 100 policy is generally more expensive than pure term insurance in the early years, it generally provides the next highest death benefit for the premium dollars spent. And because the premiums do not increase, the policy owner is likely to keep a term to 100 policy in force longer than a one-year term policy.

Some insurance companies have a term to 100 policy, or permaterm, a variation (where available) that might provide some guaranteed cash values, but only if you keep the policy in force long enough.

If you compare two similar term to 100 policies, the one offering a cash value might be the better option if there is no significant difference in cost.

If your policy has been in force for a few years and you can prove you are healthy, you might consider reapplying to the same life insurance company to see if you can obtain the same type of policy at a lower premium rate. Companies will change the pricing of their policies and you may get a better premium. If the old policy is a better deal, hang on to it. While you are at it, it is also a good idea to ensure that you have adequate coverage and the right types of insurance.

Whole Life

Whole life insurance is permanent insurance that combines lifetime with a savings component. The premiums do not increase over the life of the policy. So you may keep the insurance in force longer than a renewable term policy (where the premiums increase at the end of the term, such as every 10 years). The amount of whole life insurance coverage purchased is less than the coverage purchased for each dollar used to buy term life insurance.

Your insurance adviser will provide you with a cash value projection, which will give you some idea of the future cash value of the policy based on the assumptions used by the insurance company. But remember, there is a difference between a projection and a policy guarantee. Down the road, once the cash value of a whole life policy has started to build up, it can be accessed as a policy loan as long as the policy is in force.

Some people draw similarities between whole life and term insurance like the differences between renting and owning. Some people don't like feeling they are "throwing away premium payments" when they buy term insurance. These people might prefer whole life insurance because they feel there will be something at the end of the day that is theirs. But life insurance is not like home ownership.

If you select a policy because there is a savings component, rather than selecting it based on the amount of insurance you *need*, you could end up being underinsured.

Universal Life

A universal life policy usually has a term insurance component and a tax-deferred savings (sometimes referred to as a tax shelter) or investment component. With a universal life policy, you contract for the amount of life insurance coverage you require, pay the base premiums, and possibly pay additional premiums for more investment or insurance. The additional cash can be invested. Although the minimum death benefit is normally guaranteed, the cash value and maximum death benefit vary with investment performance. Small variations in assumptions for interest rates, rates of returns, and the actual returns earned can have a significant impact on the future value and whether or not your policy is adequately funded.

A life insurance illustration showing the total death benefit, including the savings component, is often compared with the after-tax dollars that would have accumulated in a non-registered investment account at the same point in time.

A universal life policy is often marketed as providing the flexibility to increase (subject to continued insurability) or decrease the amount of insurance coverage as your situation changes. The premiums can be increased to maximize the savings component, decreased, or even suspended (a premium "holiday") as long as there is enough money in the investment component that can be used to pay the required premiums.

Compare the cost of the premiums for the universal life product with the cost of other insurance products. Look at the guarantees (if any), the projections for the savings side, and the fees or charges. If you do not maximize the savings/investment side of the policy, or take lots of premium "holidays," this type of policy could be more expensive than term insurance over the long term.

NAMING A BENEFICIARY

On death, the policy death benefit, less the amount of any outstanding policy loan, is paid tax-free directly to the beneficiary named on the policy.

If you indicate "estate" as your beneficiary, the death benefit will be paid to your estate and be subject to probate tax, and creditors could make a claim on the amount if it is in your estate. However, if the purpose of the death benefit is to pay the final tax bill, it is practical to have the money paid directly to the estate.

There are benefits to naming a beneficiary (other than your estate).

- The death benefit is paid directly to the beneficiary named.
- Payment is made quickly (usually within 30 days of submitting proof of death).
- Since the death benefit does not go through the will, it is not included in a probate tax calculation.
- The death benefit is protected from the deceased's creditors, except what might be owed to CRA.

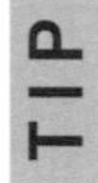

A life insurance trust can be set up with the death benefit from a life insurance policy using the same terms as any testamentary trust set up in the will of the deceased and retain creditor protection. A life insurance trust can hold the money for young or mentally incapacitated children or grandchildren.

The beneficiary designation on a life insurance policy may be revocable (it can be changed at any time) or irrevocable (it cannot be changed without the signed consent of the previous beneficiary). Irrevocable beneficiary designations are more often found in older policies.

It is important to keep the beneficiary elections up to date on all your life insurance policies, including any group policies. If you want to change your beneficiary, contact the insurance company or your insurance broker for a beneficiary change form to complete. Revocable beneficiaries can also be named in your will, but this may trigger probate tax.

LIFE INSURANCE PREMIUMS VERSUS INCOME TAX

If you leave everything to your spouse/partner, the income tax can be deferred until after his or her death when the assets pass to the next generation. But if you outlive your spouse/partner, or do not have a spouse/partner, and have a cottage, RRSP, RRIF, an investment portfolio, or a business, you could be surprised by the amount of tax owed on the final tax return. RRSPs and RRIFs are treated as if they were cashed in, and on other assets, all previously untaxed capital gains are taxed.

It is important to consider the tax bill on assets that cannot be transferred tax-free (some readers may remember when the $100,000 capital gains exemption was eliminated). You want to ensure that any particular asset, such as a cottage or a business, does not have to be sold to raise cash to pay the taxes.

Q. I've done a calculation and I'm considering buying a life insurance policy to pay the income tax that will be due upon my death and preserve the value of my estate. Will the death benefit from the life insurance policy be taxed?

A. No.

Purchasing life insurance to pay income taxes and other debts at death is not a new use for life insurance; debts have always been part of the "How much do I need?" calculation that is often used when estimating the amount of life insurance that might be needed. Estimating the tax bill at death is not an exact science—it's a moving target based on investment returns and the amount you use for your own income needs over your lifetime. But even a rudimentary calculation will give you a figure to work with. Then you need to figure out if you want to insure for it. For some people, the real question is not just "How much insurance do I need?" but "Do I want to pay insurance premiums each year?" *and* "What will happen if I do not purchase insurance coverage?"

Before purchasing life insurance to preserve the value of your estate for any grown children, you need to decide if it makes sense. If your children require more than they might receive after tax, you might be able to increase the value of your estate by purchasing life insurance for, relatively speaking, pennies on the dollar.

To purchase enough insurance to replace the tax due on your RRIF when it is treated as if it were cashed in, you need to estimate the value of your RRIF in the future.

To project the future value of your RRIF, you need to make some assumptions:

- the rate of return you will receive on your investments

- the withdrawals, both the minimum required and any additional withdrawals you might make
- your life expectancy

EXAMPLE Let's assume that your RRIF is currently worth $200,000 and that you will earn an average annual return of 5.75% (after fees, such as management fees on mutual funds) and withdraw the minimum amount required based on your age each December. The right-hand column estimates your potential tax bill at any given age, assuming your marginal tax rate is 40%. For example, if you died at 78 and your RRIF was $187,003, the tax bill on this RRIF would be about $74,801.

Age	Value of RRIF at Beginning of Year ($)	Withdrawal %	Minimum Withdrawal ($)	Value at December 31 Tax Bill ($)	Potential Value
69	200,000			211,500	84,600
70	211,500	4.76	10,067	213,594	85,438
71	213,594	5.00	10,680	215,196	86,078
72	215,196	7.38	15,881	211,688	84,675
73	211,688	7.48	15,834	208,026	83,210
74	208,026	7.59	15,789	204,198	81,679
75	204,198	7.71	15,744	200,196	80,078
76	200,196	7.85	15,715	195,992	78,397
77	195,992	7.99	15,660	191,602	76,641
78	191,602	8.15	15,616	187,003	74,801
79	187,003	8.33	15,577	182,178	72,871
80	182,178	8.53	15,540	177,114	70,846
81	177,114	8.75	15,497	171,801	68,720
82	171,801	8.99	15,445	166,234	66,494
83	166,234	9.27	15,410	160,383	64,153
84	160,383	9.58	15,365	154,240	61,696
85	154,240	9.93	15,316	147,793	59,117
86	147,793	10.3	15,223	141,068	56,427
87	141,068	10.8	15,235	133,944	53,578
88	133,944	11.3	15,136	126,510	50,604
89	126,510	12.0	15,181	118,604	47,442
90	118,604	12.7	15,063	110,361	44,144

JOINT LIFE INSURANCE POLICIES

A joint life insurance policy is a policy where the need for insurance is based on two lives. The cost (the premiums) is also based on the ages and health of two lives. There are two types of joint policies: joint second to die and joint first to die.

Joint Second to Die

A joint second to die policy, sometimes called a joint and last survivor policy or joint last to die policy, pays out the death benefit after the death of the second insured. Nothing is paid to the beneficiary until after the death of both insureds, and the policy premiums are paid as long as one of the insureds is alive.

For example, the Smiths have accumulated a significant estate (house, cottage, and business) that they want to leave to their adult children. Each has an RRSP on which he or she has named the other as beneficiary. Their other assets are registered jointly, and on the death of the first spouse, all these assets will transfer to the surviving spouse tax-free. But on the death of the second spouse, they anticipate high bills for income tax and legal fees. The Smiths want to keep the business and cottage in the family and have purchased a joint second to die insurance policy that will provide cash to the estate to pay the bills, so their estate can pass, intact, to their children.

If the purpose of the insurance death benefit is to pay the deceased's bills and taxes, naming the "estate" as the beneficiary ensures the money is paid to the estate and is available for that purpose.

The cost of this type of policy is usually cheaper for a healthy married couple than a policy with the same death benefit for a single male the same age. A primary reason is that women are likely to outlive their spouses and the benefit does not pay until the second spouse dies.

To estimate the cost benefits of a joint second to die policy, base the cost on the number of years the premiums will likely be paid. Take Keith and Catherine, both 60, who are looking at a joint second to die term to 100 policy. The premium illustration they looked at assessed the cost benefits of the policy for 20 years or, in this case, until Keith reaches 80. But according to Statistics Canada, a woman Catherine's age has a 48% probability of being alive at age 85. So an illustration based on 20 years would underrepresent the possible cost if Catherine lives to be 85. You may want to ask for illustrations to age 86 or 92 if you feel that is more appropriate for you. Ideally, the cost of life insurance over your lifetime should be less than the amount of income tax to be paid.

Are you considering purchasing insurance to preserve the value of your estate for your children? It's been suggested you get the children to pay the annual premiums if you cannot afford them. While this may be a good idea, you'll have to discuss this with them and have them buy into the idea. In my experience, people generally don't want to discuss their affairs in detail with their children or discover the children don't have the money. I've found that this idea works better in theory than in real life. But for the few families whose children all have similar interests and access to money, it can work.

Some people say "It's not my problem" and will spend money on their own retirement—and why not!—and have no interest in paying premiums to purchase additional life insurance to offset some or all of the future tax bill. You may well say, "My kids will get enough already, so why should I spend more?" There is no right or wrong answer. It's your money. I've found that people who have family members with financial needs, or where there are particular assets, such as a cottage or a business that they are particularly interested in protecting, are more interested in additional insurance than others. You get to do what makes good economic sense to you and fits your own belief system and your family's needs. In other words, you can do what you want, but a second opinion may be helpful.

Q. I have no spouse. Is it better just to let my estate pay the income taxes on my RRSP or RRIF at the time of my death or to buy life insurance to cover the income tax bill?

A. It depends on a number of factors and your personal situation. I'm interested in why you are interested in paying premiums for life insurance when you might use that money for other things while you are alive. Here are some areas you could explore:

- Can you afford the insurance premiums?
- Have you explored other ways to reduce the tax bill? For example, if you have no dependants, you could leave your RRSP/RRIF to a registered charity and receive an official tax receipt that would create a non-refundable tax credit. (See Chapter 14.)

Joint First to Die

A joint first to die policy pays out the death benefit when the first insured dies. For example, two business partners buy a joint first to die life policy together. When the first partner dies, the surviving partner receives the insurance proceeds to buy the other's share of the business from the estate.

LIVING BENEFITS

Most life insurance contracts state that the death benefit is payable only after they have received proof of death, i.e., a death certificate. But some health conditions before death create such financial hardships that the death benefit would be more of a benefit while the person is still alive.

People who are terminally ill and who have life insurance may be able to receive some of the death benefit while they are alive—basically an advance on the insurance benefits of up to 50% (maximum $50,000) of the death benefit. Insurance companies call this a living benefit.

If your policy has been in force for at least two years and you have a medical certificate that states you are terminally ill and not expected to live for more than two years, you might qualify for a living benefit, which is basically an advance of the death benefit under the life insurance policy.

Some newer policies clearly state that a living benefit is available under the contract.

If you find yourself in this situation, check with your insurance company—even if a living benefit is not expressly stated in your policy—to see if they have implemented this benefit.

To deal with their financial hardships, a few terminally ill patients have sold their policies at a discount or used their insurance policy as collateral.

Long-Term Care

Long-term care insurance is a separate insurance policy contract designed to pay out monthly benefits if someone is diagnosed with an illness and is unable to care for him- or herself. Benefits under this type of policy can go towards paying for the care in a long-term care facility or for care that make it possible for to stay in your own home for as long as possible. In order to qualify benefits under a long-term care policy, each policy will state its requirements, some of which might include the inability to perform the functions of daily living, such as bathing or thinking clearly.

Critical Illness

Critical illness insurance is a separate insurance policy contract designed to pay out a lump sum amount if you are diagnosed with a critical illness, such as a stroke, heart attack, and other life-threatening illnesses, as stated on the contract. As always, it's important to check the details of the policy. Some policies only pay out the benefit when the illness is judged to be long-term and/or severe.

SEGREGATED FUNDS

Segregated funds are similar to mutual funds; in fact, they are the life insurance industry's answer to mutual funds, a professionally managed investment product—but with guarantees. For the fine print, get a copy of an information folder, the seg fund industry's version of the simplified prospectus, and read it.

However, segregated funds have some estate planning features worth examining: a capital guarantee, the ability to name a beneficiary even on open accounts (i.e., non-registered, that is not an RRSP or RRIF account), and possible creditor protection.

Table 11.1: Comparing Estate Planning Features

	Mutual Funds vs.	Segregated Funds
Death benefit guarantee	No	Yes
Name a beneficiary on non-registered accounts	No	Yes
Probate tax/fees on death	Maybe	Not if beneficiary named
Offer creditor protection	No	Maybe

The Guarantee

Segregated funds currently offer guarantees that your capital will be worth at least 75% of the original investment and sometimes 100%, less withdrawals, after they have been held for 10 years (or 5 years, depending on the company) or on the death of the owner, whichever comes first. Some people find guarantees attractive because of the peace of mind it offers. But if you need income from these investments over the next 10 years, this holding period might conflict with your need for income.

However, if you don't think you'll be around for the next 10 years, there could be some real value from the death benefit guarantee since you don't have to worry about the direction of the financial markets to protect the value of your capital.

Naming a Beneficiary

Because segregated funds are offered through life insurance companies, you can name a beneficiary, even for non-registered accounts. The account can then pass directly to a named beneficiary and does not have to be distributed through a will. This reduces the need for probate tax, and may be a selling feature in provinces where probate taxes are high or where there is no maximum. Segregated funds held in RRSPs, RRIFs, and certain life insurance policies are exempt from income tax.

Creditor Protection

In some situations, insurance products offer credit protection not available with the other investments. Some professionals and business owners find the creditor protection offered in some situations attractive. Some brokerage firms have a disclosure form that indicates protection is valid only under certain circumstances. One factor that would negate the creditor protection would be an individual who knew he or she was going bankrupt at the time of the purchase.

SUMMARY

These benefits come with a price tag. The management fees for segregated funds are generally higher than the management fees for similar mutual funds. Some argue that the higher management fee on segregated funds pays, in part, for the guarantee.

As with any product, it is important to understand how the product works and the costs. The fees and how they are set are outlined in the information folder. The cost for the guarantee may change over time. However, for any individual, the benefits may or may not outweigh the costs.

chapter twelve

trusts

It is so hard to know if I am doing the right thing for my son. He's 20 now, and I don't know at what age he'll have the wisdom to manage all my money. I have left everything in trust for him until he is 30 and have chosen trustees who understand my wishes. I hope I've done it right.

—L.

TRUSTS HAVE BEEN AROUND FOR HUNDREDS OF YEARS. They can be used for many purposes, but they all entrust a trustee with assets and property on behalf of others. Some can be set up while you are alive (an inter vivos trust); others through the instructions in your last will and testament after your death (a testamentary trust). This chapter looks at what trusts are and how they can be used as part of an estate plan to achieve a particular objective, minimize taxes, or deal with a family need.

First, a short primer. Simply stated, a trust is a formal arrangement where the legal owner (called the settlor or transferor) transfers assets or property to a trust. A trustee is appointed to follow the rules of a trust agreement and manage the assets for the beneficiaries who will ultimately benefit from those assets, receiving income or capital or both, according to the terms of the trust.

There are three main types of trusts used for estate planning for Canadians resident in Canada:

- In a living or inter vivos trust, assets are transferred into the trust while the settlor is alive and taxed at the top tax rate.
- In a testamentary trust, assets are transferred into the trust according to the deceased's will after his or her estate is settled and are taxed at graduated rates.
- In an alter ego trust and joint partner trusts, which are living trusts that can be set up by you the settlor while you are alive. Unlike other living trusts, you pay tax on all the income earned on the assets in the trust annually at your personal graduated tax rates.

Many people consider trusts to be sophisticated estate planning tools. While they may not be for everyone, they should *not* be overlooked. A trust can be used for tax planning (although changes in tax rules continue to make this increasingly difficult) and for a variety of needs or situations, including the following:

- to manage money for children until they are older
- to manage assets for a child or spouse/partner who cannot do so because of disability, age, or mental incapacity
- to protect assets from lawsuits and creditors
- to split income with family members
- to give to charities
- to control the shares of a private corporation
- to reduce probate taxes
- to as an alternative to a power of attorney document for finances if your situation requires more formal instructions
- to provide privacy; the wording of trusts and the assets in the trusts are private, but the wording of a will and assets distributed through a will can become a matter of public record

In some ways, a trust document appears to handle the distribution of property and assets that could be handled by a will. In fact, a testamentary trust is set up in a will and there may be some situations where an individual may want to set up a trust while he or she is alive.

Before implementing any financial strategy, you need to consider the pros and cons as well as the costs and the benefits. In simple situations, a trust may not be practical or cost effective. However, in other situations, where money must be managed on behalf of a minor child or a disabled adult, the costs may be a secondary consideration.

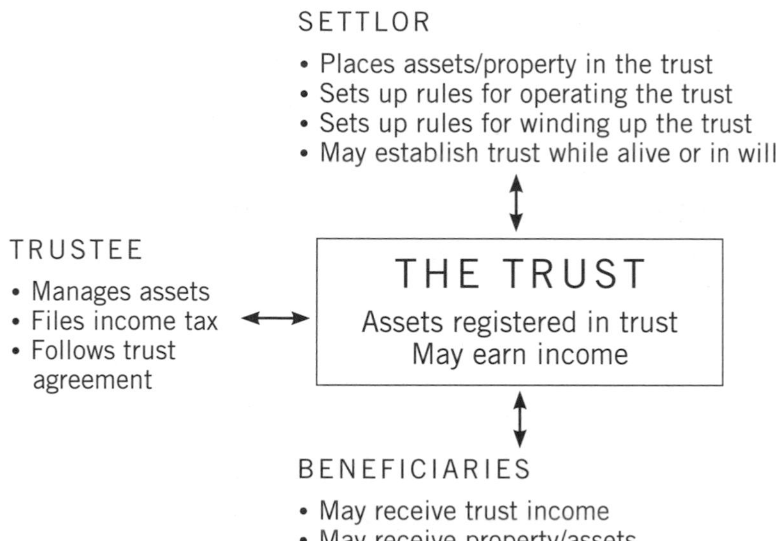

THE TRUST AGREEMENT

The rules for a testamentary trust are documented in the will. The rules for a living or inter vivos trust are documented in a separate trust agreement, sometimes called a trust deed. The terms of the trust normally specify:

- the purpose of the trust
- the assets to be held in the trust
- the beneficiaries of the trust
- the names of the trustees you are appointing
- the powers you are granting to the trustees
- the benefits the beneficiaries will receive and when
- how the assets of the trust will ultimately be distributed and to whom

Trust law allows a great deal of flexibility, and as long as the purpose is legal, the terms of the trust can be as unique as your individual situation; as limited or as flexible as you require. Any areas not specifically covered by your trust agreement will be handled by your provincial trust laws.

Your trust agreement should be prepared by an estate lawyer familiar with the type of trust you want to establish. You will require specialized expertise in this area, so don't scrimp. The correct legal wording is extremely important and can avoid tax and legal complications down the road. After a trust is established, changes to the trust agreement may be difficult, expensive, and sometimes impossible. A poorly worded trust agreement could end up costing you or your beneficiaries many more dollars in the future.

A trust may last for many years with the assets distributed according to the instructions in the agreement on your death, or on the death of the last surviving beneficiary. If all the beneficiaries are over 18, they could request that the trustee distribute the trust assets prior to the stated provisions in the trust. While this mechanism enables a trust to be dissolved when it appears to serve no further purpose, it may or may not be in all the beneficiaries' best interests to dissolve the trust at that time. (*Caution:* Beneficiaries should obtain independent financial and legal advice before requesting a trust be dissolved to ensure they are not giving up any tax or legal advantage.)

BENEFICIARIES

The beneficiaries of a trust receive benefits from the assets held in the trust now or in the future. In general, beneficiaries are classified as 1) income beneficiaries, who are entitled to receive income (such as interest, dividend, or annuity income) earned in the trust, or 2) capital beneficiaries, who are entitled (or ultimately entitled) to receive capital from the trust (such as stocks, GICs, and real estate) or both.

THE TRUSTEE

The trustee is responsible for managing the assets and property held in trust. He, she, or they are required to:

- manage and control the property according to the trust agreement and the provincial *Trustee Act*
- act in the best interests of all the beneficiaries
- perform duties with honesty, skill, and the highest level of care
- perform the duties personally and not to delegate the duties
- act without any conflicts of interest

Trustees can be held personally responsible for any financial loss if they do not carry out their responsibilities. Sometimes a trust agreement will release the trustee from personal financial liability provided the trustee acted in good faith.

The trustee is required to act impartially on behalf of the beneficiaries or, as it is sometimes referred to, with an even hand. Situations could arise where the trustee has to act impartially *and* in the best interests of all beneficiaries, and could be in a position where he or she has to make very difficult decisions.

As an example, consider three different trust agreements. The first agreement set up for a spouse stated that after his or her death, any capital remaining in the trust would be distributed equally among the children. A different agreement for a different couple provided more details and stated that the spouse would be entitled to receive only the income earned by the trust. And a third agreement gave the trustee full discretionary powers, where the spouse had no control over any of the money in the trust and was entitled to receive the income earned in the trust, but was also entitled to receive assets.

These spousal trusts would result in different incomes for the three spouses involved and, all things being equal, could create very different estates for the children.

In the extremes, the second agreement could result in that spouse not receiving enough money to maintain his or her standard of living (because what he or she would receive depended only on whatever income the trust earned).

The third agreement might provide very well for that spouse, but might leave little to distribute to the children, which some families might say is just fine. However, in complex families, this may not achieve the desired outcome.

A trustee also has to act with an even hand when considering beneficiaries of the same type. Consider the trust with two young adult beneficiaries, Kevin and Eric. Kevin needs some additional money now to complete his education. However, Eric might perceive that if Kevin accesses this money now, it might use up some of Eric's own future benefits. The trust document could clarify the settlor's intentions and provide assistance to the trustee.

The trustee you select might be a trusted family member or friend, or you might want to hire a professional trustee.

A professional trustee, such as a trust company, can be a useful choice, especially

- if the value of the assets is particularly large or complex
- if the trust will exist for a number of years
- if specialized knowledge is required
- if family members might have difficulty acting impartially
- to avoid appointing a U.S. trustee and its associated complications

You might consider naming a professional trustee and a family member as co-trustees, who have to act together. With this arrangement, you get professional advice and someone representing the family's interests.

If the trust document is prepared by a lawyer representing a professional trustee, you should seek independent legal advice to ensure the document adequately protects all parties involved.

As with most estate planning documents, name an alternate trustee. If your trustee dies and your trust agreement does not name a backup, then your trustee could end up being replaced by his or her executor.

Powers of the Trustee

A trustee's powers are authorized by the *Trustee Act* in your province (the *Civil Code* in Quebec) and as specified in the terms of the trust agreement. You may want to give your trustee very specific instructions in the trust agreement or give your trustee very broad powers to distribute income and capital and make investment decisions as he or she sees fit.

Some people place the emphasis on selecting a good trustee. Then, rather than attempting to write instructions for every possible future situation, they give their trustee broad powers to make decisions in the best interests of the beneficiaries.

Giving trustees full discretionary powers allows them to use their judgment to make decisions in the best interests of the beneficiaries now and in the future. Why might you consider this? Suppose you are putting money into trust for your five-year-old. You cannot know how much a university education might cost in 15 years. With discretionary powers, your trustee has the authority to pay the required amount, and you don't have to estimate and stipulate an amount that might be required then. Whether this strategy is appropriate for your situation depends on a number of factors, including who you appoint as trustee and who the beneficiaries are.

Prudent Investor Rule

The trust agreement should provide your trustee with investment powers that are appropriate to manage the assets and investments in the trust. In many provinces, trustees can now follow the "prudent investor rule." In other provinces, there is a list of eligible investments.

The prudent investor rule requires that a trustee exercise the care, skill, diligence, and judgment that a prudent investor would exercise in making investments. In Ontario, the criteria a trustee is required to consider when planning the investment of trust property include, among any others that are relevant to the circumstances:

1. general economic conditions
2. possible effect of inflation/deflation
3. tax consequences of investment decisions or strategies
4. the role each investment or course of action has within the overall portfolio
5. the expected total return from income and capital appreciation

6. the need for liquidity, income, and preservation of capital, as well as appreciation of capital
7. the special relationship or value of an asset, if any, to the purpose of the trust or to the beneficiaries

Since many Canadians do not have the expertise and skill required if they are acting as a trustee, it may be prudent for them to obtain the skills of a professional adviser who would be willing, in their opinion, to put in writing the implication of each of the above considerations and anything else that was considered relevant, such as costs.

TESTAMENTARY TRUSTS

A testamentary trust receives its instructions from the wording of the last will and testament. Clauses in the will name the trustee (who, in some cases, might be the same person as the executor of the estate), the beneficiaries, which assets are to be held in the trust, how the assets are to be managed, and when they are ultimately to be distributed.

The cost of documenting a testamentary trust is included in the lawyer's fee for preparing the will. The terms of a testamentary trust are changed by updating the will, either with a codicil or by preparing a new will. (See Chapter 4 for more details.)

The testamentary trust is not established until after your death, and after your estate has paid your debts and taxes. The assets earmarked for the testamentary trust are transferred from your estate into the testamentary trust.

The most common types of testamentary trusts are the spousal trust and other family trusts. Other family trusts include trusts for:

- underage children who cannot hold assets directly
- spendthrifts
- family members with special needs

10 QUESTIONS TO CONSIDER WHEN CONTEMPLATING A TESTAMENTARY TRUST

1. What would be the purpose of the trust?
2. What types of assets would the trust hold?

3. Who are the intended beneficiaries?
4. When would beneficiaries receive distributions from the trust? Will they be predetermined and/or discretionary?
5. Who would be an appropriate trustee(s)? Backup trustee(s)?
6. What types of powers and discretion will you give the trustee to deal with situations in the future?
7. What initial and ongoing costs might you expect?
8. How many years might the trust exist?
9. How and when would the trust be wound up?
10. Who would be the ultimate beneficiary?

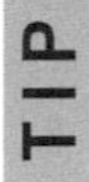

The trustee appointed for the testamentary trust is often the same person who was appointed as the estate trustee. While this is sometimes appropriate, it is sometimes by default. Not only should you consider who would be the most appropriate estate trustee, you should also consider who would be most appropriate for each testamentary trust to be set up by the will. And don't forget to ask the person if he or she would be willing and able to act in that capacity.

Spousal Trusts

A spousal trust—for a spouse or a common-law partner of the same or opposite sex—can hold property and assets for the exclusive benefit of a surviving spouse or partner and can be set up with some or all of the inheritance. The spouse could be the trustee with control over how the money in the trust is invested and when it is paid out and how much.

As we have discussed, your spouse/partner can receive assets on a tax-free basis when they are rolled over to your spouse, or when those assets are put into a spousal trust for his or her exclusive use.

A spousal trust becomes tainted and loses its tax benefits if anyone other than the surviving spouse receives benefits from the trust. If the spouse is not the only beneficiary, this can be dealt with by establishing a spousal testamentary trust for the exclusive use of your spouse (so the spousal trust does not become "tainted"), and a separate family trust.

An effective retirement planning strategy attempts to build pools of retirement income in both partners' names. However, on death, that strategy is collapsed when the assets and income from the deceased are added to the assets and income of the surviving spouse. However, if the deceased's assets are put into a testamentary trust, the pools can be kept separate and the total tax bill potentially lower.

Traditionally, spousal trusts were set up for widows who did not have the expertise to manage the assets they inherited. They now have several additional uses, including:

- Continuing to split income by reporting the income earned in the testamentary trust on a separate trust return, especially when your spouse/partner has an income of his or her own. Assume half of your estate is left outright to your spouse and the other half is held in a spousal trust. Each year, two income tax returns are filed, one for your spouse and one for the trust, which could result in less tax being owed than if all the income were combined and reported on one tax return.

EXAMPLE You have $250,000 of investments (not including the investments you have in your RRSP), which earn $15,000 of income annually. If you leave the $250,000 outright to your spouse, he or she will be required to add the $15,000 earned to his or her other income each year. Your spouse's taxes on the $15,000 earned would be $6,000 (assuming a marginal tax rate of 40%). But if the $250,000 were left in a testamentary trust for your spouse, the $15,000 earned would be taxed on a separate tax return and the tax would be about $3,300 annually, resulting in a tax saving of $2,700.

- Providing for your spouse and preserve the assets held in the trust for your children in the event your spouse remarries.
- Providing for your spouse and ensure that children from a previous marriage will receive something from your estate. A spousal trust could provide your spouse with an income for life, but on his or her death distribute the remaining assets to your children. This means that your children's inheritance is not dependent on the goodwill

of a step-parent or the terms of the step-parent's will. For example, suppose, a widower remarries and his new wife moves into the old family home. He could leave the house in a spousal trust for his wife but, on her death, have the trust indicate that the house would go to her children who had been raised in the home.

- Reducing probate costs. For example, if you leave your $100,000 bond portfolio to your spouse in your will, probate tax will be charged. Then on the death of your spouse, probate tax would be charged a second time. However, if on your death the bonds were moved into a spousal testamentary trust until the death of your spouse, they could then be distributed to your children according to the trust agreement, avoiding probate tax being charged again.
- Providing potential liability and creditor protection. Some couples register all (or most) of their assets in one name to protect them from potential professional liability. For example, suppose he is an architect and the house and their assets have always been registered in his wife's name. With a simple will, if his wife predeceases him, all the assets registered in her name would suddenly be registered in his name and be potentially exposed to professional liability. However, this could be avoided if the assets in her name were transferred into a testamentary trust according to the instructions in her will, continuing to protect them from that potential professional liability (as well as offering the potential for continued income splitting).

If many of your assets are owned jointly or have designated beneficiaries, few assets might flow into the traditional "estate" to be distributed by the will and not available for a spousal testamentary trust.

Depending on the family or matrimonial property laws in your province, you might also require a marriage contract to indicate that your spouse consented to receive the inheritance in trust

Other Family Trusts

Trusts can be set up for family members other than a spouse, most often young children or children with special needs, or as part of tax planning. The wording in your will specifies the rules of the trust that can be unique to your situation.

Trusts for Minor Children

Children cannot legally own assets or property until they reach the age of majority. If they receive an inheritance, it must be held in trust until then. If no trust is set up in the will, the inheritance will be administered by the Public Trustee (the government) until the child is of age (18 or 19 depending on where you are located). Then the child would receive all the inheritance at once. Even if your child is old enough to legally own assets, how would you feel about your 18- or 19-year-old receiving a large inheritance outright—everything you have worked your entire life to acquire?

In your will you can set up a testamentary trust specifying when and how the money is to be distributed. The instructions might state, for example, that:

- income earned by the trust is to be paid to the child annually, but the capital is to be held until a specific age, with or without discretion for special needs
- all distributions from the trust are left to the trustee's discretion
- trust income and capital can be paid out at any time as long as it is used for education

Q. *I don't want my children to receive their inheritance at 18. I'm not even sure I think they will be ready at 21.*

A. Your will could set up a testamentary trust to pay for their education and other expenses while they are minors. There are many ways to set this up. As your child becomes an adult, you could consider paying out a portion of the capital, perhaps one-third at 21, one-third at 25, and the remaining third at age 30.

Trusts for Children over 18

A testamentary trust set up for children over 18 can protect assets from your children's creditors or from a divorce settlement. You might also want to discuss with your children any liabilities they potentially face. For example, some professionals, including doctors, lawyers, and accountants, still register their home in the name of their spouse to reduce exposing their assets to creditors or lawsuits.

Trusts can be a great way to leave money to your grandchildren for their education, but, while you are alive, don't overlook helping the family set up a Registered Education Savings Plan (RESP) to obtain the annual government grant of up to $400 per year for each grandchild.

Depending on the amount, it might also create an opportunity for income splitting (similar to a spousal trust).

Trusts for Income Splitting

Grandparents might want to leave money to their grandchildren for education or other expenses, rather than leaving the inheritance outright to their own, maybe more established, children. The grandchild's parent (your child) could act as trustee if he or she can act impartially on behalf of the children.

Q. I have three grandchildren for whom I wish to hold money in trust. Can I set up one trust for all three children, or should I create three separate trusts?

A. You may do either. The purpose of three separate trusts would primarily be to file three separate tax returns and have each trust pay tax at the lowest possible tax rate. In the past, Canada Revenue Agency (CRA) has ruled that if the beneficiaries are in the same class, the income from these trusts must be taxed together. But today it does not appear to be an issue.

Setting up a trust for grandchildren could provide some income splitting for the family. The income earned on the inheritance in the trust for the grandchildren might be taxed at a lower rate than if it were left outright to the parent and taxed at their higher tax rate. However, though in principle this is an effective strategy, I do not recommend it wholeheartedly. Your own children may be offended and feel left out even if they understand your reasoning. And, remember, some parents believe their own children are better off than they really are.

EXAMPLE

If the $200,000 is held in a testamentary trust for children

Annual income earned in trust (at 5%)	$10,000	
Income taxes paid by trust (federal and provincial)*	$ 2,200	
Net income of trust (approx)		$7,800

If the $200,000 is left to a parent outright on behalf of children

Annual income earned in parent's name (at 5%)	$10,000	
Taxes paid at parent's tax rate (40%)	$ 4,000	
Net income on behalf of children		$6,000
Annual savings to family by using a family trust		$1,800

*Varies by province.

If the income can be paid out to the children for their benefit and taxed at their tax rate rather than the tax rate of the trust, it may be possible to save even more tax each year. Either way, if the children are minors, any money left directly to them will need to be left in a testamentary trust.

Trusts for Spendthrifts

A spendthrift trust, sometimes called a protective trust, is used to manage assets and property for people who may not be able to handle them on their own. Suppose you have a son who has been married twice and has declared bankruptcy once, or an adult child who is struggling with drugs. You're concerned that the money wouldn't last too long if you left it to him or her outright in your will. You also feel that a lump sum would not be the best way to help your adult child get on his or her feet and stay on them.

One option you have is to set up a testamentary trust in your will, so that your child will receive a regular income from the assets in the trust rather than receiving one lump sum.

Where did the term "spendthrift" come from? Someone at a seminar shared with me that her father had always said that a spendthrift was "someone who enjoyed spending the results of someone else's thriftiness." Now this may not be a completely fair description of the reason and needs, but the term "spendthrift" has been around for a long time.

Ensure there is a clause in the trust agreement that gives the beneficiary or beneficiaries (or the settlor if it is a living trust) the power to replace the trustee and have a new trustee appointed, should this ever become necessary.

Trusts for Family Members with Special Needs

A testamentary trust can also be used to provide funds for beneficiaries who are financially dependent on you and unable to manage their financial affairs because of disability. This could include an aging parent or someone with mental or physical disabilities. For example, someone who is physically challenged may be able to earn an income, but his or her parents might want to put money in a trust in case he or she is not able to work and get around in the future. In case any assets remain in the trust after the death of the family member with special needs, the trust should also name an ultimate beneficiary.

Whether a person will be provided for adequately depends on the value of your estate, the assets placed in the trust, and how well the assets are managed. The death benefit from a life insurance policy could be used to top up the value of the trust. The trust should have instructions for how the assets are to be distributed after the death of this family member.

Ask the trustee, or a series of trustees, if they will be willing and able to act as trustee for as long as needed. If the child is currently 20, this could be for 40 years or more. If this would create a hardship, consider using the services of a professional trust company alone or in conjunction with a family trustee.

If the family member is disabled and receives social assistance or a training allowance, an inheritance could affect his or her eligibility for assistance if it is put to the "means test." If this is the case, discuss your options with a lawyer who has experience working with families in similar situations to see if the trust can be structured as a discretionary trust similar to a Henson trust (which is based on a court ruling involving the Hensons) so it does not interfere with these benefits.

However, some provinces and territories have challenged the status of the Henson trust. All parents of disabled children should work with specialists in this area.

Q. I'm concerned that my disabled adult child will be cut off from her monthly allowance if I leave her an inheritance. But I've also heard that if I don't leave her anything in my will, the Public Trustee and Guardian could apply to the courts and rewrite my will.

Living with a special needs child has never been easy, but the legalities seem designed to complicate my life and hers. What do people in my situation do?

A. The laws for dealing with individuals with special needs continue to change and are designed to protect the financial interests of those who cannot protect themselves.

I recommend you determine what is in her best interests and speak with an estate lawyer experienced in this area. If there is no one in your local area, you may have to contact one in a major urban centre.

Congratulations on looking at the long-term financial and practical needs of your daughter. Your support group or community services may be able to provide you with additional resources. The Planned Lifetime Advocacy Network (PLAN) at www.plan.ca or (604) 439-9566 may also be able to help.

A family with significant assets might also consider setting up an inter vivos trust, which could reduce the overall family tax bill if some income were taxed at the tax rate of the disabled child and reduce probate costs in provinces where it is a significant issue.

The trust would be set up for the benefit of your disabled child (who may actually be an adult) who would receive the benefits from the trust while he or she is alive. The trust should also have instructions for distributing any assets still in the trust on the death of this beneficiary as the assets could have grown substantially. Would you want those assets to be ultimately distributed to other siblings? To charity? The choice is yours.

Q. What is a revocable trust?

A. A revocable trust is a trust in which you retain the right to change your mind about having the trust and can have the assets revert back to you. The assets in the trust would not be subject to probate taxes because, technically, the property in the trust belongs to the beneficiaries. A revocable trust can provide limited creditor protection if the creditors were not owed when the trust was set up.

With an irrevocable trust, you cannot change your mind and transfer the assets back to yourself. An irrevocable trust can have some tax advantages, but you give up personal control of the assets.

INTER VIVOS TRUSTS

An inter vivos trust is created during the settlor's lifetime and is sometimes referred to as a living trust. Living trusts can be revocable or irrevocable. Over the years they have been used to split income with family members and other financial planning purposes. Now that the tax rules have been tightened, inter vivos trusts are often used for estate planning when it is more appropriate to transfer assets to a trust while the settlor is alive, rather than through a will or a testamentary trust.

The following are some estate planning uses for inter vivos trusts:

- minimize income taxes due on death by freezing the value of investments or the shares of a business
- provide privacy for your beneficiaries, since trust assets do not become a matter of public record
- provide one individual with the use of the property, with instructions to transfer the property to someone else after death
- minimize probate tax
- charitable giving structures, such as charitable remainder trusts (see Chapter 14)
- as an alternative to a financial power of attorney, a trust agreement can provide more detail as to how the assets are to be administered
- protect the assets or property from creditors

BEARER TRUSTS

Some assets are held in simple bearer trusts for children under 18; you might have set up one at your financial institution for your child. The registration on the account might read something like "Martha Scott in trust for Mary Scott," where Mary is Martha's daughter. The *Income Tax Act* attribution rules apply to these accounts. (See Chapter 5 for attribution rules.)

This type of "trust" is not a formal trust because it does not have a trust agreement. Legally, property in a bearer trust becomes the child's property when he or she reaches the age of majority. If the amount is expected to be substantial, or if you do not want the child to access the funds until he or she is older, this is not the appropriate type of trust. Consider a formal trust agreement which outlines all the terms.

Mention this bearer trust in your will. Appoint a replacement trustee to manage the assets on behalf of the child after your death.

TRUSTS AND TAXES

When the trust has a December 31 year-end and has to pay tax or pays out income to a beneficiary, the trustee is required to file a separate T3 tax return by March 31. In most cases, the provincial tax rate paid by the trust is based on where the trustee lives.

Testamentary Trusts

When assets are transferred to a testamentary trust that is not a spousal trust, the tax on any capital gains from the "deemed" sale of those assets up to the date of death are calculated on the deceased's final tax return.

When an asset is transferred to a testamentary spousal trust (as a spousal rollover), the tax can be deferred until the death of the surviving spouse, just as if the asset had been left outright to the spouse.

Income earned on assets held in a testamentary trust is taxed at graduated rates similar to the rates used to tax the income of an individual taxpayer. When the income earned in the trust is low, the tax rate is low; when the income earned is high, the tax rate is higher. A testamentary trust cannot claim the personal tax credits or any other non-refundable tax credits. Certain expenses of the trust are deductible.

Inter Vivos Trusts

When assets are transferred to an inter vivos trust, they are "deemed" to have been sold at fair market value at the time they are transferred. For example, if the value of the asset has increased, the settlor will have to pay tax on capital gains up to the time of the transfer and report the taxable capital gain on his or her personal tax return that year.

The tax rules for living trusts are not as favourable today as they were a decade ago. Today, the federal *Income Tax Act* limits the use of living trusts for income splitting with family members. Under CRA's tax rules for attribution, inter vivos trusts are more attractive when used for children over 18 than for those under 18.

All inter vivos trusts have a tax year ending December 31, and all trust income is taxed at the top marginal rate, except for alter ego trusts and joint partner trusts. This means that up to half of each dollar of income earned in the trust goes to CRA.

Prior to 1996, an inter vivos trust could have a group of beneficiaries classified as preferred beneficiaries. If the trust agreement gives the trustee the power to use the election, and the preferred beneficiary election was used, income could stay in the trust and be taxed as if it had been paid out to the beneficiary. However, the preferred beneficiary election has been eliminated (it appears some people might have been taking advantage of this election) except for those beneficiaries who receive tax credits for mental or physical disabilities.

For all other beneficiaries, the trust income has to be actually paid out to beneficiaries to qualify for their tax rate, but capital gains and dividend income retain their character for tax treatment. So if the trust earns dividend income from a Canadian corporation and pays it out to the beneficiary, the beneficiary can declare it as dividend income.

However, an inter vivos trust cannot claim the personal tax credits or non-refundable tax credits, but certain expenses are deductible.

If an inter vivos trust can use the preferred beneficiary election, you might still be able to use the child's lower tax rate and retain control of the money if the trust income can be used to pay for the child's education and other expenses each year. Some interpretations suggest trusts may also make payments for the necessities of life, but I recommend you get up-to-date advice on this.

Alter Ego and Joint Partner Trusts

If you have enough assets to justify setting up and handling the ongoing administration of a trust, an alter ego trust for an individual (and the joint partner trust—also known as the joint spousal trust, which is similar in many ways except that it is for spouses/partners) is a unique living trust in the way it is taxed (see next section). "Partner" is part of the *Income Tax Act* and includes legally married spouses and common-law partners of the same or opposite sex.

Alter ego trusts are not for everyone, but they can offer tax and non-tax benefits, including:

- Control over the use of the property in the future
- A level of privacy that is not available with a will
- Time saved because it may be possible to distribute the assets more quickly
- Potential for creditor protection
- Minimized probate costs
- More certainty (due to trust law) than is available with the powers of attorney documents

Some people will put some of their assets into an alter ego trust as a complementary estate planning strategy to their will. The assets in an alter ego trust are distributed according to the trust instructions, not the will. You still require a will.

Some people will put some of their assets into an alter ego trust to complement their power of attorney document for finances, since they are able to set out the powers and duties of the trustee. The responsibilities of the attorney under the power of attorney for finances document by comparison are more informal and, in the hands of the wrong person without monitoring, can provide the potential for abuse of those who are incapacitated.

To set up an alter ego trust, the settlor must be 65 or older; to set up a joint partner trust, the settlor and or his or her spouse must be 65 or older. In addition:

- All income from the trust must be paid to the settlor and his/her partner during his or her settlor's lifetime
- The income is attributed to the settlor during his or her lifetime
- No one else can receive any income or capital from the trust

The trust assets are disposed of at fair market value on the death of the settlor in the case of an alter ego trust, and on the death of the last-to-die in the case of a joint partner trust, according to the instructions in the agreement.

However, by choosing an alter ego trust, you may be forgoing the tax advantages that might be achieved by setting up a testamentary trust. However, there is no reason why you could not have an alter ego trust distribute some of your assets and your will distribute other assets, except for wealth, complexity, and your objectives.

Taxation of the Alter Ego and Joint Partner Trusts

The alter ego trust and the joint partner trust have existed since 1999. They are living trusts, but the way they are taxed is an exception from other living trusts. As a bit of background, when assets are transferred into a trust while you are alive, they are normally deemed to have been disposed or sold, which triggers a tax bill for any profits resulting from that deemed disposition. As well, any ongoing income earned is taxed at the top marginal tax rate.

But if you are 65 or older and transfer assets to an alter ego trust for your exclusive personal use, this transfer occurs on a tax-free rollover basis. You are then responsible for paying tax on all the income earned on assets in the trust annually at your personal tax rate (almost as if they were still held in your own name). On your death, the profits from a sale or deemed disposition are taxed. However, the assets are distributed to your beneficiaries according to the instructions in the trust agreement, not your will, reducing the cost of probate.

A joint partner trust is similar to the alter ego trust, except that you and your spouse can receive income and capital from the trust and defer the final tax bill on any remaining profits until the death of the last surviving spouse.

Before setting up an alter ego trust or joint partner trust with your lawyer, work with your accountant to maximize your tax benefits. For example, you'll need to deal with qualified small business assets eligible for any remaining $500,000 capital gains.

It appears you can't set up an alter ego trust or joint partner trust to reduce the costs of probate or for your privacy *and* have the assets held in the trust transferred to a testamentary trust to access the graduated rates on your death. You need to weigh the benefits of using an alter ego trust to reduce probate taxes (top rate is 1.5% in Ontario) versus the annual income tax beneficiaries might save if they received their inheritance in a testamentary trust and could calculate the tax bill using graduated tax rates.

The 21-year rule is deferred until the death of the settlor or the partner.

21-Year Rule

After 21 years, trusts are required to report a "deemed disposition" of the assets at their fair market value. Tax is due on any profit resulting from this "sale," ensuring assets held in trust cannot avoid tax forever.

Until recently, trusts with preferred beneficiaries had been able to defer the deemed disposition until the death of the last preferred beneficiary, which could have lasted for generations. The deferral of the 21-year rule was eliminated in January 1999 for family trusts with preferred beneficiaries, requiring that tax be paid on any deferred capital gains at least every 21 years.

It is helpful if the trustee can ensure that the trust will have enough cash to pay the tax bill so assets don't have to be sold when the 21 years are up. For example, a prominent family had established a family trust to hold a collection of Canadian antiques. Because they had used the preferred beneficiary election, the value of the collection had increased significantly but had previously been exempt from declaring any capital gains. When the 21 years are up, the trust could potentially face an enormous tax bill on the deferred capital gains and some of the antiques will need to be sold to pay the bill. Between now and then, the trustees plan to sell some of the pieces to raise some cash and ensure that nothing has to be sold at "fire sale" prices.

If you are looking for a jurisdiction where a trust might exist in perpetuity, look at Manitoba and a few other provinces.

As another option, a trustee might consider distributing some assets outright to the beneficiaries since it may be possible to transfer assets to beneficiaries at the adjusted cost base without triggering an immediate tax bill. But first, the trustee(s) will need to review the reasons the trust was set up and the needs of the beneficiaries. Was it primarily to manage and control the assets? If so, then moving the assets out of the trust may not be desirable, since the trustee would no longer have direct control over the assets.

Ideally, a trust agreement would give a trustee the power to adapt to changing tax realities because it is not possible, when a trust agreement is written, to anticipate future tax changes. However, if the trust agreement does not give the trustee the power to adapt to changing tax realities, then the trustee could apply to the courts to formally change the terms of the trust (called varying the terms of the trust) if it can be shown that the interests of all beneficiaries, including future beneficiaries, are protected.

Q. What is an asset protection trust?

A. An asset protection trust (APT) is a trust established to protect assets from creditors or a marriage breakdown. Since assets in a trust are technically outside the settlor's control, creditors cannot access these assets to settle your debts. However, if your creditors or estranged spouse can prove that you set up the trust to avoid your legal obligation, an asset protection trust will provide you with no "protection." Suggested minimums for an offshore APT are $250,000 (preferably $500,000 to offset set-up and administration fees).

COSTS FOR ESTABLISHING AND MAINTAINING A TRUST

There are fees for setting up trusts, legal fees, bookkeeping, administration fees, money management fees, annual tax returns, and final distribution fees. If your province has written guidelines for fees, maximums are set according to the *Trustee Act* where the trustee lives. For a testamentary trust, the costs to write up the terms of the trust are included in the cost of writing the will. For an inter vivos trust, the set-up cost includes the legal fees to establish the trust agreement.

The cost to establish and maintain a trust depends on the complexity of the trust, the value of assets to be held in trust, and whether you require a professional trustee. If the trustee is a family member, the trustee fee might be waived. In general, assets of less than $250,000–$300,000 are generally not large enough to offset the cost of professional management. In fact, small trusts face a minimum fee for the services of a professional trustee, and this cost may be discouraging.

QUESTIONS TO ASK A PROFESSIONAL TRUSTEE ABOUT FEES

Yes	*No*	*Are there annual fees:*
❐	❐	for preparing the income tax return?
❐	❐	for managing the assets, based on the value of the assets?
❐	❐	for time you spend with the trustee?
❐	❐	for money management, such as an annual wrap fee or investment counselling fee?
❐	❐	based on the income earned by the trust?
❐	❐	based on the money paid out of the trust each year?
❐	❐	for distributing assets to the beneficiaries?
❐	❐	any additional fees?

If the answer to any of the above questions is *Yes*, be sure to ask to see the fee schedule and an example of how the fees are calculated.

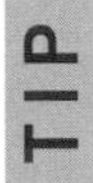

When looking for a professional trustee, you should shop around. While the services may be similar, the fees and what is included in the basic fees may vary. Remember, trustee fees can be negotiated, so don't be afraid to ask.

The annual administration fee for a living trust with $500,000 in assets earning 5% annually might be calculated as follows:

Annual fee for preparing income tax return	$ 750
Annual administration fee (½ of 1%)	2,500
Fee based on income earned and paid out (5% of $30,000)	1,500
Total (paid annually)	$4,753

However, if the annual minimum fee was $5,000, $5,000 would be charged.

The trustee, or the trust company, may also charge a final distribution fee when the trust is wound up and the assets are finally distributed to the capital beneficiaries. This fee depends on the value of the assets and the type of paperwork required to transfer ownership from the trust to the beneficiaries.

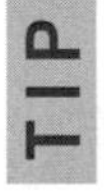

Some wills used to appoint one trust company as the professional trustee. Some people are now adding wording that would allow them to move the trust to another trust company, providing an out or exit plan in case the trust company reduces its services or charges fees that are high in relation to the income earned by the trust.

Even the public guardian, if required to act as trustee, is entitled to charge trustee fees, although for small accounts or for people on social assistance, the public trustee may waive its compensation.

DEALING WITH THE FAMILY COTTAGE

You (and your family members) may have to consider what do with the family cottage. Families explore various options—such as transferring the cottage to a trust while they are alive, dealing with it in the will, holding it in a testamentary trust—to find a solution that works for them. Some families even come to the conclusion that because of the location and the amount of upkeep, the best solution is to sell the cottage so that Mom and Dad are not tied to the property, particularly if they are finding it harder and harder to get there.

Some strategies suggested to deal with a cottage are designed to minimize the amount of tax that could be due on the death of the registered owner. Other strategies are designed to reflect the family's wishes. The following discussion briefly considers the advantages and disadvantages of some of the strategies. However, first things first.

If *you* would like to keep the cottage in the family, start by determining if it is important to other family members to keep it in the family. It may not be as important to them as it is to you! For example, Liz and Dave have three adult children, two in Vancouver and one in Toronto. They could leave their Vancouver-area cottage to all three, giving each a one-third interest in it. But how much practical benefit would the cottage have to the child living in Toronto? It might be more equitable to leave the cottage to the two children in Vancouver and bequest cash or other assets to the child in Toronto. And you should also explore with your adult children the concept of "wanting to keep it" with the reality of how much it costs to upkeep it. Your children may have no idea of what it costs to maintain the cottage and pay the annual property taxes.

Should you consider gifting or selling the cottage to your children while you are alive? Perhaps. Are you ready to give up being the owner of the cottage (and paying all the expenses) and prepared to be a guest? While it may seem simple to transfer the ownership of the cottage to your children by re-registering the title as joint tenants in common or with rights of survivorship (where allowed), there are a number of issues to consider, including:

- Could the cottage be lost if one of the owners declared bankruptcy?
- Could you end up sharing the cottage with one of your children's partners who might become his or her ex in the future?
- Would all siblings be willing to do their share of maintenance or pay for the costs of maintenance? Do you see this as a mini commune or a co-op or something else?

- What if the people can't agree on an issue down the road?
- How much tax might be due on the deemed disposition at the time the title was transferred?

There are a number of items to consider, and remember—you are not dealing with just your children. You are also dealing with your children's partners. There's a lot more to consider than just the tax.

Assuming it is a priority to keep the cottage for the next generation, it could be done a number of ways, including the following:

- Leave it as a gift to the children who want it and leave other assets or insurance to the others (watch the after-tax benefits as discussed in Chapter 3).
- Give children the "right of first refusal" to buy the cottage "in kind" from the estate at fair market value in order by age or by expression of interest based on your discussion with them. In some families, the children forget the earlier discussions and sparks can fly.
- Leave each child equal ownership of the cottage as joint tenants in common. If your family gets along, this can be effective. But if they couldn't share it while you were alive, they won't be able to share it after you and your spouse die. As well, there are other considerations. What might happen if one wants to sell his or her share but the others cannot afford to buy out their sibling? Or, as I have also seen, what if one sibling cannot afford his or her share but because of privacy issues, does not want to ask the other siblings to buy out that share?
- Place the cottage in a testamentary trust, which would protect it for minor children, and from the divorce or bankruptcy of a child. The trust agreement should set the rules to ensure fair and equitable use of the property and how operating costs are to be paid.

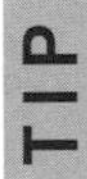

The estate is responsible for the tax bill on any taxable capital gain at the time of your death. If you want to keep the cottage in the family, your estate plan should ensure the cottage itself does not have to be sold. Life insurance might do the trick, or if you also have a house that is paid for and exempt from tax because it is your primary residence, it might provide enough cash to pay the taxes.

People used to have and use part or all of their capital gains exemption to minimize the tax on the sale of the cottage property.

The following strategies are often considered to minimize taxes by those who believe the value of their cottage will increase. These strategies involve transferring the ownership of the cottage while you are alive and deferring the tax problem on future profits to the next generation, or hoping the federal government will eventually eliminate capital gains tax sometime in the future.

- *If* you are ready to give up ownership of the cottage (and all the responsibilities that go with it), you could give or sell it to the children at fair market value and then enter into an agreement giving you the right to use the cottage. You could also hold a mortgage on the cottage to protect your own interests. Keep in mind, though, that life can be very different when you are the guest and your adult children are the owners.
- Transfer the cottage to an inter vivos trust, but remember that generally trusts have to declare and pay tax on any capital gains every 21 years.

  If the cottage has increased in value and there is a taxable capital gain from an actual or "deemed" sale, the estate is responsible for any tax resulting from the sale at fair market value.
- Transfer the cottage to a holding company or non-profit corporation. Each family member would be a "member" of the non-profit corporation; the adults could be voting members and the children non-voting members. Members would pay annual membership fees to cover maintenance and improvement costs.
- If you plan to sell your home and move into rental accommodation, another option to consider is to elect the cottage as your principal residence. While the cottage is your principal residence, any increase in value would be exempt from income tax under the principal residence exemption.
- And last but not least, do nothing—except keep good records of any renovation costs.

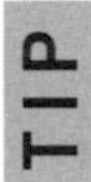

To minimize the amount of taxable capital gains on the cottage when it is eventually sold or transferred to the next generation, keep good records of all repairs and upgrades.

SUMMARY

Professional advice is required to ensure that a trust is set up properly and that the trust has enough powers and flexibility for the future to protect the trustee and beneficiaries, whether they stay where they are or move to another province.

This chapter has touched on only some of the uses of trusts. A trust can be an effective estate planning tool, but it can also add cost and complexity.

chapter thirteen

business succession planning

If you fail to plan,
you plan to fail.
—Old saying

IF YOU HAVE ACHIEVED YOUR PERSONAL VISION of success, congratulations.

For the business owner or entrepreneur, I have one additional question for you: What might be the most appropriate way for you to maximize the value of your business? Should you sell it as a going concern to a group of employees over time, transfer it to a family member who is groomed and ready to step into your shoes, or sell it to another interested buyer, such as a senior employee or an outsider, to name just a few options?

If you have put off thinking about the succession plan for your business, you are not alone. And if you are thinking about retirement some day, you have realized that you need to think about a succession plan. However, for business owners I think an estate plan depends on their retirement plan because the business is often their largest asset or the asset that produces the greatest amount of annual income. But until you have figured out the what, when, and how of your retirement, the actual succession of your business will not happen unless you are faced with death or disability first. And from my business experience, business owners are not the first ones to think about retiring!

When considering your succession plan for your business, what are your key issues?

1. create an appropriate income; this could be done a number of ways, including selling the business and using the capital received from the sale, drawing an income from the ongoing operations under the new owners
2. maintain the value of the business for eventual sale down the road or for hand-off to family member(s)

Of course, regardless of what you actually do, you would also want to make sure you pay no more in tax than is necessary and that family members are treated fairly.

But the ideal business succession requires that you, as senior management, spend some time considering certain "What if" scenarios for your business and personal situation. You owe it to yourself, your family, your employees, and your customers.

Maybe these aren't the right questions for you. Perhaps you built the business because you loved doing what you started out doing, and now you have a business that could provide you with a comfortable, interesting retirement, a legacy, or a firm where your children could always be employed.

It's your responsibility as senior management to ensure that you have an appropriate succession plan in place, and to ensure that the business will have enough cash available to continue to pay its liabilities, such as paying its employees and income taxes. By working with your accountant and financial consultants, you may also be able to minimize any taxes that may be due at the time of your death.

This chapter is limited to businesses that are closely held, such as the following:

- a business or practice owned and operated by partners, where there is (or should be) a partnership agreement
- a business or practice owned by an individual that might employ family members or others
- a business operated by family with the intention to be left to the family

There are also some consulting practices where the intellectual capital of the owner or the value of the goodwill dies with the owner. A practice that is not incorporated may have assets that are actually personal assets that are dealt with in an individual's will.

Some consultants or professionals have independent practices and employees who work with their clients to help them achieve their objectives. When looking for an appropriate successor, these practices may want a successor who shares their approach when working with clients and holds similar professional designations. In addition to these "matching" characteristics, there is also the matter of price and terms and conditions. Some may have a family member who has entered the business and the business will eventually be his or hers. But they also want to treat all family members equally, regardless of whether they are active in the business.

If they have no family members interested in joining them in the business, they may put in place a written partnership agreement to formalize their succession plan.

The business owner's business succession plan and personal estate planning should be integrated, especially if there are family members who are part owners of the business and family members who are not.

In the beginning, businesses go through two key phases: start-up and growth.

A business in the early years, the start-up phase, is highly dependent on the owner and is in a high-risk phase. The business may not survive the loss of the key owner in this phase.

During its growth phase, the business normally becomes more established and issues start to arise that did not exist in the start-up phase. If the business is family based, one or more family members may be involved in the business, while other members are not. If so, revisiting the family wills and considering the ownership structure and opportunities for tax minimization may become important. However, people often become too busy to put it high on their agenda when it should be an important item.

When the issues have been considered, details of the succession plan can be put on paper.

Your business succession plan—the one that envisions the future of your business without you—is difficult, but even the most successful business owner cannot run a business forever.

The Canadian Association of Family Enterprise (CAFE) was founded to support family businesses with business succession planning and other issues. The programs include mentoring, personal advisory groups, education, and networking for family business members. For information, or to locate one of the 15 chapters closest to you, call the CAFE National office at 1-866-849-0099 or refer to www.cafemembers.org/cafenational/.

Some business owners say they don't plan to retire—their plan is to spend less time at the office. However, there are differences between an estate plan and a retirement plan. I can say with certainty that you need an estate plan. I just don't know when. But I believe your estate and business succession plan should be done sooner rather than later.

IS YOUR BUSINESS HIGHLY DEPENDENT ON YOU?

One "What if" scenario to consider in a business succession plan is what if you or someone vitally important in keeping your business up and running were not in the picture because of death or disability. Losing a key person can be detrimental to the ongoing operation of a successful business. If you think the company should be liquidated when you die, you might want to provide advance directions to your executor(s).

The insurance industry offers "key man" or "key person" insurance to cover the services provided by a key individual, enabling the business to hire someone to fill in for a period of time to keep the business up and running. A business might have more than one key person: you might be the only one. Perhaps an industry consultant could help maximize the value of your business by keeping it running.

Do you need this type of insurance? Here's a better question. Is it important to keep the business running to maximize its value? Then making money available so your survivors can hire someone experienced to manage the business (this person may not come cheap) on your death until it can be sold or someone groomed to take it over may be a worthwhile business expense. Of course, if the business has sufficient financial reserves of its own, this person's salary might be funded from investments held inside the business, rather than from key man insurance.

KEY PERSON CHECKLIST

Evaluate your business situation.

Yes *No*

❒ ❒ Are you key to the operation of the business?
If yes, what might it cost to replace you for six months? $_____

Do you have any employees in sales who are key to the business?
❒ ❒
If yes, what might it cost to replace them for six months? $_____

Do you have any employees with relationships with suppliers or creditors who are key to the business?
❒ ❒
If yes, what might it cost to replace them for six months? $_____

Do you have any other employees who are key to the business?
❒ ❒
If yes, what might it cost to replace them for six months? $_____

How much might any additional special training cost? $_____

Are there sufficient funds in the business to cover these potential expenditures?
❒ ❒

Any questions that raise questions or concerns require further investigation to ensure that your business is never short a key person, or the funds to hire a key person on a temporary basis.

SELLING THE BUSINESS

If you do not believe the business would survive your death, and keeping it in the family is not a viable option, you may want to consider selling the business.

Even if you're not planning to sell in the near future, understanding the factors and issues that go into valuing your particular type of business can help your estate maximize its value (and perhaps help you to maximize its current profitability). You may have capital assets, real estate, inventory, and/or goodwill. Your accountant or an outside consultant could offer some insight in this area.

If you are the primary asset of the business, the business would likely have a higher sale value while you are alive and able to help a new owner get established (maybe through a management contract). Giving up control is often a difficult decision, and this suggestion may be good only in theory, especially if the business is your main purpose in life.

If selling is the most viable option for your situation, then your final choice will be somewhere between the best successor for your business and the best price. Most deals do not allow you to have both. However, you can groom your business three to five years before you actually plan to exit the business to attract a higher price than you might if you had not groomed it.

If you sell the business but do not receive the full sale price in one year, you may be able to claim a capital gains reserve, which allows you to match the amount of taxable capital gains with the amount you receive each year (for up to five years after the sale). For example, you might sell your business for $300,000 and receive the sale price in instalments over three years. In year one, the amount of capital gains declared would be $100,000 and the remaining amount would be held as a capital gains reserve reducing over the next two years. You might also structure a retiring allowance with the sale to transfer the maximum allowable amount tax-free to your RRSP.

If selling the business is not an option, and there are no successors, either family or employees, some owners simply wind up the business or never actually do anything formal, but continue to go to the office or factory every day for fewer and fewer hours until they are no longer able to.

KEEPING IT IN THE FAMILY

Your business may be your single largest asset and you may want to see your family continue your legacy, but many businesses are actually sold to non-family members for a variety of reasons.

However, when the business can stay in the family, there are many questions to be answered over time. Who will operate it? If you need to take money out of the business to retire, what impact would it have on the financial health of the business and those running the business?

Do you intend to divide the value of the business among your family members, i.e., your children? Would you leave it to your spouse and defer these questions for a few more years?

Would you leave the business equally to all your children, or to just one? Although you may want your children to work together, it does not happen this way in most families. If one child runs the business, he or she may have different objectives than the children who are not-so-silent partners.

If your intention is to treat all your children as equally as possible but only one will inherit the business, you might try to equalize the benefits in some way for those who are not active in the business by:

- naming them as the beneficiaries on life insurance
- leaving them personal or non-business assets
- leaving them non-voting shares in the business
- finding some other way that fits your family and personal situation

In some families where one or two children are interested in the business and have been integral to the business' success and growth, it can be important to reward them for their efforts at the time, rather than just through the instructions in your will. You may want to call a family and/or succession meeting to discuss the future of the business.

If your spouse is not interested in running the business and the business is your primary asset, you need to determine how to provide adequate support for your spouse/partner after your death. You may have heard of situations where the spouse of the deceased became an active partner in the business—much to the dismay of the other partners—because of inadequate estate planning for support or family laws.

Potential for Family Conflict

Consider the family of four siblings, two brothers, 25 and 20, and two sisters, 23 and 18. Their father died young at 50, having started a business four years earlier, leaving a spouse, a little life insurance, and some debts. There was not enough to provide an income for his widow, and the only family asset was the growing business. Since selling the young company would have generated little cash, the best option at the time was for one or more of the children to step in and run the family firm.

There was no succession plan—indeed, it would have been difficult to have had a clear plan given the ages of the children at the time. The widow started working in the business, and the eldest son and daughter pitched in, but the eldest son had other career aspirations he wanted to pursue. Over time, the other two children tried to help out, but one did not have the aptitude for the business and the other found it difficult to work with his family and left.

Ten years later, the widow retired, and today her "pension" is dependent on the success of the business. The eldest daughter and her husband are still actively running the firm. The other three children, who are not at all involved in its operation, still see "Dad's" business as part of their rightful entitlement.

This case has the intrigue of a modern-day soap opera: misfortune, fate, luck, ambition, conflict, and success. If this were your business, how would you want it to turn out? Should your son-in-law be rewarded for his major contribution to the success of the business with a partial ownership? Or should he be treated as just another employee? Should all your children share in the profits, even though your daughter was clearly responsible for building and nurturing the company after the founder's death? Should the children share in the success of the business that occurred after your death?

Clearly, there are no easy answers. It doesn't matter if the business is a family campground, a french fry company, a successful retail operation, or a garage.

TAX PLANNING

If it is your wish to keep the business in the family and its value has grown, you need to estimate the income taxes that would be due from a "deemed" sale of the business on death. If you leave the business to your spouse, you have not eliminated the need to plan—you've just postponed the tax bill until the death of your spouse.

As with all financial planning, reducing taxes should not be the driving motivation when looking at what to do. First, you have to decide what you want to have happen. Then, by considering the tax rules, you may be able to structure the plan to minimize the tax bill—the icing on the cake, so to speak.

Estate Freezes

An estate freeze is a strategy used to minimize the income taxes due at death. A number of techniques can be used, but basically they all focus on locking in the value of the business by issuing new shares (to be held in a family trust so you retain some control over them) and passing future growth or profit to the next generation. By locking in the value you know the potential tax impact on death because it has been fixed (frozen).

If you sold or gifted shares of the business to an adult child, you would also lock in the value of those shares at today's value. Another way to implement an estate freeze is to transfer your business assets to a holding company or do a corporate reorganization.

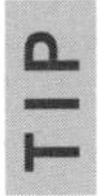

If your business is a small business corporation, the sale of your shares in the business may qualify for the $500,000 capital gains exemption. If you and your spouse both own shares in the business, you may qualify for up to $1 million in capital gains exemption.

To qualify for the $500,000 capital gains exemption, a business must have qualified small business corporation shares and pass the 50% test and the 90% test during the 24 months prior to the sale of shares:

1. Only the shareholder (or related shareholders) held shares of the corporation.
2. More than 50% of the fair market value of the business assets were assets used in an active business carried on primarily in Canada (50% test).
3. All or substantially all of the value of the Canadian-controlled private corporation's assets were used primarily in carrying on an active business in Canada (90% test).

Performing an effective estate freeze is complex and requires professional financial, tax, and legal advice. In my opinion, anyone considering an estate freeze should regard it as permanent since it is difficult and costly to reverse (although it may be technically possible). You also want to ensure that you do not create any adverse income tax implications today and that you have considered all implications, as well as alternative techniques that may be more appropriate.

To satisfy CRA, it is important to get an independent valuation of the fair market value of any property, asset, or business for audit purposes.

Before considering an estate freeze, ask yourself the following questions:

- Does your business continue to have good growth potential?
- Are you psychologically ready (don't answer this too quickly!) to give up control of your business and pass it all on to the next generation? If you are still actively building the business or a new area of it, you may not be ready to give up the benefits of your efforts.
- Would an estate freeze create a capital loss/gain and result in any immediate taxes?
- What might be the most appropriate time to do an estate freeze?
  a) When the market value of your shares are down, there could be less immediate tax consequences.
  b) When you have completed building the new business opportunity?
  c) Would it be better to wait a few years?

- What legal and accounting costs are involved? Do the benefits outweigh the costs?
- Have there been any tax changes that affect how and when an estate freeze might be set up?

While an estate freeze might reduce the income taxes on death, this should not be the only reason for putting in place any technique. It should also make good business sense!

Estate Freeze through a Holding Company

An estate freeze can be completed by transferring assets from an old corporation to a new holding corporation without changing the value of the company.

Typically, the parent/owner would hold the preferred shares and the children would hold the common shares. All future growth in the company would then occur through the common shares held by the children. (The shares might be held in trust.) The holder of the voting preferred shares could still control the company.

Estate Freeze by Reorganizing a Corporation

An estate freeze can also be completed by reorganizing the share structure of an existing company (sometimes referred to as a section 86 freeze). The shares of one type are exchanged for another type. For example, the common shares of a business would be reorganized into two new classes of shares, the preferred shares and the common shares. The business owner would hold enough preferred shares (with voting rights) to maintain control and the next generation would hold the growth shares of the company.

In some cases, the reorganization of a business is accomplished with some combination of estate freezing techniques, including but not limited to:

- transferring an active business to a holding company (under section 85 of the *Income Tax Act*)
- using the remaining shares to reorganize the business capital so that after the estate freeze the children hold the growth shares and the parent holds the preferred shares

NEEDS OF BUSINESS PARTNERS/ SHAREHOLDERS

The death of a major partner or private shareholder can represent a major risk to the future of the business and the surviving partners and shareholders.

In addition to the issues a family business faces, the person with partners or shareholders has some other questions to address:

- Under what conditions would the business continue?
- Would there be enough cash flow to operate the business?
- If your main asset is the business, will your family members be joining the partnership?
- Are your partners or shareholders willing to welcome your spouse or children into the business? Would you be willing to accept theirs?
- If your business can be run only by a professional, what arrangement should you make? A physician, for instance, might want to arrange with another doctor to take over the practice by some business agreement, or take on and groom a younger doctor.
- Can any of the business assets be sold to provide for your family so that they do not need to be actively involved in the business?
- Are there restrictions in any existing agreements that need to be considered?

A business owner could give his or her executor useful additional powers under the will, such as:

- the ability to reorganize the shares of a business
- the ability to enter agreements with shareholders and partners
- the right to hire key people to keep the business up and running

Although this chapter focuses on estate planning for your family and business partners or shareholders, you might also want to consider these issues should one of your partners or shareholders predecease you. Do you want the first right to buy out their shares, or are you willing to have their family members become your partners or shareholders? In many cases, it makes sense for the surviving partners or shareholders to purchase the business interest rather than a stranger or competitor. The terms of such an arrangement would be found in a shareholders' or partners' agreement.

BUY-SELL AGREEMENT CHECKLIST

Yes	*No*	
❒	❒	Has a formula been established to determine a purchase price?
❒	❒	Have you entered into a formal buy-sell agreement or partnership agreement?

What is the most economical way to fund the agreement?

- ❒ Savings
- ❒ Sell assets
- ❒ Bank loan
- ❒ Life insurance
- ❒ Other: ____________

What method of buy-sell funding are you using?

- ❒ Promissory note
- ❒ Redemption of corporate shares (if a corporation)
- ❒ Criss-cross
- ❒ Other: __________
- ❒ Unsure __________

The value of a business may not be not easy to determine. It is based on a number of factors, including the market value of the business, the financial position of the business, and earnings potential according to some formula.

There may be an independent valuation of the business—to put a price on it. The remaining partners or shareholders would have to have some way to acquire the business at a fair price from your estate. There are a number of ways to fund a buy-sell agreement including:

- Using the partners' personal cash or corporate reserves. Often, the personal funds will not be enough. A more mature business may have built up reserves inside the business to provide all or part of the necessary funding.

- Buying out the deceased's interest with a loan to the spouse if the business can afford this expense annually until the debt is paid. Under Ontario's *Family Law Act*, a surviving spouse is entitled to a minimum of 50% of the value of the family assets up front if they elect. If your business partners cannot afford to buy out your interest, they may end up with your spouse as an active, if unwilling, partner.
- Borrowing the funds. The loss of a partner/shareholder often represents a major risk to the future of the business and a bank manager may be uncomfortable lending a large amount when a key individual is no longer involved. You know it is easier to borrow money when you don't really need it!
- Using life insurance to buy out the estate's interest in the business or some combination of the above.

Once determined, the value of each shareholder's interest should be reviewed periodically to ensure that the other shareholders still have the ability to finance the buyout of a deceased's share.

Partnership Agreements

A partnership agreement documents the rules for operating the business partnership, including how partnership assets will be transferred on the death of one of the partners. From an estate planning perspective, the buy-sell agreement should also specify on death, or in the event of disability or retirement, who will purchase their interest, how the price will be determined, and how and when it will be paid.

Shareholders' Agreements

A shareholders' agreement documents the rules between private shareholders and covers many areas of the business agreement, including how a shareholder's shares in the business will be handled on the death of that shareholder and how any shareholder loans would be paid off.

At the very minimum, even a family business should have a buy-sell agreement specifying who will buy the business or the shares, how the price of the deceased's interest in the business will be determined, and how the proceeds are to be paid.

Using Insurance to Finance a Buyout

If life insurance is determined to be the most viable option to finance a buy-sell agreement, there are two major ways to use it.

- If there are two principals in the business, each would purchase an individual policy on the other's life sufficient to buy out his or her interest in the business in the event that one individual predeceases the other. Because individual insurance is based on the health and age of the person being insured, one principal could end up paying more for this coverage than the other.
- Use corporate-owned insurance and have the business pay the premiums. On the death of one of the principals, the corporation would use the insurance to buy the deceased's portion of the business from the estate. Again, because this insurance is generally based on the health and age of the person being insured, an insured who is much older or in poor health may receive a greater premium "subsidy" from the corporation than the other shareholders. If this is not considered fair, you could work out some formula to equalize the subsidy.

Q. Is it better for the corporation to pay the life insurance premiums or for me to pay them personally?

A. Sometimes the discussion of whether the premiums should be paid by the individual or the corporation centres around which is the more tax-effective. But the corporation can ensure the insurance premiums are paid. Some businesses choose to pay the premiums because individuals sometimes forget.

QUESTIONS TO CONSIDER ABOUT THE FUTURE OF YOUR BUSINESS

Evaluate your business situation.

Yes	*No*	*Unsure*	
			For family-owned and -operated businesses
❐	❐	❐	Are you the owner/operator of the business?
❐	❐	❐	Are any other family members currently active in the business?
❐	❐	❐	Would you like to see the business continue if you are not able to work?
❐	❐	❐	If you have a spouse/partner, is he or she interested in operating the business? For how long might this be practical? ___________
❐	❐	❐	If you have children, are any or all of them interested in operating the business?
❐	❐	❐	If not all the children will be active in the business, have you considered how you will distribute your estate fairly?
❐	❐	❐	Do your children have the aptitude for running the business?
❐	❐	❐	Are you prepared to groom them to run the business?
❐	❐	❐	Could the business be sold as a going concern?
❐	❐	❐	Have you estimated the value of the business?
❐	❐	❐	Have you determined ways to maximize the value of the business?
❐	❐	❐	Are you really interested in selling the business or is it really your retirement hobby?
			Additional considerations if you have employees or partners
❐	❐	❐	Do you have any employee(s) who have the skills and aptitude to manage and operate the business?

Yes	*No*	*Unsure*	
❒	❒	❒	Do you have partnership or shareholder agreements in place? Is there any wording in these agreements that restricts selling the business?
❒	❒	❒	Have you estimated the tax liability due if the business was sold and how it would be dealt with?
❒	❒	❒	On your death, might your spouse have to make an equalization claim against the estate and the business?
❒	❒	❒	On your death, would the business have to be sold or wound down? What employee and/or tax obligations would there be?
❒	❒	❒	Have you and your partners/shareholders reviewed your agreements to ensure they are up to date?
❒	❒	❒	Are you in agreement regarding the current valuation of the business?
			Additional considerations
❒	❒	❒	Are there any issues or restrictions that might keep you from realizing the value of the business?
❒	❒	❒	Are you ready to sell the business?

Not only are some of the questions very difficult, they may also have no clear answers. But the very survival of your business and the needs of your family may depend on reviewing your business succession and estate plan with your professional advisers.

IF YOUR BUSINESS IS A FARM

When your family business is a farm, you have both business and family estate planning issues. You may need or want to reduce your hours from full-time to part-time, hire part-time help, retire from the business, bring in a (family) successor, or even sell the farm.

Q. We have four sons and feel fortunate that we were able to send them all to university. Like most of our neighbours, only one is interested in carrying on the farm. He has moved back home with his wife and two young children. We want him to take over the farm and carry on the family business. If he inherits the farm, there are few other assets in our estate for the other children. We want to be fair to all our boys, but we also want the farm to continue. How do other people solve this dilemma?

A. This is a tough question for many farmers, especially when the farm is your most significant asset. While there is no magic answer, some farmers have taken one or more of the following steps:

- Purchase life insurance and name the other children as the beneficiaries.
- Have the son operating the farm pay income from the business to his siblings. To ensure that the farm can continue as an operating concern, you may want to set a maximum amount that can be paid out in any one year, and tie it to a percentage of annual profits.
- Sell off a portion of the land to raise some capital for the other children.

A farm can be rolled over to a child, grandchild, or great-grandchild without triggering taxable capital gains, helping to keep the farm in the family for generations.

Congratulations on raising four great kids. If it helps, I can tell you at least one real-life story where a farmer had four sons. He gave one son one-quarter of the farmland while the other three, in his words, "don't deserve anything." Now the three just want to get back at this brother since he has received this land well in advance of anything they might receive. This couple is putting off their estate plan when they really need to have it in place in my opinion. There are the financial issues of estate planning and then there are the hothouses of family emotions.

SUMMARY

A key to running a successful business is planning.

The key to a successful succession plan is planning.

Whether you decide the business should continue after your death—in which case, your executor and any partners will need to know enough about its day-to-day operation to keep it up and running—or whether you decide it should be sold, planning will help with the transition and potentially maximize its value.

The death of any key individual in a business can be difficult to plan for, but without estate planning and professional advice, the continued success of a business without its owner is uncertain.

chapter fourteen

gift planning

I have tried to teach people that there are
three kicks to every dollar:
one when you make it ... two when you have it ...
and three when you give it away.
—Paraphrased from William A. White, writer
(1868–1944)

TODAY'S CHARITIES HAVE MORE WORK to do but are receiving less government support.

Gift planning is personal. You get to decide which charity or charities you want to assist through your charitable donations. You get to decide who you think will do a better job with your money—the government through tax dollars, or the charity or charities of your choice. While the *Income Tax Act* determines how much tax you have to pay, you can decide if you want to pay those dollars as tax or make a charitable donation in a way to get the maximum tax benefit. You can control, or at least direct, some of what you cannot keep.

Gifts can be made while you are alive, deferred until death, or a combination of the two. They are called "planned" gifts because you have the opportunity to plan when to make the gift and when the related tax savings will most benefit you, and then build that into your estate plan. Some of the strategies in this chapter work for gifts of any amount; some work better for larger gifts.

Planned gifts can be made using cash, stocks or bonds, life insurance, artwork or manuscripts, real estate, or other assets of value if they are acceptable to the charity. A gift of cash or life insurance could be made today or promised for the future, and some of these promises can even provide tax savings today. Assets can be given outright or through a legal structure, such as a trust, corporation, or private foundation.

Some individuals plan to make significant donations on death, but may not be able to take advantage of the non-refundable charitable tax credits that may be available to them.

If your initial thoughts are to make all your charitable gifts on death (such as through your will, beneficiary designation on your RRSP/RRIF, and/or life insurance), you may want to estimate the amount of tax due on your final tax return to see if your estate will be able to use all the non-refundable tax credits. If you find that your final tax return will not be able to take advantage of all of them, you may want to revise your plan to see if there is a better way. Some people find that a combination of giving some now, some over time, and some at the end of the day works well.

Suppose your estate will be in the 40% tax bracket and you do not have a spouse or partner to roll your RRSP over to. If your RRSP is worth $100,000, and your estate had to pay tax in the 40% tax bracket, your estate could face a tax bill of about $40,000 on the value of the RRSP. However, if you were to designate a charity as the beneficiary of your RRSP, your estate would receive a charitable receipt of $100,000. That charitable receipt would create a non-refundable tax credit that would offset some of the tax that would otherwise result from your RRSP. Not a bad way to make a difference!

However, the best way for you to make a difference depends on your value system. You can also work with your adviser to maximize the value of your gift.

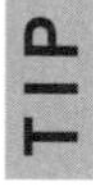

To update a beneficiary election on your RRSPs, RRIFs, or life insurance policies, it is not enough to tell the financial institution or send them an email. You must sign a written beneficiary designation with the institution or document it in your will. Otherwise your change will not be effective.

MAXIMIZING THE TAX BENEFITS OF GIFT PLANNING

Saving tax is usually not the first consideration when you make a planned gift, but it does not hurt. It goes without saying that the larger the gift, the more important it is to maximize the available tax benefits. Planning can help you can get the maximum tax benefit from a gift, but it should not deter you from making a charitable gift or bequest today.

To issue a valid tax receipt (an official donation receipt), the charitable organization or foundation must be registered and have a charitable number.

The amount of the receipt depends on the market value of the gift at the time it is made. If the gift is a financial asset (such as cash, stocks, bonds, or the cash value of an insurance policy), the value is relatively easy to determine. If the gift is personal property (such as art or manuscripts) worth over $1,000, it needs to be appraised independently by a professional appraiser, valuator, or an individual qualified and knowledgeable about the specific property to support the amount of the receipt. If a market value cannot be determined, the charity cannot issue a receipt. And so there is no misunderstanding, you should discuss it with the charity and confirm the amount that will show on the charitable receipt before you make the gift when the gift is not cash.

The Canada Revenue Agency (CRA) does not issue a refund cheque specifically for charitable donations. Instead, the charitable receipt creates a non-refundable tax credit. In 2006, the non-refundable federal tax credit was 15% on the first $200 of donations and 29% on amounts over $200. The tax benefit is not as small as you might think. The donation saves both federal and provincial tax and any surtaxes that might have been due. For example, a charitable donation of $1,000 would reduce income taxes by approximately $393, depending on where you live.

EXAMPLE *Non-Refundable Tax Credit for a $1,000 Charitable Donation*

Total amount of gift	$1,000
First $200 of charitable donation ($200 at 15%)	30
Amount over $200 ($800 at 29%)	232
Federal tax credit	$ 262
Provincial tax credit* (assuming 50% of the federal amount)	131
Total amount of tax saved based on non-refundable tax credit	$ 393

* The provincial tax rate varies across Canada

While this non-refundable tax credit reduces the amount of income tax payable, it doesn't reduce the income amount used to determine the Old Age Security (OAS) benefit clawback.

Annual Donation Limit

The total charitable donation you can claim for the non-refundable tax credit while you are alive in any one year is limited to 75% of your net income, except for certain gifts, such as gifts to foundations (see "Gifts to Foundations" later in this chapter). While you are alive, if your net income is low, any unused portion of the charitable receipt can be carried forward for any of the next five years.

EXAMPLE Louise made a charitable donation of $120,000 in 2006. Her net income for the year was $40,000. The maximum she could claim as a charitable donation for the non-refundable tax credit in 2006 was $30,000 (75% of her net income). Assuming her net income for the next four years continues to be $40,000, she would be able to claim the whole amount of the charitable donation over the four years. But if Louise died in 2007, a significant portion of the tax benefit could go unused.

Donation Limit at Death

In the year of death, all eligible gifts, including those made through the will, can be claimed. Charitable gifts can be claimed for up to 100% of your net income, or under proposed legislation, gifts made in the year of death, including those made through the will plus any unclaimed gifts made in the previous five years. Any unused amount cannot be carried forward (since this is the last income tax return), but your executor can apply the unused donation to your income tax return for the previous year (up to the 100% net income limit for that year).

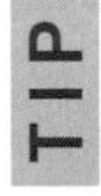

Spouses can pool their charitable receipts on one income tax return even if the receipts are not in both names. This can maximize the tax benefit, since $200 of the combined total would be calculated at 15% (rather than $200 for each spouse).

Exceptions

Have you ever bought a lottery ticket to support a charity that gives you a chance to win a car, house, or a cottage? These tickets are not considered charitable gifts and are not eligible for charitable receipts.

Suppose you purchased a ticket for a charitable event that included dinner and entertainment. You may receive a charitable receipt for the part that does not reflect any personal value you received. So if you paid $150 for a fundraising event that included a $50 dinner, the charitable receipt would be issued for $100.

You can use a charitable receipt received from a Canadian charity to claim a non-refundable tax credit. Generally, foreign charities are not eligible to issue official tax receipts that can be used on Canadian income tax returns.

WAYS TO MAKE PLANNED GIFTS

You might want to give to a particular charity in return for some help you or someone close to you received, or because of some affiliation you have with that organization. For example, someone who:

- received a scholarship many years ago might want to set up a scholarship fund
- was helped tremendously by a hospital might want to give some of his or her estate to the hospital in gratitude
- enjoys the arts may want to make a donation to an arts group

- is affected by a disease might want to fund research

People also make gifts to do something for their community, or because of their personal or religious convictions.

Gifts of Cash

Every year, many Canadians give cash, write a cheque, or donate to charity through payroll deduction. The donation might be made at the office or through one of the various campaigns or events that charities use to raise funds throughout the year. The gift may be planned or unplanned and one of the simplest ways to give. It allows the charity to benefit immediately, but most charities do not give receipts for donations under $10. Some charities accept your donation on your credit card—letting you collect loyalty or mileage points. Just make sure you don't have to pay any credit card interest.

A gift of cash is easy, but if you have any qualifying investments that have increased in value, you might want to consider the after-tax benefits of "in kind" donations.

You can maximize your tax savings by considering the asset you give. While giving or bequesting cash may be simple, a gift of publicly traded shares or bonds that have increased in value has significant tax advantages. Cashless stock options appear to be an exception.

Gifts through a Will

A charitable gift is a bequest made in a will and while you may be tempted to leave all of your money to charity and not to your family, this wish is limited by the family or succession laws of your province. Lawyers call this a restriction on testamentary freedom. Governments see this as a way to keep your family off public support or for you to live up to your family obligations. However, some donors may have no family and may elect to leave their entire estate to charity.

Review your will and your charitable intentions. A charitable donation through your will might offset some of the taxes due on death.

The amount the charity receives should not be left to the discretion of your executor. To claim the charitable receipt, the charity must be named and the amount of the gift, or a formula to determine the amount of the gift, must be specified in the will and the asset given in kind. (See "Bonus on Gifts with Capital Gains" later in this chapter.)

Table 14.1 lists some types of bequests that might be made in a will. The wordings here are not the full legal wordings; many charities will provide your lawyer with sample language to properly document your wishes in your will.

Table 14.1: Types of Bequests Made Through a Will

TYPE OF BEQUEST	SAMPLE WORDING
Gift of a specific sum of money	
• for general use	"I give A the sum of $ __ to be used for general purposes."
• for a specific use	"I give B the sum of $ ___ to be used for [purpose]."
Gift of a specific asset	"I give C my collection of ___."
Gift of all/or part of the residue	"I give D 30% of the residue of my estate."
Contingent gift	"In the event my spouse does not survive me, I give E ___."
Trust remainder bequest	"I give X what's left in the trust after the death of the last beneficiary of the trust."

Tax benefits
Charitable receipt

Other considerations
Works for gifts of any value
Probate taxes could apply
Gifts are not confidential
Relatively easy to change
Gift could be contested if you do not provide adequately for certain family members

Bonus on Gifts with Capital Gains

Capital gains on charitable donations of appreciated securities was completely eliminated in 2006. Publicly listed stocks, bonds, mutual funds, segregated funds, and certain other investments with otherwise taxable capital gains are effectively tax-free when donated to charity as an "in kind" gift. When a qualifying gift is made, CRA treats the gift as if the asset were sold on the day the charity receives the gift in order to determine its market value for the charitable tax receipt and tax purposes. Unless there are restrictions to the contrary, the charity manages the asset(s) as it sees fit and may sell the gift if it determines it is appropriate. This saves the donor or the estate from having to deal with the sale.

Just because you see donations of millions of dollars announced in the media doesn't mean you can't make a more modest gift.

If you sold qualified assets, such as a mutual fund, that have increased in value (perhaps to make a cash gift), you would have to include 50% of the capital gain on your personal tax return. But if you donated the units of that mutual fund to charity, you wouldn't have to.

Part 1 of the following example considers the benefits if Bob sold some investments and donated the cash to charity. Part 2 consider the benefits if Bob donated the investments "in kind" to the charity.

EXAMPLE

Part 1

Bob has 160 Bank of Montreal shares that are now worth $10,000, which originally cost him $2,000. If he were to sell the shares and donate the cash to his favourite charity while alive or through his will, $4,000 of taxable capital gains (50% of $8,000) would be added to his tax return in the year the gift was made. Assuming he is in the 40% marginal tax bracket, approximately $1,600 in tax would be due.

However, he would also receive a charitable receipt for $10,000 that would create a non-refundable tax credit of approximately $2,872. This could be used in the current year to offset his tax bill, and he would receive a net tax benefit of approximately $1,272 ($2,872 – $1,600) for himself and the charity would have the donation.

Part 2

Effective May 2, 2006, capital gains tax on charitable donations of appreciated securities was completely eliminated. Talk about a win for registered charities and a win for investors.

Bob can donate the same $10,000 of Bank of Montreal shares with the same $8,000 profit directly to the charity—and not pay any tax on this profit (see Part 1). The non-refundable tax credit for Bob would be approximately $2,872 and the charity would benefit from the donation.

And if you really like the investment, you can repurchase it for your portfolio, since there are no superficial rules. This would increase your adjusted cost base on that investment, although you would have some additional transaction fees.

Give your executor the appropriate powers in your will to determine which assets (cash or appreciated assets) to donate to maximize the tax benefits of your gift. For example, you might want your executor to be able to donate a portion of an investment (sometimes referred to as a 50–50 strategy) to the charity and sell others within the estate to maximize the value of the charitable receipt.

Building a Portfolio

A number of mutual fund companies and financial firms have set up investment programs available through financial advisers that are designed to help investors realize their charitable intentions by initiating a regular savings investment account and then donating the capital gains in the future.

GIFTS THROUGH LIFE INSURANCE

A life insurance policy can be donated to charity. You could purchase a new policy or use a policy you no longer need for your family. Donating a life insurance policy has some advantages:

- the amount of the gift may be larger than you might otherwise afford

- if privacy is important, the gift can be kept outside the will

The following are some of the more common options.

Changing the Beneficiary

One way to use life insurance is to name the charity as the beneficiary on the policy so that the death benefit would be paid directly to that charity. This strategy could avoid probate taxes or fees on the amount of the gift and provide confidentiality. But there are no immediate tax benefits when you change the beneficiary.

However, on your death, the death benefit is paid by the life insurance company directly to the charity and the charity issues a tax receipt that can be used on your final tax return.

Say you have a life insurance policy with a death benefit of $10,000 and no cash value; you want to leave $10,000 to your local hospital and receive the maximum tax benefit. One option is to name the charity as the beneficiary on the life insurance policy.

Tax benefits

On death, the insurance proceeds qualify for a charitable tax receipt.

Other considerations

No probate taxes or fees
Gift is confidential
Gift is difficult to challenge
The previous beneficiary, if "irrevocable," might have to give signed consent before the beneficiary can be changed
You retain the right to change the beneficiary

Assigning an Existing Life Insurance Policy

If you have an old life insurance policy you no longer require for your personal needs, you could gift or assign the policy to charity while you are alive rather than cancel it. The charity would receive the life insurance proceeds on your death. If the policy has an irrevocable beneficiary, you would also have to obtain the written consent of the beneficiary.

EXAMPLE Brian has a whole life policy with a death benefit of $25,000 and a cash surrender value (cash value less any outstanding loan) of $10,000. When he assigned the policy to the charity and named the charity the beneficiary, the charity issued an official tax receipt for $10,000. Since Brian also decided to continue to pay policy premiums, he can receive an additional annual tax receipt for those premium payments.

When you absolutely assign a life insurance policy to a charity, you transfer the legal ownership of the policy to the charity. If there is any cash value at the time of the assignment, you may be entitled to receive a tax receipt for a charitable donation for that cash value, but your estate does not also receive a receipt for the death benefit. If you continue to pay premiums to keep the policy in force after it has been assigned, they might also qualify for a charitable receipt.

Tax benefits

Official tax receipt for the cash value of the policy at the time of the transfer

If premiums continue to be paid, they qualify for an additional official tax receipt each year, if approved by the charity

Other considerations

No probate taxes or fees

Gift is confidential

Gift is difficult to challenge

Change is impossible to undo

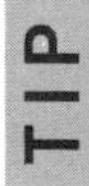

If the policy had an unpaid loan when it was assigned, the *Income Tax Act* states that you could qualify for an additional tax receipt if you paid it off. However, from a practical perspective, it might be more beneficial to write a cheque directly to the charity. Then the charity would have the money immediately and you would still get an official tax receipt.

Purchasing a New Policy

You can make a planned gift by purchasing a new life insurance policy if you are insurable.

The cost for any new insurance policy depends on a number of factors, including your age and your health. If you are considering this option, shop around for the best rates from quality insurers and be sure that you can afford to pay the premiums. Some charities will help you arrange this directly through their own insurance programs, or you can arrange it through your own insurance adviser.

Tax benefits

Official tax receipt for premiums paid in the year, if approved by charity, or official tax receipt for the insurance proceeds on death

Other considerations

No probate taxes or fees
The cost of the policy
Gift is confidential
Gift is difficult to challenge

Q. I have a $100,000 life insurance policy that has a cash value of $25,000. I'm wondering if it would be better to assign the policy to charity (and get an official charitable receipt that I could use now) or to bequest $100,000 to the charity in my will.

A. The larger your potential tax bill on death, the more you might benefit from the non-refundable tax credit resulting from the $100,000 charitable receipt on death.

Assuming your estate will not be challenged by family or creditors, the choice is yours. Reduce your tax bill today by using the charitable receipt for $25,000, or reduce your tax bill on death as well as maintain the insurance policy because you never know what the future may hold.

GIFTS TO FOUNDATIONS

While the term "foundation" makes some people think they need to have millions of dollars, most foundations can be considered charities. For example, we have hospital foundations and community foundations.

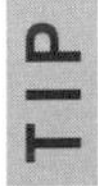

If you are interested in setting up a private foundation, it may not take as much money as you think (generally $250,000 or more). However, while private foundations are an effective planned giving tool, they have some tax planning restrictions. It also takes more than money to run one effectively. You also need to consider how the money will be managed and allocated as long as the private foundation lasts.

Crown Foundations

Many universities, museums, hospitals, libraries, and other quasi-government agencies have crown foundations. Like other charities, the amount that can be claimed for the non-refundable tax credit in any one year is limited to 75% of the donor's net income while alive, and is increased to 100% of the deceased's net income when the gift is made through a will.

Community Foundations

The mandate of most community foundations is to enhance the quality of life within the local community. There are now more than 50 community foundations in Canada and over 500 in North America. The Vancouver Community Foundation (established in 1942), the Montreal Community Foundation, and the Community Foundation for Greater Toronto (established in 1983) are just three examples of community foundations supporting the arts, education, health, social services, and/or the environment in their local communities.

A gift to a community foundation would be eligible for the non-refundable tax credit for up to 75% of your net income while you are alive, and up to 100% if made through your will.

In addition to accepting donations of cash, other assets, and life insurance, community foundations are able to set up relatively inexpensive trust funds for scholarships or memorials.

GIFTS TO GOVERNMENT

Donations of Ecologically Sensitive Land

Donations of ecologically sensitive land—ecogifts, ecological gifts, and ecologically sensitive land—are important for the preservation of Canada's environmental heritage.

Environment Canada can be involved in determining the value of the gift before it is made. There is no income limit, and you may claim charitable receipts of up to 100% of your net income and carry forward any amount not claimed for up to the following five years while you are alive.

There are also proposed guidelines on split-receipting that can be found in the *Income Tax Technical News*, no. 26.

For more information, contact the Ecological Gifts Program, Environment Canada, by email at ecogifts@ec.gc.ca

Gifts of Cultural Property

If you donate certified cultural property of "significant benefit to Canada" to a designated public institution (such as a public art gallery, historic site, or museum), that public institution may issue a charitable receipt, which you can claim for up to 100% of your net income.

Cases of abuse and fraud related to gifts of cultural property have been uncovered and CRA is being vigilant in this area, especially in cases where the value of the gift increases significantly in a short time and has not been appraised by a professional valuator.

If you are considering donating cultural property, contact the public institution of your choice to determine if the gift meets the criteria of providing a "significant benefit to Canada."

Other Gifts to the Government

Want to help pay down the country's debt? If so, you can write a cheque payable to the Receiver General and send it with a letter to the Receiver

General, Place du Portage, Phase III, 11 Laurier Street, Gatineau, QC K1A 0S5, stating that you wish your gift to be used to service the public debt. It will then be used to reduce the federal Debt Servicing and Reduction Account.

But most people I've met feel they are already "donating" too much!

OTHER TYPES OF GIFTS

Other types of gifts allow the donor to gift the asset to charity, but to continue to receive income or to even continue to use it. These gifts might include a gift annuity, a charitable remainder trust, or a gift of residual interest. They are not made through your will.

This type of gift is promised today, but completed in the future. The amount on the tax receipt will be based on the projected value of the gift at the time of death. This residual value is determined using a number of factors, including the current market value of the gift, current interest rates, and the current ages of you and/or your spouse. The older the donor is at the time of the gift, the greater the potential tax advantages. However, if no residual interest value can be determined, no official receipt can be issued.

As with all of the strategies described in the book, it is important to discuss the benefits and the tax implications with your advisers and to make sure your own needs are met before signing anything.

Some charities have affinity credit cards that raise dollars for their organizations. You may also be able to donate miles or points through some loyalty programs.

Gift Annuity

With a gift annuity, you give a charity a gift of cash, investments, or real estate in exchange for a guaranteed income for a fixed number of years or for life. The charity invests the funds and receives any remaining value in the annuity on your death. In many ways, a gift annuity is similar to an annuity issued by an insurance company, except that any amount left over goes to the charity, not the insurance company.

The annuity income can provide attractive after-tax income. The portion of the payment that is considered a return of your own capital is tax-free. The amount of income is based on actuarial calculations and depends on the value of the gift, your age, interest rates at the time of purchase, and any options you request. The income from the annuity is typically guaranteed for a fixed number of years or for the rest of your life, or for the lifetimes of both you and your spouse under a "joint and last survivor" option.

A number of charities issue their own annuities. Some reinsure the policy or will refer you to an insurance company. While the charity may require a minimum gift to set up an annuity, some minimums are very low. Before you make your gift, you should determine the amount of income you would receive, the income that would be taxable each year, as well as the amount of the charitable tax receipt.

The key when considering a gift annuity is the amount of after-tax income (otherwise, you would probably make an outright gift of cash). If the income quoted will not meet your current and future income needs, then this is likely not the right option for you at this time.

Charitable Remainder Trust

A charitable remainder trust (CRT) involves transferring investments or property to an inter vivos trust that allows you and/or your spouse to continue to have the right to use those assets or to receive all income they earn. On death, the trust will be wrapped up, and the charity knows that because they are the capital beneficiary they will receive the remainder value of the trust assets.

Once you make the gift and transfer the assets to a charitable remainder trust, you cannot dip into the capital to top up your income, even if you need additional money. The assets are transferred irrevocably into the trust and the income is paid to you (or you and your spouse) during your lifetime. While you are alive, the charity cannot access the investments or property.

But because you give up control of the asset, you may be eligible to receive a tax receipt. The amount of the receipt would be based on your current age (the older you are, the bigger the receipt), the asset donated, and actuarial projections of the value of the asset on your death.

EXAMPLE Margaret Nelson wants to make a donation to her favourite charity and reduce her taxes today. She is planning to transfer her cash and fixed income investments worth $500,000 into a charitable remainder trust. She expects to receive about $20,000 of income each year, assuming an annual return of 4.5% less fees to administer the trust (50 basis points, or half of 1%). On Margaret's death, the charity will receive the assets remaining.

The official tax receipt Margaret receives will be based on the present value of her gift that factors in:

- her life expectancy
- the current value of the assets
- a discount factor
- the type of gift

As with any trust, the assets to be held in the trust should be large enough to offset the cost of setting up the trust, as well as the annual administration and trustee fees. From a practical point of view, if the assets to be held are less than $100,000, then another method of gifting might be more appropriate.

This gift structure is less common in Canada (but it is growing in popularity) than in the United States, where U.S. taxpayers have to pay an estate or wealth tax based on the value of the property they hold at death. The less property Americans hold, the lower their estate tax. (The term "property" is used in a very general sense. It could be cash, investments, or real estate.) The trust document should be prepared by your lawyer.

Benefits to you and your estate
Tax receipt now for charitable donation
Assets in the trust are not subject to probate
Continuing income or use of the property for the rest of your life or the life of your spouse
Beneficiaries cannot contest the trust
Can be tailored to your own situation
Confidential, since the gift is outside the will

Disadvantages to you

You lose control of the asset

You cannot access more income or capital from the trust once it is set up

The trust is irrevocable

There are annual administration and trustee fees

You continue to pay tax on any income earned by the trust

Benefits to the charity

Receives title to the property

Knows the gift will eventually be received outright

Can use the trust assets as collateral to borrow money

Gift of Residual Interest

A gift of residual interest is created when you transfer the ownership of property to a charity according to a formal agreement with the charity, but retain the right to use the property (rather than receive income). For example, you might want to gift your home, but retain the right for you and your partner to live there for the rest of your lives. This can be great in theory, but many people do not feel comfortable giving away the home that provides them with a sense of security.

Be clear about your emotional need to own any asset outright. Never give away something you are not prepared to give up, even if it is in name only. This type of a gift also works for other types of real estate.

Benefits to you and your estate

Tax receipt now

Assets are not subject to probate

Continuing use of the property outright for the rest of your life and the life of your spouse

Confidential, since the gift is outside the will

Disadvantages to you

You lose control of the asset

The gift is irrevocable

Benefits to the charity

Receives title to the property

Knows the gift will eventually be received

Q. Will naming my chosen charity as the beneficiary of my RRIF cancel out the income tax?

A. From a tax point of view, the RRIF is treated as if it were cashed in. However, if you designate the charity as the beneficiary of your RRIF, your estate would also receive an official tax receipt. This will create a non-refundable tax credit that can be used to reduce the tax bill on your final tax return.

THE PROCESS OF GIFT PLANNING

Before making a gift to any particular charity, you want to ensure that it is registered as a qualifying charity and can issue an official tax receipt.

Canada Revenue Agency (CRA) maintains an online list of Canadian registered charities, which is searchable, at www.cra-arc.gc.ca/tax/charities/online_listings/canreg_interim-e.html

You might want to ask the charity how much of the donation would go directly to its programs and how much would be used in administration. Unfortunately, there have been scams by unscrupulous charities, but the government has been tightening the information filing that charities must do.

If the donation is not cash, ask the charity if they can accept the type of gift you are considering. Many charities can provide you with sample language to include in your will or other documents to formalize your wish. Some larger charitable organizations also have staff dedicated to assisting potential donors with their decisions. However, you should never feel you are being pressured to make a decision or a donation during these discussions.

Q. I want to give $5,000 to charity this year. Given some of the tax benefits available for planned gifts, am I better off to write a cheque for $5,000 or to donate my mutual funds, which are now worth $5,000 (they cost me $3,000)?

A. There are tax advantages to giving these investments directly to your charity rather then selling them (assuming there is no redemption fee) and giving cash to the charity.

If you were to sell these mutual funds, you would have to report a taxable capital gain of $1,000 (50% of the $2,000 profit) on your income tax for the current year. The tax bill would be about $1,600 (assuming you were in the 40% tax bracket). But if you donate these mutual funds directly to the charity, under the rules that became effective May 2, 2006, there would be no taxable capital gain. It is to your advantage to donate the mutual funds "in kind."

Either way, you will also receive the official tax receipt from the charity.

You may want the charity to use your gift as it sees fit. However, if you have some specific instructions or conditions regarding how you want the gift used, be sure to discuss your wishes with the charity and obtain their input. For example, some people who donate to their local hospital make their gift for general purposes. Others specify that their donation be used for a specific purpose, such as the neonatal or neurosurgical unit. Certain restrictions or conditions make it hard, sometimes impossible, for the charity to accept the gift. On the other hand, the charity may be able to suggest an alternative so that your gift can be accepted and honoured in a way that is as close as possible to your wishes.

If you have a specific use in mind, also consider giving the charity the right to use the gift in a more appropriate way at a future time, so it can be adapted to changing needs and used effectively.

Some charities have ways to recognize donations (such as placing the donor's name on a plaque), with the donor's permission, even when they may not receive any benefit until after your death. Being recognized can help others to consider making their own contributions, but it is not a requirement. Your gift can be private if you wish. However, any gift made in a will that is probated will become a matter of public record.

When naming a charity in your will or in a life insurance policy, use the full legal name of that charity. There are now more than 80,000 registered charities in Canada, and some have similar names. You want the right one to receive the benefit—and not leave your estate with a dispute to settle.

SUMMARY

While saving taxes may not be the prime motivation for making a planned gift, there can be significant financial benefits.

When planning the gift, be sure to consider:

- the needs of the charity or charities you wish to assist
- ways to maximize the tax deduction
- the financial needs of your family
- your own financial needs so you don't give away too much too soon

It is important to many people to know they have made a difference, whether their name is published or put on the side of a building or not.

chapter fifteen

documents concerning health care

I was responsible for my mother right to the end and I had to make some tough decisions. I discussed the options with my sister, but she refused to be involved. I did the best I could for Mom, but to this day, even though I know I made the right decisions, I feel guilty.

If my mother had let me know what she wanted, it would have helped. But it still would not have made it easy.

—*S.*

WHILE SCIENCE AND MEDICAL TECHNOLOGY may be able to prolong or sustain life, there may be times when you may be in a temporary or long-term situation in which you may not be able to give or withhold consent for medical treatment.

If you have not yet prepared your will, then you probably have not yet prepared a document that allows you to choose who will make decisions for you in the event that you are not able to make medical or health care decisions on your own behalf. In general, the person you appoint is called upon only if and when you become incapable of making these decisions yourself. I think that it is difficult for some people to think that they might be alive but in a position at some point when they might be ill or very old and not be able to make their own decisions. Remember, this could happen to anyone. Thinking about this now is one of the reasons it is sometimes referred to as "advance care planning."

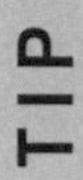

If your will is in place but you are missing one of the two pre-estate planning documents, your estate plan is incomplete. In this chapter, we discuss one of the pre-estate documents, the power of attorney for personal care.

You could be in a position where you become incapacitated and unable to make your own health or personal care decisions, perhaps from a stroke, disease, age, or drugs. If you prepare a document in advance that appoints someone to make decisions for you should this happen, this person will be able to speak for you and represent your wishes. People can and do get sick, and medical science cannot provide the answer for everything.

In the event that you become incapacitated some day, I believe it is important to prepare a document regarding your future personal medical and personal care 1) so that you have legally chosen someone you trust to make these decisions on your behalf, and 2) and provided surviving family with guidance to help them to carry out your wishes.

Provincial legislation across the country now gives you the legal right to appoint someone to make decisions on your behalf in the event that you become unable to make these decisions for yourself. The person should be someone you trust, understands your personal values, will follow your instructions, will make decisions that he or she believes are in your best interest—and will stand up for your wishes. If you name more than one attorney, they are required to make decisions on your behalf together, unless you state that they may act jointly and severally.

Advance health care directives include living wills, power of attorney documents for personal care, and health care proxies. Although the document in each province has a different formal style, you can name someone to make decisions on your behalf related to your personal and health care, which could also affect where you will live and what medical treatment you will receive.

In most provinces, this document is separate from the power of attorney for financial matters. Even in provinces where they can be combined, many lawyers prepare two separate documents for added privacy. Some lawyers include the advanced health care directive, or living will, in the document for personal and health care; in some provinces, others prepare a separate document for a living will.

POWER OF ATTORNEY FOR HEALTH OR PERSONAL CARE

In some provinces, you may appoint someone to make decisions for your personal or health care on your behalf. This person may be called a health care proxy, representative, agent, guardian, or a power of attorney for personal care, depending on the province you live in. Naming a power of attorney means that someone of your choice—not a government official—has the right to make personal care decisions for you when you cannot.

Even without a power of attorney for personal care, immediate family members may be able to make health care decisions on your behalf, such as in a medical emergency, but not on a long-term basis. However, practices and laws could change. Health care facilities, such as long-term care residences and nursing homes, seem to be moving in the direction of requiring this type of document, even when a family member could technically act without it.

If you are asked if you would be willing and able to take on the responsibilities by acting as the power of attorney for health or personal care, and you are not sure what might be involved, refer to Appendix III for a List of Duties for Your Representative When Making Personal and Health Care Decisions on Your Behalf.

In Ontario, under the *Substitute Decisions Act*, the power of attorney for personal care incorporates a living will and the attorney to make personal and health care decisions for you (hence "substitute decisions"). The attorney for personal care does not have any authority to make these decisions for you unless he or she reasonably believes that you are no longer capable of making a required medical decision yourself. To help prevent potential abuses, several groups of people who have certain relationships with you—for example, in Ontario, teachers, doctors, nurses, landlords, or social workers—are excluded from acting as your attorney for health care decisions on your behalf, unless he or she is also your spouse.

If you live in B.C., you can appoint a person to represent you if you become incapable of making your own decisions regarding your health care or other personal care matters. B.C. residents can, if they want, name a monitor to oversee the actions of their named representative in order to determine whether or not they are performing their duties.

If you live in Quebec, the mandate for health care may be very specific, or may only provide general guidelines regarding your instructions for your health care. If the mandatary is considering consenting to any treatment that could have serious medical risks or permanent side effects, court approval may be necessary before treatment.

While you are not required to prepare these documents, the alternative, should you become unable to make your own decisions, is to have someone from the office of the provincial public guardian or trustee make these decisions or oversee the decisions made by your family.

The person you appoint is referred to by different names, depending on the province in which you live. This person may be called a health care proxy, representative, or a power of attorney for personal care. See Table 15.1 for the term used in your province.

Table 15.1: Power of Attorney for Health or Personal Care

PROVINCE	NAME OF DECISION MAKER	NAME OF DOCUMENT
Alberta	agent	Personal Directive
British Columbia	representative	Representative Agreement for Health Care
Manitoba	proxy	Health Care Directive
New Brunswick	attorney for personal care	Power of Attorney for Personal Care
Newfoundland	substitute decision-maker	Advance Health Care Directive
Northwest Territories	attorney	Ensuring Power of Attorney
Nova Scotia	deemed guardian	Authorization to Give Medical Consent
Nunavut	attorney	Enduring Power of Attorney
Ontario	attorney	Power of Attorney for Personal Care
Prince Edward Island	proxy	Health Care Directive
Quebec	mandatary	Mandate Given in Anticipation of Incapacity
Saskatchewan	proxy	Health Care Directive
Yukon	proxy	Enduring Power of Attorney

For information related to naming someone to manage your financial affairs, see Chapter 7.

LIVING WILL

If you are mentally competent, you have the right to refuse medical treatment. For example, some people wish to refuse treatment if they believe the outcome will not provide them with the quality of life they want. However, if you become mentally incapacitated or unconscious, you are assumed to have given consent to all medical treatment that the medical establishment considers necessary.

A living will documents your instructions for the refusal or consent to medical treatment. With personal care documents, the instructions that might have been in a separate living will are now built into the power of attorney document, giving your representative the legal authority to speak and carry out your wishes even when you cannot speak for yourself. If, for example, you want to be an organ donor, you should make it clear that you can be left on a ventilator for that purpose.

Your living will instructions are misnamed: they are *not* a will and they deal with your dying, not your living. The living will is an advanced health care directive in which you can indicate, based on your own values, your wishes as to the types or degree of health care or medical intervention you would like to receive or refuse when you are unable to speak for yourself. However, some instructions may be prohibited by law and you may not be able to document them.

The more clearly you indicate your wishes, the easier it will be for your health care providers to follow your wishes in the spirit you intended.

Some documents include wording similar to "If it is anticipated that I cannot enjoy a reasonable quality of life after recovery or remission, I request that I be allowed to die and not be kept alive by artificial means or heroic measures." For example, it is a good idea to specify what you mean by "quality of life," such as not wanting to live hooked up to machines when there is no hope of survival.

One of my clients had worked with her lawyer and had signed her will and her general power of attorney. But she had difficulty with the wording that had been used in her power of attorney for personal care, and this document was still in limbo, even though she had the wording developed and accepted by the legal system. I tried to interpret this for her from a personal perspective, although I did not provide new wording for her document. I said that to me this wording meant that if I were ever at a point where I had no control over who I was and had no hope of having any quality of life, then the wording meant that I would want to be allowed to die and not be kept alive by machines. She then felt ready to visit her lawyer and execute the document.

Don't assume your family or representative understands or shares your wishes. Discuss your beliefs and wishes with your family and health care providers. The more specific you can be (without being overly detailed), the more they will be able to respect your wishes.

If you are scheduled for major surgery, your surgeon may ask you to make sure that your affairs are all in order and that your family knows your wishes regarding the quality of life you wish (i.e., Would you want to spend the rest of your life in a vegetative state?) and your wishes regarding organ donation. Then, in the event that it becomes necessary on the day of the surgery to make a life or death decision, your family will be as prepared for making the decision as anyone could be.

It is never easy to hear this from a surgeon. First and foremost, you are reminded of the potential risk of the surgery. As well, you have a limited amount of time to ensure your affairs are in order. And if you think that your days are numbered, you really don't want to spend them doing paperwork—you'd probably rather spend them with the people who are important to you. You don't go into surgery thinking, "Boy, am I glad my paperwork is in order and that we've reduced the amount of tax that will be due by as much as possible." You go into that operating room, hopefully, feeling loved.

Unless you have just put your estate plan in place, you may want to ensure that your affairs are in order. Since you are probably under physical and emotional stress, you may want a trusted friend or adviser to help you locate all your papers and make sure they are all stored together, if they are not already. And telling your family your wishes will provide them with the guidance they need should a representative of the transplant team approach them.

There may be circumstances under which you do not want to have your life prolonged. Perhaps you cannot imagine living if you cannot take care of yourself or if you were to be sustained by medical intervention in intensive care. Or perhaps you have a terminal illness and are willing to accept treatment to minimize the pain, but do not want any aggressive treatment or to have your life sustained by artificial means or through medical intervention. If you watch any of the medical shows on television today, you may hear actors and actresses facing terminal illness say "DNR" or "I'm DNR all the way." DNR stands for "do not resuscitate."

The Dying with Dignity Association provides information and counselling services. They can be contacted at (416) 486-3998 or through www.dyingwithdignity.ca

Q. Must my physician follow the instructions in my living will?

A. Yes and no. According to the Centre for Bioethics, the Canadian Medical Association supports living wills in principle, but some professionals may be reluctant to follow advance directives on medical treatment when those instructions involve assisting with a suicide, for fear of being charged under the *Criminal Code*.

The legal status of living wills varies from province to province. The lack of legislation has not stopped the courts from recognizing living wills as valid documents. Even if you live in a province where a living will is not yet formally recognized, putting your wishes and beliefs in writing provides guidance for your family and medical professionals during difficult times regarding your medical care and the quality of life you desire.

Compassionate Care Benefits may be paid to eligible individuals under Employment Insurance (EI) who are absent from work in order to care for a gravely ill family member. You *do not* have to be named as a power of attorney for personal or medical care to be eligible for these benefits. Eligibility is based on earnings and your relationship to the family member. In addition, a number of provinces have also added their own compassionate-care legislation, including Ontario and British Columbia.

Like other estate planning documents, a living will or advanced care directive should be reviewed regularly and updated if necessary to reflect your current wishes and medical condition. It should also be reviewed if you move to another province as the provincial laws vary.

CONSIDERATIONS WHEN PREPARING POWER OF ATTORNEY FOR PERSONAL CARE

The document can be prepared by anyone who is mentally competent and, in most provinces, at least 16 years old. Remember, once teenagers reach a certain age, they no longer require their parents' intervention when seeking medical treatment. However, the person you appoint to act as your attorney, proxy, or representative must have reached the age of majority.

Selecting Your Attorney

The person you appoint as your power of attorney for personal or health care is generally only called upon when and if you become incapable of making your own decisions on these matters, or when it appears you are no longer capable of making a required medical decision yourself. The person or persons you appoint do not have to be a lawyer.

Some people appoint the same person for the financial decisions as for their personal and health care decisions, although you can appoint different people. If you appoint more than one person to act as your attorney, they are required to make decisions on your behalf together unless you state they may act "jointly and severally," that is, they can make decisions together or act independently.

The person you appoint should be someone you trust, who understands your personal values and who will follow your instructions or, if you have not left detailed instructions, will make decisions based on what he or she believes is in your best interest and will stand up for your wishes. You should not just assume that they are willing and able to carry out your wishes. Be sure to ask them if they will act on your behalf if necessary.

Once you've made your selection, make sure the attorneys named in the document know your wishes and the location of the document. Depending on the situation, it may be appropriate for each representative to have an original copy of the document.

It's a good idea to include the name of a substitute or backup attorney, who is willing and able to act on your behalf in the event the original attorney cannot when the time comes. If your first choice becomes unwilling or unable to act, or unable to continue to act, and you don't name an alternate or backup attorney, your power of attorney document could be revoked. Then the decision maker of last resort—someone from the office of the provincial public guardian and trustee—would make or oversee the decisions taken on your behalf.

Authority of Your Power of Attorney for Personal Care

The decisions related to personal care could include where you will live, what you will wear, who you see, and what you eat. The decisions related to medical care range from consenting to medical tests and major surgery to withholding consent for medical treatment.

Unless restrictions are specified, a power of attorney document authorizes your attorney to act on your behalf for all personal and health care decisions, including selecting a physician to determine whether or not you are mentally capable to make these decisions yourself.

Your representatives do not have to make exactly the same decisions you would make if you were able; they only have to make decisions that are in your best interest. Of course, it could help your representative(s) if you discuss your wishes while you are mentally capable.

Your power of attorney for health and personal care may be involved in making some of the following decisions on your behalf, including but not limited to:

- arranging regular medical and dental checkups
- consenting to medical tests, including exploratory surgery
- consenting to major surgery

- arranging palliative care
- withholding consent for medical treatment you might not want
- participating in medical research studies or experimental treatments
- releasing information related to your medical records and history
- deciding where you live, what you eat, wear, etc.
- prohibiting prolonging your life if there is no reasonable expectation of recovery, such as during the last stages of a terminal illness
- releasing information related to your medical records and history

Unlike a general power of attorney for finances, the document for personal and health care decisions generally is not effective until you become incapable of making these decisions for yourself.

Compensation

In addition to considering reimbursing your attorney for all reasonable out-of-pocket expenses related to looking after your personal and health care, you can also consider if you want your representative or attorney to receive any compensation for his or her time and services.

SUMMARY

Provincial legislation for advanced health care directives is evolving. Law makers are attempting to balance the needs of all involved to:

- give patients the power to make their own medical decisions
- give individuals the right to appoint someone to make decisions
- provide those named as substitute decision makers with the legal authority to follow those instructions
- provide a legal framework that protects all parties involved, including the individual, the medical providers, and government officials who may become involved, without unnecessary red tape or high administration costs

No one knows what the future will hold. My husband has the following words in his power of attorney for personal and health care:

> *Death is as much a reality as birth, growth, maturity, and old age. It is the one certainty of life. If the time should come when I can no longer take part in the decisions for my own future, I hereby direct that this statement be allowed to stand as an expression of my wishes made while I am mentally competent.*
>
> *This request is made after careful consideration. It may appear to place a heavy responsibility on those individuals whose care I am in. However, it is with the intention of relieving you of such responsibility and placing it wholly upon myself in accordance with my strong personal convictions that this statement is made.*
>
> *If the situation should arise where my attending physician(s) has determined that there can be no recovery by me from a physical and/or mental disability and that my death is imminent, I hereby direct that I be allowed to die. It is my desire not to be kept alive by artificial means or heroic measure, which would only serve to artificially prolong the process of dying. I do not fear death itself as much as the indignities of deterioration, dependence, and endless pain. I request that I be allowed to die naturally with only the administration of medication and the performance of any medical procedures deemed necessary to provide me with comfort and/or to alleviate suffering, even though this may hasten the moment of my death.*

These words will provide me and his doctors with guidance if I should ever have to make a health care decision on his behalf, as well as our discussion in which he told me his wishes.

It can be even more difficult for some people to prepare this document than a will. We all know we won't live forever, but it can be more difficult to anticipate being incapacitated and not able to make our own decisions. This document allows you to appoint someone you trust and who cares about you to make health care decisions that are in your best interest.

chapter sixteen

the final gift

How do you say thank you?
—M.

THE MESSAGE COMES ACROSS loud and clear. An organ transplant can greatly improve the life expectancy, productivity, and quality of life of the recipient. People die waiting for an organ that can be transplanted because not enough people, or their families, are willing to donate their organs.

Each province has legislation, such as Manitoba's *Human Tissue Amendment Act*, which gives you the right to indicate your wish to be an organ or tissue donor. A donation on your death can help someone who might otherwise die.

The Trillium Gift of Life Network in Ontario is one not-for-profit provincial government Organ and Tissue Donation Agency that promotes and supports organ and tissue donation across Ontario. As of September 2006, there were 1,750 people on the waiting list year-to-date and the total number of transplants that had been performed was 295 (source: www.giftoflife.ca). Across Canada, there were over 4,000 people waiting.

On your death, you may want to donate your organs to save someone else's life or donate your body for medical research. We have to consider our own values and personal issues for this individual decision.

Q. Will my family know the names of the people I helped?

A. No, the donation after death is confidential. However, your family will receive a letter within a few weeks informing them which organs and tissues were transplanted. There may be an option of communicating with the recipients by anonymous letter, and families are encouraged to initiate this correspondence.

ORGAN AND TISSUE DONATIONS

There are people waiting for almost every major organ—including the heart, kidneys, lungs, liver, pancreas, and bowels—every organ, in fact, except the brain. And it is not only organs that can be transplanted and improve the quality of life for the person in need. Many types of tissues can also be donated, including skin, bone, heart valves to replace a faulty one, and corneas for those whose sight has been damaged. You could be both an organ donor and a tissue donor. Different organs could be transplanted and help a number of different people.

Some donations can be made while you are alive, including blood and bone marrow. Living donations of a kidney or a portion of the liver are possible if there is a close biological match.

If you are going in for major surgery, your surgeon may ask you to ensure your family knows your wishes regarding quality of life and/or organ donation. Even if you are not asked, I think it's a good idea to discuss this with your family because at death, decisions regarding donation need to be made quickly while the organs are usable.

One individual in his early 20s had fractured his ankle. Because of the location of the fracture, it still had not healed even after a year and it was deteriorating. He was put on a waiting list for a replacement ankle bone and stayed in town with a pager. Within the year, the pager went off and he reported to the hospital, where his surgeon transplanted the new ankle bone, improving the quality of his life.

Even if your wishes to be an organ and/or tissue donor are known, your doctor's first priority is to care for you and, if you are not able to speak for yourself, to carry out your wishes according to the instructions in your power of attorney for health care document or as expressed by the individual named in the document.

Before being considered as an organ donor, the individual must be declared brain dead but still have a beating heart. Brain death is the end of all brain function and is irreversible. Because the donor is on a ventilator and the heart is still beating, the body's organs continue to receive oxygen and stay functional.

You can donate your eyes even if you wear glasses. For more information, contact http://eyebank.med.utoronto.ca/donation.htm

Organ donation is now being considered after cardiac death in some hospitals, which is a relatively new approach in Canada. But organ donation in this situation has been practiced in some countries for decades.

Although we would like to think all donations can be used, the suitability of a donor's organs and tissues for transplant depends on the donor's health at death and the cause of death. But don't be the one who counts yourself out. The oldest organ donor in Canada was over 90 and the oldest tissue donor was 102 (source: www.giftoflife.on.ca).

A family may volunteer or be offered the opportunity to give consent to donate their deceased relative's organs. With the shortage of organ donors, medical providers will increasingly approach families who have just lost a loved one to ask if they would be willing to provide consent. To increase the probability that your wishes and rights will be honoured, let your family know what they are.

Q. When can the body be released to the family?

A. After the declaration of death, the organ donation process generally takes up to 24 hours: eight hours for the medical tests to be completed, two to eight hours for the surgery to remove the organs (leaving no visible disfigurement), plus eight hours if an autopsy is required. Your body would be released to your family as quickly as possible.

Signed Donor Cards

Each province runs its own organ donation and transplant program, and maintains a database of people who are waiting for a transplant. While Canada currently does not have a national program, the provincial programs coordinate their services.

One way to indicate you would like to be an organ or tissue donor is to sign an organ donor consent card or the consent form on the back of your driver's licence, or to state this in your documents for health and personal care. If you do not have a driver's licence, you can obtain a consent form from your province's transplant program.

You should also discuss your wishes with your family to help them understand what you want and to make it easier for them to carry your wishes out. A family member may also be required to sign a final consent form at the time of your death. Decisions have to be made quickly—or ideally have already been made.

Q. Can I donate my organs and still have a funeral?

A. Yes. The organs, bones, and tissues are removed in a sensitive manner, and it would still be possible after the donation to have an open casket at the funeral service if that was the family's wish.

DONATING YOUR BODY FOR MEDICAL RESEARCH

Here lie the cremated remains of those who, in the interests of their fellow man, donated their bodies to medical education and research.

—*From a stone in the University of Toronto section of St. James's Cemetery*

Are you interested in donating your body for educational purposes or scientific research? There are at least 16 medical, dental, or other health profession schools that need a certain number of bodies every year. Future medical professionals can learn a certain amount of anatomy from a textbook or computer simulation, but at some point, they need to work on a real body to add another dimension to their experience.

If you are interested, contact your local medical school for more details. If your body is accepted, the school will normally arrange for transportation of the body, but the estate or family may be required to pay for the cost.

The school will keep the body for between six months and three years and then cremate it. Different schools have different options available after cremation. For example, at the University of Toronto, the cremated remains may be released to the family or the estate for a private burial (at the expense of the family or estate), or they may be buried by the university at the university burial service held each spring. For more information, contact the school in your area.

If your body is accepted for medical research or education, many people believe that it is still important for those close to you to recognize that a death has occurred. Family and friends may wish to hold a memorial service around the time of death, even though no body is present.

Some people visited the Body Worlds2 show when it was in Toronto and may be interested in donating their body and being "plastinated" for the research and possible exhibit. For more information regarding the process, see www.bodyworlds.com

SUMMARY

Organ and tissue donation is a way to give the gift of life, even at a time of death. A recipient's life, or quality of life, depends on this gift. And while it will not reverse your death or the death of a loved one, the gift may be a way for something positive to come out of even the most tragic of deaths, no matter what the age of the deceased.

chapter seventeen

planning your funeral

Death is just a distant rumour to the young.
—*Andy Rooney*

AS DIFFICULT AS IT IS FOR MOST people in Canada to face death, planning your funeral, either formally or informally, is part of an estate plan. I suppose if you are still trying to find reasons to put off writing your will, you probably aren't ready to consider your funeral.

Funerals, like marriages or bar mitzvahs, are a rite of passage, a way to recognize a significant stage of life or the significance of life. The successful Disney movie *The Lion King* had an award-winning song called "The Circle of Life." More people are now thinking about death as a natural part of life, part of the ongoing cycle. Nevertheless, death is never easy. Many people are reluctant to consider the final decisions that need to be made, either by them or by family on their behalf.

Think about the time and effort that goes into planning another rite of passage, a wedding. Some traditional funerals are as elaborate as the most formal wedding, and yet, with a death, there are only a few days to prepare, days when your family is most vulnerable, both emotionally and financially.

Some people feel that significant amounts of money are required to pay tribute to the deceased. There is no one way to celebrate a life. It can be celebrated simply or elaborately. I believe a life is not enhanced or diminished by the amount of money spent on a funeral. Some elaborate, expensive funerals have been arranged by people who later realized that the money spent did not appease the guilt, mixed feelings, stress, or the grief they were feeling at the time.

There are few "rules" regarding what funeral arrangements are necessary. Funerals range from the traditional to the irreverent. For example, Hunter S. Thompson's wishes were carried out when his ashes were fired from a cannon.

EXECUTOR'S RESPONSIBILITY

You can leave specific instructions or provide general guidance regarding your wishes to assist your family and executor, but the final responsibility for arranging your funeral lies with your executor, and he or she may legally override your oral or written instructions if they are not appropriate. For example, if you prearrange, but not prepay, for an elaborate funeral that your estate cannot afford, your wishes are not likely to be carried out. On the other hand, if your wish is for a very simple funeral, your instructions may provide the needed guidance to your executor and family, who might otherwise have felt they needed to spend more.

You can put instructions for your funeral in your will. I suppose that some people do this thinking that this means they don't have to discuss their wishes with their family or executor ahead of time. Unfortunately, timing is everything and if your will is not located until after your funeral, your wishes will not be followed unless you had told your family and executor of any special requests you had regarding funeral arrangements or cremation. (Or your wishes may not be followed until sometime in the future as in Sweden, where one town has been considering freeze-drying its population!)

Although the funeral home might provide some forms and guidance to the executor, it is the executor's job to follow through on his or her duties to ensure that all items are completed. There is a list of duties for an executor or estate trustee in Appendix I.

COSTS

Funerals are big business and can be expensive. Costs range from around $4,000 to more than $15,000, depending on the arrangements and the pricing policies of the funeral home, memorial society, or non-profit organization. The prices for individual items or packages of items and services vary from one location to another. Some expensive caskets can be purchased at the funeral home or through an outside provider (this is occurring in the U.S., so it may not be too long before this service is available in Canada); others can be rented. There is a wide range of products available between the most expensive and the least expensive.

The most basic service is called a transfer service or immediate disposition service, and involves the transfer of the deceased's body from the place of death to the cemetery or crematorium. It may be arranged for around $1,400. Any burial or transfer service can be complemented by a memorial service. However, if the family will be spending time with the deceased, it is important to consider not just the cost but also the final visual memory that will be left with the family. This should be discussed with the funeral director.

I've found some people become particularly interested in preplanning their funeral after they have been involved in making funeral arrangements when someone close to them has died—a spouse, a friend, or a close family member.

When you are discussing your options with a funeral director or counsellor, consider what you would want. You may have strong wishes regarding the type of funeral or service. Some people make notes of what they like and dislike at the funerals of friends and relatives. You may have a special piece of music, or there may be a part of a ceremony that you think would be particularly appropriate. There may also be a part of the ritual you would not want to be recreated at your funeral or memorial service.

Look for a funeral home that gives value for the dollar and has a sensitive funeral director. There should be no pressure from anyone you speak to. If you live in a small community, you may not have many options to choose from, but by preplanning, you can reduce costs or pressures on your family.

The funeral or memorial service is for the living. The Trillium Gift of Life Network has a Grief Library at www.griefwords.com/library/default.asp with resources for mourners and ideas for creating meaningful funerals. I've been to funerals for teenagers where the friends of the deceased had the opportunity to speak, creating a very moving service for everyone there.

You may want to arrange other details, such as the newspaper notice, who might be invited, the flowers, and the reception after the service. While some people may find making these details morbid, others find great comfort in making their own arrangements. My grandmother wrote her own obituary and kept a book with the details that were important to her. It was amazing to see her memories in her own handwriting You, on the other hand, might just want to indicate to your family that you want them to do what they think is best, or that you don't want anything fancy.

PREPLANNING

Preplanning your funeral may minimize the stress families can experience when members come together. Funeral homes often suggest we should preplan our funerals. Preplanning involves determining your funeral wishes in advance. It does not require any payment in advance or any other financial obligation, but you can comparison-shop, consider how you would like to be remembered, and ultimately make it easier for your executor to carry out your wishes. On the other hand, a funeral home's preplanning services can attract and help it anticipate future business.

I asked one couple I worked with if they had discussed their funeral wishes. She assumed that her husband would want a funeral with a burial in accordance with their traditional religious beliefs. He, however, wanted to be cremated, as he believed this to be more environmentally friendly. They had some work to do.

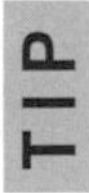

The funeral home can also help your survivors find grief counselling services and your executor complete some forms necessary for his or her responsibilities.

A funeral can be a major expense. When you have the luxury of time, you can compare the costs of the various services and supplies, and plan the funeral or service you would like, taking into account your budget, wishes, and the traditions of your community.

Q & A

Q. How do I preplan a funeral?

A. Ideally, visit three or more funeral homes and obtain their information and price lists. Most funeral homes will arrange an appointment to discuss your options and answer your questions without obligation or any sales pressure. Your plan will be a written file with the preferred funeral home—or verbal instructions to your executor—regarding your wishes. It can be relatively informal without any money being committed.

In some provinces, the arrangements for the funeral and burial, cremation, or interment can be made through the same place. However, in Ontario, for example, funeral homes and cemeteries are required by law to operate separately, although many have associations with the other.

In 2004, 56% of Canadians who died were cremated, according to the Cremation Association of North America. The percentage across Canada ranged from a high of 78% of deaths in B.C. to a low of 2.2% in Nunavut.

When planning your funeral or memorial service, you may want to decide if you want it to be:

- non-denominational, non-religious, or to reflect your religious beliefs
- simple, elaborate, or something in-between
- with or without a service
- a burial or cremation
- in an open or closed casket that will be bought or rented

Preplanning is on the rise. One funeral home in Toronto told me it is preplanning an average of two funerals a day. The demographics of the Canadian population, increased awareness through articles and advertising, different cultural traditions, and concern about controlling funeral costs contribute to this trend. Many nursing homes require that a funeral be preplanned before a resident moves in, or that they have the name of a funeral director to contact when necessary.

PREPAID FUNERALS

Prepaid arrangements involve a signed contract that itemizes the arrangements and services that are paid for in advance, either by cheque or by arranging a life insurance policy.

Most provinces have legislation dealing with prepaid funerals. The funds paid are held "in trust" for you, either by the funeral home or a provincial organization. If you've prepaid your funeral, be sure your executor knows, so he or she will not arrange and pay for another funeral!

Some contracts state that funds held in trust will go toward the actual cost of the funeral (with an unwritten implication that the family or the estate will pay any additional amount owing at the time of the funeral). Some contracts now state that if, at the time of the funeral, the cost of the details that were prepaid is greater than the amount paid, the funeral home will be responsible for paying the difference.

The contract should include a clause that states what will happen if the amount prepaid is more than the actual cost. Perhaps the excess might be returned to the estate, as well as a clause stating what will happen if the funeral is not handled through that home.

Q. Can funeral expenses be deducted on the final tax return?

A. No.

Suppose you prepay $4,400 and your contract guarantees that the selected funeral services will be fully paid for and any excess refunded. The funds earn the current interest rate each year, and at the time of death, the amount in trust is $5,390. If the actual cost of the funeral in three years is $5,000, the estate will receive a refund of $390. But if the cost of the funeral is $5,900, the contract states that the additional cost will be covered by the funeral home. Your family will not have to write an additional cheque (unless they want any additional services that were not prearranged under the original contract).

If you prepay a contract with a purchase price of less than $15,000 (which is much more than the cost of the average funeral), the interest on the funds grows tax-free unless it is not used for the prepaid services.

As with any contract, you should determine how flexible the funeral or cemetery contract is with the money.

- What might happen if you move?
- Can you obtain a full refund?
- What does the contract say about cancellation if you change your mind?
- What happens if your executor arranges your funeral somewhere else?
- Can you cancel within 10 or 30 days of signing and obtain a full refund? Or at any time? If not, what amount would be withheld?

Before signing any contract, be sure you read and understand each clause and that you will be protected if you move or change your mind.

Your province may have regulations regarding refunds. For example, in Newfoundland, under the Prepaid Funeral Services Regulations, 2000, if you cancel the contract, the funeral home deducts the lesser of $250 or 10% of the money paid under the prepaid funeral contract before refunding the money paid for the contract.

In British Columbia, the money paid can be refunded within 30 days under certain circumstances. However, once a pre-need contract has been completed, the funeral home is entitled to retain up to 20% of the contract, as well as the cost for any unique pre-ordered items.

Q. I've purchased a double burial plot. The resale value is now about $10,000. I want to take an extensive trip and be cremated. Can I sell my plot?

A. Refer to the contract that you signed. It should say how cancellation of the contract is to be handled and specify any fees to be withheld.

In some provinces, funeral homes operate separately from cemeteries and crematoriums. If you decide that you wish to buy a burial plot, you might have to arrange this separately.

Besides prepaying the funeral, some of the more common ways to pay a funeral bill are the following:

- a joint bank account with someone who will be responsible for paying for the funeral and burial costs from that account (but not in Quebec)
- for your executor to pay for the funeral from your bank account if the bank approves the request to provide the funds
- for a family member to pay the expenses and for the estate to reimburse him or her
- a small insurance policy

Break-ins have occurred while family members attended a funeral. It would be prudent to have someone house-sit during the funeral.

Whether you preplan or prepay, you can take the initiative as part of your estate plan. Remember, even telling your family your wishes is a form of preplanning. Now go out and live your life as you would like it to be remembered!

chapter eighteen

you can't take it with you

If you don't think every day makes a difference,
read the obituary column.
—*Mike McKinley*

ESTATE PLANNING CAN BE FAIRLY straightforward or very complicated, depending on your personal and financial life. It will evolve and grow as your life and your family does. Your plan will affect those people closest to you, your community, and perhaps people you don't even know.

Your estate plan should reflect what is important to you. It should meet your needs while you are alive and consider the tax issues, legal issues, and family matters. It can help to ensure there is enough money to pay the taxes and, if your family was dependent on you as a breadwinner, you can build insurance into your plan to replace your income if something should happen to you prematurely.

Estate planning also includes preparing powerful legal documents; even naming a beneficiary on your RRSP is part of a plan. Doing nothing is not a responsible option! It is not in the best interests of your family, business, or other relationships.

As I mentioned in the Preface, thirty years ago estate planning was fairly simple. The relevant laws and personal finances were relatively straightforward. But today, I believe that estate planning—or not having an estate plan—has a greater impact on Canadians than ever before. We have the opportunity to keep the government out of our lives wherever we can and, through our estate plan, we can make our wishes known and distribute our assets as we wish.

STEPS IN DEVELOPING YOUR ESTATE PLAN

1. Determine your objectives and goals.
2. Review your personal and business situation and your family dynamics.
3. Assess your estate planning issues.
4. Determine the appropriate estate planning strategies.
5. Discuss your plan with those affected, including your family, your executor, guardian, and powers of attorney.
6. Prepare and keep good records.
7. Prepare or update your pre-estate and estate documents.
8. Review your estate plan periodically.

With that said, you do not want to unnecessarily complicate your estate. The roots of your estate plan are your own personal objectives.

- Whom do you want to benefit from your estate: yourself, your beneficiaries, or Canada Revenue Agency (CRA)?
- Are you creating a major legacy and leaving as much as possible to your beneficiaries? Or leaving only what is left over after you have enjoyed it? Or is your primary purpose to keep as much as possible from the CRA?

This book has discussed some of your options for meeting your objectives.

By planning, you will be able to benefit your beneficiaries the way you envision.

GETTING ORGANIZED AND KEEPING RECORDS

Throughout the book, we've been discussing wills, power of attorney documents, trusts, taxes, and other relatively complex estate planning considerations.

There is also a relatively simple but very important aspect of estate planning that is often overlooked—being organized. When someone dies, all the important documents need to be found—the will, birth certificate, life insurance policies, company benefits information, safety deposit box and key, bank accounts, pension plans, RRSP and RRIF accounts, ownership papers for specific assets and property, and other important papers.

You can assist your executor and spouse (and make it easier for your family) by writing down where they will find your will and important personal papers. I have a file that contains a copy of every financial paper I receive. In my family, my husband knows where to find the information he needs (and vice versa). The more account numbers, addresses, contact names, and other information you provide, the more you help your executor do his or her job. And if your power of attorney for finances needs to step in before your death, being organized will also help him or her. If your power of attorney and/or executor needs to access your computer for your personal or business records, he or she will also need the necessary passwords.

Not a problem, you say. But Canadians have enough trouble locating their own papers to complete their income tax each year! One family was trying to settle the father's affairs after he died. He had been very secretive all his life about his money. Not knowing where to find even a list of all his accounts and property dragged out settling his estate. And just when they thought that it was all settled, something new was uncovered.

Simplify, Simplify, Simplify

While you are getting organized, it may be useful to remove some of the complexity from your financial matters. You could look at your overall financial affairs and consider if they are more complex than they need to be. Do you really need four RRSPs, five bank accounts, and three brokerage accounts?

This is more important than you might think. What may make life simpler for your estate might also make your own life simpler and easier to manage if you don't give up any investor protection. Could your estate be settled more quickly if you deposited the share certificates currently sitting in your safety deposit box in with your other investments in your investment account? Then, on your death, your executor would *not* have to send the original certificates, along with the documentation required—which could include a copy of the will, a copy of the death certificate, and a copy of the grant or letters probate—to the representative or trustee of each company (to be registered in the name of the estate or transferred to a beneficiary).

If the shares were registered in an investment account, the monthly statement would provide a handy inventory of your investments. The executor would only have to send the supporting documentation once (to the brokerage firm) to arrange for the account to be registered in the name of the estate.

Q. My spouse and I have signing authority for our safety deposit box and my daughter knows the location of the key in case something happens to us. Is there anything else we should do?

A. Yes. The key alone is not enough. Your daughter has no authority to go into your safety deposit box unless she has signing access. To give her authority (if this is what you want to do), have her name and signature added to the safety deposit box signature card.

At the back of this book, you will find an order form for the *Estate Planning Workbook* with additional forms and checklists to help you:

- take a snapshot of your current financial situation
- determine your estate planning objectives

- identify questions for your lawyer, financial adviser, accountant, or other professional
- instruct your advisers
- make it easier for the executor of your will and the person named in your power of attorney documents to follow your instructions, find all the people mentioned in your documents, and locate the details of your personal and financial life.

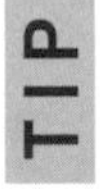

Someday you've got to get organized. Keeping good records is one of the cheapest (if not the simplest) estate planning strategies to implement. Where are your personal documents? In a drawer? In a box in the basement? In such a "safe" place that even your executor won't be able to find them?

TAX PLANNING

Throughout the book, I have assumed that you do not want the CRA to "benefit" from your estate any more than absolutely necessary. You may also have strong feelings with regard to the size of CRA's share of your estate.

Estate planning can reduce the taxes and fees that your estate will be required to pay on your death, and result in a smoother transition to your beneficiaries with less family conflict. Making informed decisions will help you to determine the most effective ways to manage your financial affairs, and ensure that you do not send the CRA any more than is necessary, or any sooner than necessary.

Because you can transfer assets tax-free to your spouse on death, it makes sense to consider which, if not all, assets to leave to your spouse. And if you have survived your spouse, then you should review your own plan to make sure that as much as possible goes to the next generation and not to the government. There are tax considerations when assets are left to a spouse (same-generation planning) and other considerations when assets are left to children or grandchildren (inter-generation planning) or charity.

Taxes are never simple, and no matter how well you structure your estate plan, it is likely that governments will collect some tax and perhaps try to get more in the future. Recent tax changes, including the elimination of the personal capital gains exemption and increases in provincial probate fees, are just two examples of the direction governments are heading.

WORKING WITH PROFESSIONALS

I believe there is no substitute for professional advice. But many people find it challenging to find and work with competent professionals they feel they can trust. Professionals cannot make your decisions for you, but they can give you advice tailored to your particular situation (which a book cannot do), direct you on the most efficient course of action, and ensure that you have taken care of all the details. You might be working with a team of professionals who are all experts in their particular area. The team might include: a trust officer; financial adviser or planner; business valuator; life insurance representative; a lawyer specializing in family, corporate, or estate law; and an accountant, to name just a few.

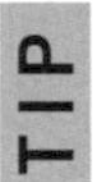

Members of the Society of Trust and Estate Practitioners (STEP), which offers the TEP designation, have experience in estates and trusts and estate planning matters. Visit www.step.ca for more information.

One of the best ways to locate a good professional is by word of mouth. Remember, finding a good adviser is a lot like finding a good family doctor: it takes competency and the right chemistry as well. You should feel comfortable with the individual and feel he or she cares about you. If you are not comfortable with this person, you may not take the advice, or you may take the advice without questioning it, and neither is good for your financial health. None of your advisers should intimidate you.

Take advantage of the free initial consultation offered by many professionals (although there is a trend to charge for this meeting if advice is given). Be prepared to discuss your situation, your concerns, your values, and your goals. If you are used to being very private about your financial affairs, you may at first feel a bit awkward discussing your family and financial situation. This initial meeting will help you to determine whether you feel comfortable with the adviser on a personal level, as well as give you an opportunity to assess his or her competency.

The adviser should look comprehensively at your financial health, understand your needs, answer your questions, and ensure confidentiality in your relationship. Look for experience, credentials, high ethical standards, community involvement, and dedication to clients. While not all advisers currently consider their clients' estate planning needs, I expect this will be a growing area of specialization as the population of Canada ages.

Q. *The person I've been working with for my investments has not advised me on my estate planning needs. What should I do?*

A. Determine if he or she can provide you with the estate planning you need. They should ask to see your will, powers of attorney documents, along with your tax return, RRSP, and investment statements. If they are not comfortable helping you with your estate planning, start by asking them to refer you to someone who is an expert in estate planning.

Sometimes, your advisers may ask you questions that make you examine your own decisions. For example, if you are naming your eldest daughter as your power of attorney for finances, the lawyer might ask whether you are sure you can trust her. Their questions are designed to help protect your interests. Think through your decisions a second time, but don't stop relying on your own judgment if it has served you well over the years.

YOUR ESTATE PLANNING PRIORITIES CHECKLIST

This checklist is designed to help you with the "Decide" step of estate planning. It will help you identify your estate planning priorities. As you work through your estate plan, you can refer to this checklist to ensure your estate plan reflects your long-term goals and objectives.

I agree/disagree with the following statements:

	Strongly Agree	*Agree*	*Neither Agree nor Disagree*	*Disagree*	*Strongly Disagree*	*Not Appli-cable*
I want to enjoy my money while I am alive.	❒	❒	❒	❒	❒	❒
I want to leave everything to my spouse or partner.	❒	❒	❒	❒	❒	❒
I want my common-law partner treated as if we were married.	❒	❒	❒	❒	❒	❒
I want my spouse or partner to enjoy the same standard of living after my death.	❒	❒	❒	❒	❒	❒
I want to appoint a guardian for my children under 18 or 19.	❒	❒	❒	❒	❒	❒
I want all my children to benefit equally from my estate.	❒	❒	❒	❒	❒	❒
I have children from a previous marriage. I want to keep their inheritance separate.	❒	❒	❒	❒	❒	❒
I would like to help pay for my grandchildren's post-secondary education.	❒	❒	❒	❒	❒	❒

	Strongly Agree	Agree	Neither Agree nor Disagree	Disagree	Strongly Disagree	Not Applicable
I want to make sure my children/ grandchildren don't receive their inheritance too early.	❒	❒	❒	❒	❒	❒
I want to minimize the final tax bill to CRA.	❒	❒	❒	❒	❒	❒
I want to minimize the final taxes sent to another tax jurisdiction, such as the IRS.	❒	❒	❒	❒	❒	❒
I want to minimize all costs and fees required to settle my estate.	❒	❒	❒	❒	❒	❒
I want to maximize the tax benefits of my charitable donations.	❒	❒	❒	❒	❒	❒
I want to be remembered with a simple funeral or memorial service.	❒	❒	❒	❒	❒	❒
I want to keep all my assets until I am sure I don't need them—that is, after my death.	❒	❒	❒	❒	❒	❒
I want to leave my beneficiaries as much as possible.	❒	❒	❒	❒	❒	❒

	Strongly Agree	*Agree*	*Neither Agree nor Disagree*	*Disagree*	*Strongly Disagree*	*Not Appli-cable*
I need outside professional advice to develop a succession plan to keep the business in the family.	❐	❐	❐	❐	❐	❐
I want to keep our vacation property in the family.	❐	❐	❐	❐	❐	❐
I want to integrate my estate plan with my retirement and tax plan.	❐	❐	❐	❐	❐	❐
I believe in organ and tissue donation.	❐	❐	❐	❐	❐	❐
I want to choose who will make decisions on my behalf should I become incapacitated.	❐	❐	❐	❐	❐	❐
I want to ensure my estate plan cannot be challenged.	❐	❐	❐	❐	❐	❐
I will organize my financial affairs so my representatives can act with the minimal amount of stress.	❐	❐	❐	❐	❐	❐
Other __________	❐	❐	❐	❐	❐	❐

chapter nineteen

it's an ongoing process

NOTHING STAYS EXACTLY THE SAME.

Estate planning is an ongoing (but not frequent) process. Tax, trust, family, and succession laws continually change, as do the market values of property and other assets. For example, tax laws can change and affect the tax savings of giving certain assets to charity. You may have "earned" some capital losses or received an inheritance that requires a review of your estate plan. Family members come and go, and family obligations can be opted into in certain provinces. If you are raising a family and have not yet accumulated significant savings, one of your primary concerns may be to create an estate for your dependants through life insurance.

And as you consider life in retirement and the assets you have accumulated, you'll want to ensure that your estate plan is up-to-date and will carry out your wishes.

For example, I wrote my first will in 1980 shortly after our first son was born. But if I had not taken the time to update it and my estate plan, I would not have addressed these important changes:

- additional children
- changes to Ontario family law

- the increased size of our assets
- the increased sophistication in the types of investments in my portfolio
- the use of spousal trusts
- changes to the personal circumstances of our named guardian and her ability to act in that capacity
- the needs related to my growing business
- the needs of my children as they became adults, including that they no longer needed a guardian
- updating the named executors
- making modest but tax-effective charitable gifts.

And if we had not talked as a family and documented our powers of attorney for financial matters and personal care, we would not have had our documents in place, just in case.

MOVING THROUGH THE STAGES OF LIFE

While it may be dangerous to attempt to generalize the needs Canadians have at different stages of life, we will look at some strategies to be considered at various times. As we mentioned at the beginning of the book, estate planning is not something reserved for the elderly—it applies to the full life cycle. It is as much about life as it is about death.

Of course, not everything here will apply to everyone. There may also be items not included here that your personal adviser will recommend for you. These are simply ideas and guidelines to make sure you are on the right track.

Single

No Kids

This is a broad category, covering everyone from those who are just attaining adulthood to those older who do not have the responsibilities of children. But this doesn't mean there are no responsibilities. You may have parents who need your help.

You may not need much life insurance, but at a minimum, you should prepare a will. If you die intestate, your parents will inherit your estate. Maybe they need it, but maybe they don't. If they don't need your estate, then you could leave it to your brothers or sisters, or nieces or nephews, or to charity rather than your parents.

You also need a valid power of attorney for financial matters and for health care. Even if you don't have much, you don't want your family and friends to have to deal with the public trustee.

With Kids

If you are in this situation, then you have full responsibility (but you already knew that). In your will, you need to make sure you have named a guardian to look after the children who are minors as well as a trustee to manage any money they may inherit. If you are divorced, it may make sense to name your ex as the guardian and to make sure your will has been updated since your divorce.

If you die before the kids are launched, having enough insurance in place might make the difference between the kids getting the upbringing and education you would want for them, or not.

You also need the pre-estate documents, such as the powers of attorney for health care and finances.

Married

Not every spouse is interested in estate planning issues, but every surviving partner is.

No Kids

Even though you may have set up your estate planning and named each other as joint tenants with rights of survivorship and each other as beneficiaries on your pension, RRSP/RRIFs, and life insurance, you still need a will if only to cover the "What if you both die in a common disaster?" and the pre-estate documents, such as the powers of attorney documents.

With Kids

By now, you know that wills and powers of attorney documents are needed.

You also need to ensure that there is enough life insurance in place so that the survivors could continue their current standard of living in the event of your death.

As the children mature, you will want to:

- ensure your will covers a distribution of your estate to your grandchildren, in the event a child predeceases you
- determine if a testamentary trust is an appropriate vehicle to use
- encourage them to have their own estate planning documents in place once they are adults
- deal with any special needs
- update your beneficiary designations on your RRSP if you had named your children
- discuss your estate plans with them

Second Marriages

Marriage always requires a person to reflect on estate planning. Couples in second marriages have additional considerations that may include children from previous marriages, marriage contracts, and other issues.

Many husbands and wives leave everything to the other in their wills, and then on the last death, everything is to their children. This strategy may not work in a second marriage if you want to ensure any children you have from a previous marriage receive some inheritance (especially if the new spouse is only a few years older than the children). Rather than waiting for the new spouse to die, or trusting him or her, some of the more common estate planning options for this situation include:

- leaving your children a portion of their inheritance on your death and the balance to your current partner
- purchasing a life insurance policy with your children named as the beneficiaries

The planning techniques you incorporate will depend on the size of your estate, the ages of your children, and the family dynamics, to name just a few considerations. You may also need to consider if any support payment obligations continue after your death.

Your executor should be someone who is willing to wade through any family feuds.

Same-Sex Partners

Spouses and partners can have different rights, depending on your province and the documentation you have in place.

I wouldn't wait for laws to change to cover your estate planning needs. There are steps you can take now to protect your partner.

Be sure to prepare wills that clearly state your instructions and name your partner as the beneficiary on RRSPs/RRIFs, life insurance, annuities and pension plan, where appropriate. Also prepare your power of attorney.

Consider registering assets as joint tenants with rights of survivorship (not in Quebec) or, for added privacy, setting up a living trust prior to death.

If there are children involved, set up testamentary trusts for any assets they might inherit and name the appropriate guardian in your wills.

Don't die intestate.

Close to Retired or Retired

In addition to making sure you have enough income to provide for you for the rest of your days:

- ensure the income is tax-effective and will be there when you need it
- consider your gift planning or charitable donations
- review your will and power of attorney documents
- discuss your estate planning with your executor, family, and friends who are named in your documents
- review your plans to minimize taxes and expenses on death, as well as probate tax

- ensure that your spouse will be comfortable with your financial planner/adviser and with handling the money after you are gone
- consider setting up a spousal trust for ongoing income splitting

Q. I really want to die broke, but I also don't want to run out of money before then. Is this something Canadians can do?

A. Almost. You might look into a reverse mortgage on your house. If you live long enough, the payments you take out, plus the accumulated interest, may use up most of the value of the house. If you are prepared to purchase a life-only annuity, the payments will stop on death. And don't forget about spending your money and enjoying it, or giving it away just before you expire.

Elderly

What happens when you or a family member is no longer able to cope with all the day-to-day aspects of life? The mail may not be picked up or the grass is not being cut.

You may need to arrange for community services, such as social worker visits, and private support, such as a housekeeper or gardener, other quality of life matters, as well as making arrangements to handle the financial matters. Nursing home care may also be required, and if you cannot make decisions related to your own health or personal care, the power of attorney may need to be exercised on your behalf.

If you can't or no longer want to manage your money on your own, the power of attorney document for financial affairs may have to be exercised on your behalf so that your finances are managed properly and protected. At this stage of life, money can be a source of worry, even if you have enough to be comfortable. Talking with a trusted family member may be a source of comfort.

THE SIX D'S REVISITED

I wish I could tell you that you only had to do estate planning once and never have to consider it again, but that would be untrue. I would like to leave you with some thoughts that I hope you will find helpful when you are thinking about your estate plan. It really boils down to six D's: decide, design, develop, discuss, document, and detail your personal records.

- Decide what you want to do. Consider your goals and objectives for your estate plan. Do you want to leave as large an estate as possible, or spend as much as you can during your lifetime? Decide who you would like to act on your behalf as your executor, as guardian for your children, and as your trustee.
- Design and develop your estate plan. Take a look at the ways you can set up your estate plan (since there are many). Have you considered ways to reduce the fees and taxes on your final income tax return? What is the best way to register assets? If you have a family business, how can you meet the needs of your family as well as the needs of the business?
- Detail your personal records. Consider what your executor and family will need to know to put together all the personal and financial details of your life. Or what your representative or power of attorney would need to know to make decisions on your behalf. By preparing a personal inventory of all your assets, liabilities, and contact information, someone else will have the necessary details so that nothing will be overlooked
- Discuss your plans with your family and those people to whom you will be assigning responsibilities, including your executor, guardians, and trustees. They do not have to know all the details of your estate plan, but they should know enough to tell you if they are willing to act on your behalf when the time comes. Remember, you will not have the opportunity to explain your decisions after your death. Take the time to ensure those involved appreciate your decisions, even if they do not agree with you.
- Document the plan. This means you actually have to prepare the formal legal documents and ensure your executor knows where to find the necessary paperwork so that he or she can do the job. If you do not have your documents in place, the government has rules it must follow. It is not enough just to discuss your estate plan.

The legal documentation in your estate plan might include:

- a will
- a power of attorney for finances/mandate
- a power of attorney for health care/mandate, which includes the wording for your living will
- a living trust and/or an alter ego trust/joint partner trust
- an organ donor card
- beneficiary designations on RRSPs/RRIFs, life insurance, annuities, and company pension plans
- buy-sell agreements

As taxes increase and legislation becomes more powerful, it is important to ask the correct questions to achieve financial success. Tax and investment decisions also have implications for your estate, and estate planning strategies are key to a successful financial plan, but are often overlooked! One of my objectives in writing this book was to help you ask the correct questions so that you, with your advisers, can determine and implement strategies that are appropriate for your situation.

TALKING WITH YOUR FAMILY

Talking about money, incapacitation, and death is never easy. But discussions can create an understanding and provide the information so that others can assist when it is necessary. It can relieve stress for both generations. The younger generation wants to know their parent(s) have done their estate planning and whether or not they will be able to manage financially. The older generation wants to ensure they have done what is necessary.

Estate planning cannot be done effectively in isolation from your values and your life goals, or from the life goals of your beneficiaries.

Not all families will be able to have an open, frank dialogue about their situation and wishes. But the more you can share, and talk about the role and the value of money, the more you can be sure your estate plan meets your needs and the needs of your family.

Your children may not want to discuss this with you—after all, it means they have to deal with the fact that you won't be here forever. And you don't have to provide more details to your family members than you are comfortable with.

Some people want to help out while they are alive and choose to distribute some of their estate as gifts to family members or friends, or make charitable donations. Other people prefer to distribute their assets after death, just to make sure they don't give away money or assets they might need. They can be sure they won't need them any more after death. There is no one "best" or perfect estate plan, only the one you have prepared with the best information you have at hand.

Challenges

Challenges, if they arise after death, can involve the whole range of legal process from negotiation, mediation, arbitration, and all the way to a full-blown court case where the family's issues are aired in public. This is not necessarily the time when people are the most reasonable. Family battles that have been brewing just at or under the surface may become full-blown feuds.

Not every family is pleased with the will they read after the death of a family member. Sometimes they assumed they had been promised something and then after the death, discover that the distribution of the estate favoured a particular family member—that age-old problem, jealousy, or a new spouse, or something that creates the potential for a lawsuit.

To prevent controversy (not that some people don't do this on purpose), one step the deceased could have considered or tried would have been to prepare the family by discussing anything controversial with them while he or she is still alive.

Sometimes assets are registered as "tenants with rights of survivorship" as a way to avoid probate tax and are put in the name of one child without supporting documentation. This may be appropriate when there is only one child and it is clear that the asset is part of this child's inheritance. However, this could set the stage for family conflict if that child decides to keep the asset as a "gift" and there are other children in the family who know and/or believe the asset(s) should really have been part of the estate and that they should have received a share of that asset as part of their inheritance.

Another way to prevent controversy is to consider alternative ways of distribution and keep certain assets out of the estate. As we have previously discussed, these include, but are not limited to, making a gift before death, naming a beneficiary, setting up an inter vivos trust, and using a life insurance policy.

Mediation

Issues, or estate disputes, happen for a number of reasons. Some of these reasons are because the instructions in the will are unclear or because family issues come to the surface. Mediation provides an opportunity for these issues to be resolved, hopefully in such a way to prevent the family from being ripped apart any further.

Mediation is a non-binding process used in many types of disputes (estates, separation and divorce, business, landlord/tenant, etc.) where the people involved—I think of this as a family conference—attempt to work out their own settlement with the assistance of a trained mediator. The key idea behind estate mediation is that the parties involved are attempting to work out *their own* solution privately without having one imposed on them, as is often imposed by a judge as the result of the court process. A mediator is an individual trained in mediation and acts as a neutral facilitator during the meeting.

A number of provinces have introduced estate mediation sessions—some may be mandatory (as in ordered by the court) and some may be suggested by one of the lawyers or notaries involved—in an attempt to:

- resolve estate challenges
- minimize costs that would otherwise be involved in a drawn-out court case with a judge
- maintain the confidentiality of the family
- allow reasonable parties who are all going through a difficult time

an opportunity to work together to try to sort out their problems, with the assistance of a professional mediator

- keep family issues out of the court system, if at all possible

Unlike the adversial process where each party is represented by his or her own lawyer who is looking out to maximize the rights of the client, a mediator in a mediation does not represent any one person or party. The mediator's role is to be neutral and to help those involved identify the issues, the problems, and ideally reach a solution they can all find acceptable.

If those involved in an estate mediation can come to an agreement, it can avoid the costs and stress of an expensive, adversarial court process. It may be too much to hope for, but perhaps it could even leave the family members with no more issues than they came to the table with, and perhaps leave the door open for future family communication.

If you are concerned about a potential estate challenge by a family member, you could consider a distribution outside your will and working with a lawyer to ensure that you were of "sound mind."

PERSONAL AND/OR FAMILY DISCUSSION CHECKLIST

How many people actually talk about their personal or business succession plan with their family, what they want done in the event they are unable to manage their own money, where they would like to live, and how they want their estate distributed?

Take this quiz. Any *No* or *Unsure* answers may require special attention.

Yes	*No*	*Unsure*	
❐	❐	❐	Does your spouse/child(ren)/executor know where to find your will and power of attorney documents?
❐	❐	❐	Does your spouse/child(ren)/executor know where to find your financial records, income tax returns, bank accounts, safety deposit box, and insurance policies?
❐	❐	❐	Does your power of attorney for finances know what you want him or her to do if it is necessary?

Yes	*No*	*Unsure*	
❐	❐	❐	Have you provided adequately for all your dependants?
❐	❐	❐	How much is enough to leave, or how much is too much? If your beneficiaries' needs are looked after and they have a healthy work ethic, have you considered leaving a legacy through a charitable donation?
❐	❐	❐	Would it be more useful to give your children some of their inheritance now rather than later? Has everyone considered the positives and negatives of this strategy?
❐	❐	❐	Have you discussed your reasons, if you are leaving your beneficiaries unequal shares on an after-tax basis?
❐	❐	❐	Do you need to explain any wording you've put in your will to protect your child's inheritance from divorce or bankruptcy so your child can benefit from it?
❐	❐	❐	Should you leave your beneficiaries their inheritance outright or in a testamentary trust?
❐	❐	❐	Are your children prepared to inherit? Do they know how to manage the money wisely?
❐	❐	❐	Should you consider re-registering the ownership of any assets?
❐	❐	❐	Does your family know your specific wishes regarding your funeral and what you really mean if you say "as cheaply as possible"? Do you understand what that means and what celebration of your life might be missed?
❐	❐	❐	Does your family know if there are any specific funds set aside for your funeral?
❐	❐	❐	Have you discussed your specific wishes regarding organ and/or tissue donation?

Yes	*No*	*Unsure*	
❐	❐	❐	Does your family and your power of attorney know your wishes regarding medical intervention and treatment, or the withholding of treatment?
❐	❐	❐	Do the guardians you have named for your children share your values, and are they willing and able to raise your children according to those values to the best of their ability?
❐	❐	❐	While you are having these discussions, have your beneficiaries taken steps to plan their own estate (and protect their inheritance)?
❐	❐	❐	If your family has told you they want you to enjoy and spend your own money, did you really listen?
❐	❐	❐	Does your family know the names and contacts of your financial adviser, lawyer, funeral home, accountant, friends, and doctors?

The purpose of this conversation is to make sure your family and friends know what really matters to you. The first conversation may lay the groundwork for a future discussion.

It may take some time to implement your estate plan. You may choose to discuss your estate plans with your family to ensure that you organize your affairs in the best way possible for all concerned. For example, you may have trouble deciding which of your three children should inherit the cottage when in reality none of them wants it at all. Your family may be genuinely concerned for your future, and in fact they may even experience a sense of relief knowing that you have thoroughly considered your options and documented your wishes. In other families, relatives may just want to know how much they will be getting.

Warren Buffett said that, "[the perfect inheritance] is enough money so that they feel they could do anything, but not so much that they could do nothing."

Inherited money can be a mixed blessing: on the one hand, it can be a great opportunity; on the other hand, it can destroy character.

Q. I need to talk to my family about my estate plans, but I'm having difficulty raising the topic. Any suggestions on how to get started?

A. Some stages of life naturally raise the issues related to estate planning, such as marriage, births, divorce, and the death of a family member. You could introduce the subject by letting them know where they will find your important papers when they need them. You can also raise the topic by mentioning that you are having difficulty deciding who would be willing to handle all the duties of an executor. If you still have trouble getting started, you could ask a family friend or trusted professional whose opinion they value to raise the issues.

Estate planning is not easy because it makes us face the fact that we are mortal. As you plan your estate, you may struggle with what you have or have not accumulated during your lifetime, with your family relationships, with making the "right" decisions. You may even be dealing with professionals for the very first time. I hope that by now you feel a little more comfortable and ready to discuss how some of the strategies may fit your personal situation. Don't implement or pay for strategies you don't need.

NOW DO IT!

It is not a matter of "if" you should do estate planning. The integration of today's needs, retirement and tax planning, and investment management will help ensure your financial security and peace of mind. None of these aspects can be adequately dealt with without considering the others. Estate planning is just part of the puzzle.

When your estate plan is in place, you may experience a sense of relief that everything is in order and organized in an effective, efficient manner to meet your own needs and to benefit future generations.

My hope is that the information in this book, and your "homework," will save you money today and pay big benefits, now and in the future.

After all, you can't take it with you!

final words

ARE YOU READY?

What would happen if you were in a serious car accident tonight? Life is what it is. Estate planning, in my opinion, involves ensuring you have representatives in place to make the important decisions regarding your health and finances in the event you are not able to make these decisions for yourself *and* it involves ensuring you have an up-to-date will to settle your estate.

You should also discuss your medical wishes with your family so that when the time comes, either suddenly or gradually, they know what is important to you and will have the strength to carry out your wishes on your behalf.

I hope your estate plan will be the simplest, most-cost effective solution that will achieve your objectives. It should also have enough features built into it (such as backups for executors, attorneys, etc.) so that it will wear well for as long as possible regardless of the value of your assets, debts, or tax bill.

If your plan is so complex that even you have trouble following it, you might want to try to make it less complex so your executors and powers of attorneys can follow your instructions and achieve your goals and objectives. Estate planning is a personal process, but it is not a do-it-yourself one.

I think of building an estate plan as putting together a 3-D puzzle:

- One dimension considers your *personal situation*, your wishes, your family dynamics, your assets and debts, your cottage, business, and anything else.
- The second dimension considers the different *strategies and techniques* available.
- The third dimension deals with all the *laws and rules* across the country, including the *Income Tax Act*, trustee acts, family laws and Acts related to funerals, organ donations, intestacy, etc.

There are a lot of pieces that can fit together in many different ways to make a very powerful estate plan.

I hope the previous pages have been informative and helped you appreciate some of the ways to build an estate plan. Individual legal advice can help you put together an estate plan that considers all these dimensions and how they interact so that your estate plan will speak for you.

Dream as if you'll live forever;
live as if you'll die tomorrow.
—*James Dean*

appendix 1

list of duties for an executor or estate trustee

PEOPLE USED TO CONSIDER IT AN HONOUR to be asked to be an estate trustee or an executor for a friend or family member. Anyone who has ever acted as an executor will confirm that it is a job, and sometimes not a well-paid job at that. An executor has to be prepared to write lots of letters and deal with lawyers, Canada Revenue Agency, insurance companies, real estate agents, business valuators, former employers, creditors, accountants, beneficiaries, and other interested parties, as well as the deceased's professional advisers.

If you are the executor of an estate, the following checklist outlines some of your duties and some that may not be applicable to your situation, as the administration and settling of estates varies across the country. The following is for educational purposes only and is not to be considered as tax, financial, or legal advice.

However, many people who have started with this checklist have told me that they have found it to be very useful.

Started	*Completed*	*Not Applicable*	
General			
❒	❒	❒	Arrange the funeral / cremation / burial of the deceased.
❒	❒	❒	Obtain death certificate and certified copies.
❒	❒	❒	Locate the original will and review its instructions.
❒	❒	❒	Meet with the lawyer who will represent the estate in all legal matters.
❒	❒	❒	Submit an application to the provincial court for the Probate Certificate, Grant of Probate, or Certificate of Administration.
❒	❒	❒	Pay probate fees or taxes to the provincial court.
❒	❒	❒	Locate all beneficiaries, including charities, and notify them that they have an interest in the estate under the terms of the will.
❒	❒	❒	Explain your role to the beneficiaries.
❒	❒	❒	Notify the surviving spouse of any entitlement he or she may have under family law, and recommend that the spouse receive independent legal advice.
❒	❒	❒	Deal with any claims dependants may have under provincial dependant relief provisions.
❒	❒	❒	Keep the beneficiaries informed as to the progress of administering the estate.
❒	❒	❒	Review all personal papers of the deceased to help locate the deceased's assets and debts, key contacts, tax information, etc.

Started	*Completed*	*Not Applicable*	

Deal with Government Benefit Programs

❒	❒	❒	Cancel Old Age Security benefits.
❒	❒	❒	Contact the Income Security Office to ensure that all monthly Canada Pension cheques (or Quebec Pension Plan cheques) have been paid, and then to stop them.
❒	❒	❒	Apply to CPP/QPP for any death benefits the deceased qualifies for.
❒	❒	❒	Apply to CPP/QPP for any surviving spouse and dependant pension benefits.
❒	❒	❒	Contact Human Resources Development Canada to cancel the deceased's Social Insurance Number (SIN).
❒	❒	❒	Contact the U.S. Social Security office to stop benefits.
❒	❒	❒	Apply to the U.S. Social Security office for any death or survivor benefits.
❒	❒	❒	If the deceased is retired from the military, contact the appropriate veteran's office to receive any application benefits.

Obtain All Benefits Payable to the Estate

❒	❒	❒	Contact all service clubs and veterans' clubs for death benefits that may be payable to the estate.
❒	❒	❒	Obtain all unpaid wages and other benefits from the deceased's former employer.
❒	❒	❒	Contact all of the deceased's employers (current and former) to determine if any pension or survivor benefits exist.

Started	*Completed*	*Not Applicable*	
❒	❒	❒	Determine any amounts payable to the estate under life insurance policies, and the payment options.
❒	❒	❒	Determine any options for remaining pension plans or annuities, and whether the monthly income should continue or any commuted value paid.

Identify and Manage the Assets of the Estate

Started	*Completed*	*Not Applicable*	
❒	❒	❒	Prepare a detailed inventory of the deceased's assets, including the contents of the deceased's safety deposit box.
❒	❒	❒	Locate all bank accounts of the deceased, and determine the balance on deposit for each account. Notify the financial institutions of the death.
❒	❒	❒	Search for any unclaimed bank accounts.
❒	❒	❒	Open a bank account for the estate and transfer the deceased's bank accounts to the estate bank account.
❒	❒	❒	Re-register the accounts and assets of the deceased into the name of the estate, for example, "The estate of ..."
❒	❒	❒	Obtain statements showing the value of the deceased's investments as of the date of death.
❒	❒	❒	Obtain statements showing the value of the deceased's RRSPs/RRIFs as of the date of death.
❒	❒	❒	Cancel any pre-authorized savings programs (PACs) or systematic withdrawal programs (SWIP), as well as any pending securities trades.

Started	*Completed*	*Not Applicable*	
❐	❐	❐	Review the investment strategy, and adjust if necessary. Manage short-term cash prudently.
❐	❐	❐	Arrange for the storage of assets as required, and advise insurers of any physical assets of the deceased. Arrange for any insurance coverage required.
❐	❐	❐	Review all real estate documents, including deeds, mortgages, and leases.
❐	❐	❐	Arrange for valuations of any assets of the estate, such as personal property, real estate, cars, etc.
❐	❐	❐	Cancel the deceased's driver's licence, newspaper, and magazine subscriptions, telephone, cable TV, Internet subscription, as well as any club memberships.
❐	❐	❐	Arrange with the post office for mail to be redirected, if necessary, and notify all interested parties of the change of address.
❐	❐	❐	Obtain deeds for real estate, and arrange to sell the real estate if necessary.
❐	❐	❐	Obtain share certificates for bonds, stocks, or GICs not held at a financial institution.
❐	❐	❐	Close the safety deposit box.
❐	❐	❐	Transfer or cancel any insurance policies on the house, car, boat, etc., when appropriate.
❐	❐	❐	Sell any estate assets that must be sold, and those that the personal representative chooses to sell (provided this power is given to the executor in the will).

Started	*Completed*	*Not Applicable*	
Settle the Bills of the Estate			
❒	❒	❒	Identify the outstanding balances of all personal debts.
❒	❒	❒	Arrange for publication of the notice of "Advertisement for Creditors and Others" in a local paper to locate parties who may have a claim against some or all of the estate and would be paid prior to a distribution to any of the beneficiaries.
❒	❒	❒	Settle all legitimate claims and debts of the deceased, including credit cards, consumer debts, and mortgages.
❒	❒	❒	Cancel all credit cards.
❒	❒	❒	Settle the legitimate bills of the estate: creditors, funeral expenses, and other expenses.
❒	❒	❒	Estimate if there will be sufficient assets in the estate to pay all liabilities and income taxes before making any interim distribution to the beneficiaries. You do not want to take on any personal liability for the tax bill.
File the Tax Returns			
❒	❒	❒	Prepare and file the tax returns for any years prior to the date of death that have not yet been filed. Refile if necessary.
❒	❒	❒	Identify opportunities, and make the appropriate elections to reduce the tax bill of the deceased, including using the spousal rollover, applying capital losses, and contributing to a spousal RRSP.

Started	*Completed*	*Not Applicable*	
❐	❐	❐	Prepare and file the final tax return for the deceased, as well as any optional returns.
❐	❐	❐	File estate tax returns (T3) for each year the estate exists, if necessary.
❐	❐	❐	Prepare and file the tax returns for GST/HST.
❐	❐	❐	Pay all income taxes due or obtain an income tax refund.
❐	❐	❐	Obtain the tax clearance certificate from Canada Revenue Agency.
❐	❐	❐	File any tax returns required for assets held outside of Canada, including those required by the IRS.

Distribute the Assets of the Estate

❐	❐	❐	Assess any immediate need for cash that the surviving spouse may have.
❐	❐	❐	Distribute the assets, real estate, and personal property of the estate to the beneficiaries according to the instructions in the will.
❐	❐	❐	For accounts registered jointly with rights of survivor, request that the account be transferred to the surviving tenant.
❐	❐	❐	Arrange to have the RRSP/RRIF transferred or rolled over to named beneficiaries.
❐	❐	❐	After the tax clearance certificate is obtained, transfer title and distribute any remaining assets or property in the estate.
❐	❐	❐	Discuss any "in kind" distributions with the beneficiaries.

Started	*Completed*	*Not Applicable*	
❒	❒	❒	Complete the paperwork necessary to transfer stocks and other securities to the beneficiaries.
❒	❒	❒	Establish any testamentary trusts, according to the instructions in the will.
❒	❒	❒	Obtain receipts and/or release forms from all beneficiaries.
Other			
❒	❒	❒	Prepare an accounting of the estate.
❒	❒	❒	Calculate the fees payable to the executor.
❒	❒	❒	Obtain reimbursement for all necessary and reasonable expenses incurred in the administration of the estate (with receipts).
❒	❒	❒	Pay legal fees and all other outstanding fees relating to the administration of the estate.
❒	❒	❒	Pass accounts before a provincial court judge, if necessary.
❒	❒	❒	Close the estate bank account.

appendix 2

list of duties for your representative when making financial decisions

THE PRE-ESTATE DOCUMENT IN WHICH you appoint those you wish to make financial decisions on your behalf, in the event that you cannot make your own decisions, is not a simple document. This document may give the representative very broad powers and the authority to make any and all financial decisions on your behalf (except those related to estate planning, such as writing a will). Other documents may be more specific and limited. There are also variations across the country.

Unlike the duties of the executor, who is required to act upon the death of the deceased to wrap up the estate, the duties of the representative or power of attorney for financial decisions might last for a short period of time or for many years, ending when the individual regains the capacity to make his or her own decisions, revokes the authority of the representative or power of attorney for financial decisions, or passes away.

The following list outlines some of the duties of the personal representative or power of attorney for financial decisions, whether they are called to act for a short period of time or longer.

General

1. Always act in the best interests of the individual who appointed you.
2. Obtain original copies of the document if you do not already have them. Ideally, you will have been told where they are located.
3. Review the instructions in the document, your powers, as well as any restrictions.
4. Keep the individual's assets, accounts, and bills separate from your own.
5. Obtain an assessment of the individual's mental capacity if required.
6. Review all personal papers to help identify and locate his or her assets, liabilities, sources of income, and bills.
7. Notify all financial institutions that you are acting as the individual's representative. Provide them with the appropriate documentation.
8. Use your best judgment.

Collect All Income

9. Identify current and potential sources of income and benefits.
10. Obtain all unpaid wages and other benefits from the individual's current and former employers.
11. Apply for any insurance benefits, including disability, long-term care coverage, critical illness, or living benefits if applicable.
12. Apply for any government benefits the individual may be entitled to receive, such as CPP/QPP disability benefits, CPP/QPP retirement benefits, and Old Age Security benefits.
13. If the individual was previously in the military, contact the appropriate veterans' office to receive any applicable benefits.

14. Apply to the U.S. Social Security office for any benefit entitlement.

<u>**Pay All Bills**</u>

15. Identify all the liabilities of the individual, including the outstanding balances of all personal debts, and make the required payments.
16. Locate all of the individual's bank accounts and notify the banks that they will be dealing with you.
17. Pay all expenditures that are reasonably necessary for the individual's support and care, including food, clothing, accommodation, utilities, subscriptions, dental and medical care, and other personal needs, according to the individual's financial resources.
18. Pay expenditures that are reasonably necessary for the support, education, and care of the individual's dependants.
19. Pay expenditures necessary to satisfy any legal obligations the individual has.
20. Adjust the cash flow for changes in the individual's needs, such as moving into a nursing home, death of a spouse, etc.
21. If the individual is also not able to make his or her own decisions regarding personal care, work with the representative or power of attorney for personal and health care to determine how much and when income is required.

<u>**Manage Assets**</u>

22. Use a prudent standard of care for managing the individual's assets. Adjust the investment strategy if necessary.
23. Review and, if necessary, cancel any pre-authorized savings programs (PACs) or systematic withdrawal programs (SWIPs), as well as any pending securities trades.
24. Safeguard the assets, arrange for storage if required, and ensure there is adequate insurance coverage.
25. Review all real estate documents, including deeds, mortgages, and leases.

26. Buy, sell, or mortgage real estate if necessary.
27. If the matrimonial home must be sold, and the document does not provide the power to sell it under family law, apply to the courts.
28. Buy, sell, or gift personal property.
29. Buy or sell stocks or bonds, or execute any other security transaction.
30. Borrow money on behalf of the individual.
31. Review the contents of the individual's safety deposit box.
32. Make contributions to or withdrawals from registered plans.
33. Make retirement elections for employee pension plans.
34. Manage any sums of money received, such as an inheritance, divorce, or injury settlement.

Tax and Legal

35. File the individual's tax return on an annual basis.
36. Pay all income taxes due, or obtain an income tax refund if applicable.
37. File for an income tax reassessment if necessary.
38. Act as the individual's personal representative with the Canada Revenue Agency.
39. Act on the individual's behalf regarding claims and lawsuits.
40. Mediate or arbitrate disputes on the individual's behalf.
41. Represent the individual's interest in any estate or trust claims.
42. Sign legal documents on behalf of the individual.
43. Pay legal fees and all other fees for the individual.
44. File any tax returns required for assets held outside of Canada, including those required by the IRS.

Other

45. If more than one person has been appointed, work together to make decisions on behalf of the individual who appointed you.
46. Obtain legal, tax, or financial advice.
47. Receive reimbursement for reasonable out-of-pocket expenses related to performing your duties.
48. Reimburse the representative for reasonable out-of-pocket expenses related to performing his or her duties.
49. Calculate your compensation, if any.
50. Maintain full and accurate records of all activities, receipts, and disbursements made on behalf of the individual.
51. If someone has been appointed to monitor or oversee the decisions you make, provide this person with a full accounting of all your activities as required.
52. If possible, review the will so that you better understand the individual's wishes.
53. If the individual regains the ability to manage his or her own affairs, transfer the accounts to him or her. On death, transfer the accounts to the estate executor and trustee.

appendix 3

list of duties for your representative when making personal and health care decisions

THE INSTRUCTIONS IN THE DOCUMENT in which you appoint someone to make decisions for you when you cannot make decisions for yourself may be very specific, or they may be very broad and leave decisions that need to be made at that person's discretion.

In general, your representative will be called upon only when and if you become incapable of making your own decisions for medical or personal care, or when it is reasonable to believe you are no longer capable of making a decision that would be in your best interest.

There are variations across the country, but the following partial list outlines some of the duties and responsibilities of the personal representative for health care (or power of attorney for health and personal care), whether he or she is called upon to act for a short period of time or longer.

General

1. Always act in the best interests of the individual who appointed you, as they are known to you.
2. Obtain original copies of the document if you do not already have them.
3. Review the instructions in the document, any restrictions, and special requests.
4. Obtain an assessment of the individual's mental capacity if required.
5. Notify the individual's doctor, dentist, and other health care providers that you are the power of attorney for personal and health care matters.
6. Identify all expenditures that are reasonably necessary for the individual's support and care, including food, clothing, accommodation, utilities, dental and medical care, and other personal needs.
7. Determine the location of the individual's driver's licence.
8. Work with the representative or power of attorney for financial decisions to determine how much income is available.
9. Ensure that medical receipts and bills are forwarded to the financial representative.
10. If more than one person has been appointed as the power of attorney, work together to make decisions on behalf of the individual who prepared the document.
11. Apply for a disability tax credit certificate if applicable.
12. Use your best judgment and obtain professional advice whenever appropriate.

Decisions Related to Personal Care

13. Decide where the person will live, including whether or not he or she needs to move into an assisted-living or long-term care facility.

14. Make day-to-day decisions regarding what the individual will wear and who may visit.
15. Consider the individual's dietary restrictions when planning his or her menus.

Decisions Related to Medical Care

16. Arrange regular medical and dental checkups.
17. Consent to appropriate medical procedures, including exploratory surgery and major surgery on behalf of the individual.
18. Release medical records and history when required.
19. Consent to participate in medical research studies or experimental treatments if appropriate.
20. Withhold medical treatment that you believe the individual would not want.
21. Do not allow the individual's life to be prolonged if there is no reasonable expectation of recovery, such as during the final stages of a terminal illness, if it would have been his or her wish.
22. Arrange for palliative care.
23. Take legal action on the individual's behalf if necessary, related to the powers you have been granted.

Other

24. Contact the power of attorney for financial decisions for reimbursement for all reasonable out-of-pocket expenses related to performing your duties.
25. Calculate your compensation, if any.
26. Maintain full and accurate records of all activities made on behalf of the individual.
27. If someone has been appointed to monitor or oversee the decisions you make, provide this person with an accounting of all your activities.

Your duties end on the death of the individual, or when he or she again becomes able to make his or her own personal and health care decisions.

glossary

adjusted cost base — Used to determine capital gains tax. The amount paid for an asset or property, plus commissions and other expenses.

administrator — Person appointed by the provincial court to carry out the duties of the executor when a person dies intestate, or with a will that does not name an executor.

advanced health care directive — A document, or clauses in your personal care document, that indicates your wishes regarding the refusal of, or consent to, medical treatment and who should decide for you if you are unable. It often lists a number of specific scenarios, and for each scenario, the specific medical treatments you wish to be used, or wish not to be used.

affidavit of execution — A document signed by your witnesses certifying that the signing and witnessing of your will followed proper procedures.

alter ego trust — A living trust to which you can transfer your personal assets if you are age 65 or older to minimize probate fees and taxes.

attribution rule — From CRA's perspective, the person who is responsible for paying the tax on income earned, even after certain assets are given away.

beneficiary — A person or charity named in the will, life insurance policy, RRSP/RRIF, segregated funds, pension plan, or trust to receive benefits.

buy-sell agreement Agreement between business owners or partners dealing with buying out their portion of the business in the event of death, disability, or retirement.

Canada Revenue Agency Formerly Revenue Canada.

capital gain A profit on an asset or property.

CRA Canada Revenue Agency

charitable remainder trust A gift made to a registered charity using a living trust where the donor continues to receive income/benefits from the assets donated and gets a charitable receipt up front.

codicil A legal change to a will.

committee The legal guardian of an adult with developmental or mental disabilities. Used in B.C., Manitoba, New Brunswick, and PEI.

curator The term used in Quebec for legal guardian. Similar to tutor.

deemed disposition When CRA considers that assets and property are sold at fair market value even if no actual sale took place. Happens on death and when people emigrate from Canada.

dependants Family members who are dependent on you for financial support.

devise A gift made in the will.

donor A person making a gift, such as to charity, or through an organ donation.

escheat The process, if you die without a will and have no living relatives, whereby the provincial government becomes the beneficiary of last resort.

executor Person or trust company named in the will to follow out the instructions in the will when the person who made the will dies. Female is called an executrix. Also liquidator, estate trustee, or personal representative.

family trust A trust set up for family members, such as for underage children who cannot hold assets directly, or for family members who cannot handle money or who have special needs. Also see "spousal trust."

fiduciary Person acting on behalf of another who has an obligation to act in good faith and fair dealing, such as an executor, trustee, or financial adviser.

guardian The person responsible for the care of a child under the age of majority or for someone who is incompetent. A legal guardian is appointed through the courts.

heir Person receiving an inheritance through a will. Also called a beneficiary.

holograph will A will written completely in a person's own handwriting and signed at the end by the person writing the will. No witnesses are required.

in kind Something given as a good, service, or commodity, such as a stock or car, rather than cash.

inter vivos trust A living or inter vivos trust where assets are transferred into the trust while the settlor is alive and generally taxed at the top tax rate.

intestate Dying without a will.

IPP Individual pension plan, as opposed to a group pension plan.

irrevocable That which cannot be changed or cancelled.

joint tenancy Assets or property that is owned jointly with others. May be joint tenants, with rights of survivorship, or joint tenants in common.

letters probate Paperwork issued by the provincial court when the will and the paperwork submitted by your executor are in good order. In Ontario, letters probate are referred to as "the certificate of appointment of estate trustee with a will," i.e., the certificate of appointment of your executor under the will.

life insurance policy One aspect of estate planning. A contractual agreement with a life insurance company to pay your beneficiaries a tax-free death benefit, in exchange for your premium payments.

liquidator Executor in Quebec.

living trust Inter vivos trusts, or living trusts, are established primarily for family, tax, or estate planning reasons and are set up during the settlor's lifetime. Taxed at the top tax rate.

living will An advanced health care directive that indicates your wishes regarding the types or degree of health care or medical intervention you would like to receive or refuse when you are unable to speak for yourself. A living will may be part of your power of attorney for personal and health care. It is misnamed because it is not a will and it deals with your dying, not your living.

mandate In Quebec, a power of attorney document.

medical directive A document, or clauses in your personal care document, that allows a person to indicate the types of medical treatments they would like, or not like, applied for their situation.

minor Someone who has not yet reached the age of majority.

palliative care Medical care provided for the terminally ill to make them comfortable by relieving symptoms.

per stirpes Where a beneficiary (such as a child) predeceases you, the gift that would have been theirs passes on to the next generation (your grandchildren, their children).

power of attorney for property A document in which you appoint a person to make financial decisions on your behalf. The authority given is valid only while you are alive—it stops on death. The person(s) named may be the same person as your executor, but he or she gets authority from completely separate documents. They are referred to by different names in different provinces.

probate The process in which the provincial court reviews your will after death, declares it valid, and collects a probate fee or tax. If everything is in order, probate gives your executor the authority to settle your estate, commonly referred to as "letters probate."

probate fee or probate tax Amount charged by the province or territory on the value of the assets when a will is probated.

public guardian The public guardian (also called the official guardian or children's lawyer) in your province who, among other things, makes decisions on behalf of minor children who do not have a parent or legal guardian, or on behalf of individuals who cannot make decisions for themselves unless they have appointed a substitute decision maker.

residue The portion of the estate remaining after all taxes, bills, bequests, fees, and expenses have been paid.

segregated funds The insurance industry's answer to mutual funds.

spendthrift trust A trust for a spendthrift, someone who is not a good money manager, who "spends the results of someone else's thriftiness."

spousal trust	A testamentary trust set up under a will to hold property and assets for the exclusive benefit of a surviving spouse. It may be established using some or all of the inheritance.
tax clearance certificate	A certificate from CRA (or the Minister of Revenue in Quebec) issued on request.
testamentary trust	A trust set up in your last will and testament. No assets or property are in the trust until after the estate is settled.
testator	A person who prepares a "last will and testament."
trust	A formal arrangement where the legal owner (settlor or testator) transfers assets or property into a legal entity (the trust) to be managed on behalf of the beneficiaries.
trustee	A person or institution appointed in a trust agreement to manage the assets for the beneficiaries.
U.S. situs	Located in the United States.
will	An estate planning document that indicates the instructions of the deceased for distributing assets and property to his or her chosen beneficiaries and the name of the executor.

index

A

B

ORDER FORM

THE *ESTATE PLANNING WORKBOOK* can be ordered through www.amazon.ca or using this order form, subject to availability.*

The *Estate Planning Workbook* is full of checklists, worksheets, and sample documents to help you record and organize your documents, plans, and wishes.

Estate Planning Workbook ______ copies @ $16.50 each = ________

Shipping and handling (for one book $6.95, for two copies $8.50) = ________

SUBTOTAL = ________

GST/HST = ________

AMOUNT ENCLOSED = ________

____
Name

____
Street Address Apt./Suite

____
City Province Postal Code

(___)____________________ (___)____________________
Phone Number Fax Number

____
Email

❒ Enclosed is a cheque or money order for $________ payable to Headspring Consulting Inc.

Mail your order with your cheque or money order to:

Headspring Consulting Inc.
1370 Don Mills Road, Suite 300
Toronto, ON M3B 3N7

*While quantities last. Availability will be posted at www.amazon.ca and www.whosmindingyourmoney.com

about the author

SANDRA FOSTER is a consultant, author, speaker, and educator in the financial industry. Her main areas of interest are Canadians and their relationships with money and their advisers, the changing nature of financial advice, and retirement and estate planning.

She is a sought-after speaker and one of Canada's leading experts on personal finance and the issues facing the financial services industry.

Prior to founding Headspring Consulting Inc., Sandra was a vice-president at a Canadian brokerage firm, where she developed a highly successful financial advisory practice that attracted high net-worth families and entrepreneurs.

She is the author of a number of national bestselling books, including:

- *You Can't Take It with You: Common-Sense Estate Planning for Canadians*
- *Estate Planning Workbook*
- *Make the Most of What You've Got: The Canadian Guide to Managing Retirement Income*

- *Who's Minding Your Money? Financial Intelligence for Canadian Investors*
- *Buying and Selling a Book of Business: What Every Financial Advisor and Planner Should Know*
- *Partez l'Esprit en Paix*

She has won numerous awards, served as a judge for several years for the Advisor of the Year Award, and has been an active member on a number of industry boards and committees.

Sandra has also written numerous articles. In addition, she is a regular guest on radio and TV programs, and is a frequent contributor to many publications.

She holds a number of designations, including Trust and Estate Practitioner (TEP), Certified Financial Planner (CFP), Canadian Investment Manager (CIM), Fellow, Canadian Securities Institute (FCSI), Registered Financial Planner (RFP), and Certified Human Resources Professional (CHRP). She maintains active memberships in a number of professional associations.

She may be reached at:

email:
fosters@headspringconsulting.com

For more information visit:
www.whosmindingyourmoney.com

www.headspringconsulting.com